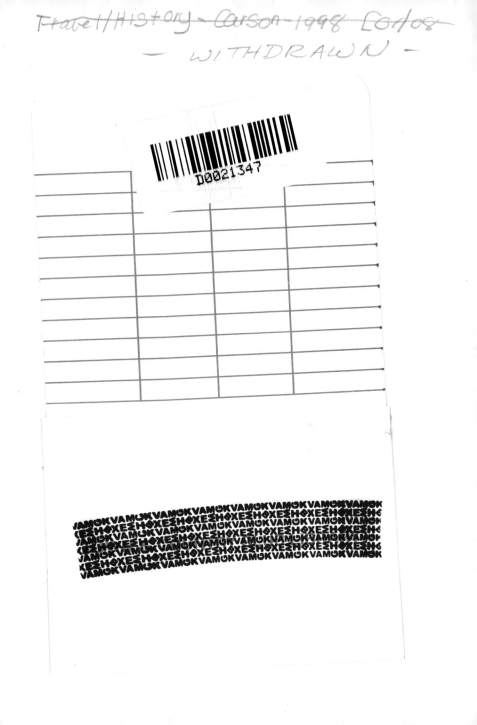

D0021347

A Gift to the

Town & Country Club

Library

from

Harold and Barbara Levine

in

Remembrance of

Carol Pearce

Jan. 2008

THE STAR FACTORY

THE STAR FACTORY

CIARAN CARSON

ARCADE PUBLISHING · NEW YORK

First U.S. Edition 1998

Library of Congress Cataloging-in-Publication Data

Carson, Ciaran, 1948–
    The star factory / Ciaran Carson. —1st U.S. ed.
        p.   cm.
    Originally published: London : Granta Books, 1997.
    ISBN 1-55970-465-9
    1. Carson, Ciaran, 1948–   —Homes and haunts—Northern Ireland—
Belfast. 2. Belfast (Northern Ireland)—Social life and customs. 3. Carson,
Ciaran, 1948–   —Childhood and youth. 4. Belfast (Northern Ireland)—
Biography. 5. Poets, Irish—20th century—Biography. I. Title
PR6053.A714Z467   1998
821'.914—dc21   98–24719

Published in the United States by Arcade Publishing, Inc., New York
Distributed by Little, Brown and Company

10 9 8 7 6 5 4 3 2 1

PRINTED IN THE UNITED STATES OF AMERICA

Acknowledgement

I am grateful to Tess Gallagher for
her many editorial suggestions

CONTENTS

CONTENTS

RAGLAN STREET

It is cold and dark, and I am standing facing my father, who is seated on the 'throne' of the outhouse. I am the age where our heads are level with each other. I am there because I did not want his call of nature to interrupt the story he'd been telling me. So he continues, phrasing it between puffs of smoke; and the red glow of his cigarette-end, as he draws on it, illuminates his face sporadically. Brief looks of dialogue are exchanged before we vanish again, overtaken by the realm of his voice, which extends beyond the cramped dimensions of the outhouse into the space of memory and narrative. As the words unreel from him, his cigarette becomes a visual aid, and its animated lipstick blip draws time-lapse squiggles on the 3-D blackboard dark; or, as a continuo between these imaginary pictures, he makes curvy waves of possibility which punctuate or illustrate the story's rhythm and its tendency to gather into ornate runs and turns. I see it like some instant-recall hologram in all its cursive loops and spirals of DNA red neon. The writing fades as instantly as it is written, but our too-slow brains retain its after-image on our retinas, just as the words of the beginning or a middle section linger on throughout the predetermined narrative: predetermined, yet always new, because each telling of the story is rehearsal, and gains different subtleties of emphasis each time round – the cistern whispering, for example, at some appropriate Cold War moment, or the Niagarous flushing which signals the end of an important episode, where the hero falls into a waterfall.

It reminds me of the ancient magisterial importance of the chamberpot, where courtiers and Privy Counsellors await the outcome of His Majesty's deliberations like a plot, and perfumes of Arabia are sprayed discreetly round the room from pomander bulbs squeezed by underpaid underlings. Or, one ponders the alternative hologram of the city described by its ubiquity of plumbing and its labyrinthine sewers, the underworld of culverts plunged in Stygian gloom. So, as children, we believed that sewer covers were the portals to a parallel sub-universe; embossed with arcane lettering and numerals, their enormous, thick, cast-iron discs proved impossible to lift. Sometimes, though, boiler-suited emissaries from the Corporation would materialize and insert long metal keys with T-shaped handles into the two slots of the submarine hatch and heave it trembling from its disturbed circumference of mossy dirt, and we would get a glimpse of ladder rungs descending into well-dark depths.

For, although much of the world was withheld from us, we had premonitions of its depth and breadth from these occasional insights: squinting through the eye-knot of a creosoted pine fence, for instance, I can see the rusted strewn sculpture of abandoned factory machinery, all axles, counterweights and cogged wheels; or, passing by an open pub door in summer, the aroma of warm beer and porter emanates a palpable extension of its nicotined interior, where blurred men speak to mirrors in a tipsy babble. Sometimes the gates in factory porticos were opened to admit a Clydesdale-drawn cart, and the inner courtyard was revealed like that of a medieval castle, smelling of straw and dung. The rhythm of the horses clopping on the cobbles in their tasselled club-footed hooves rang out against the opaque noise that beat against the factory windows from within, where I'd imagine doffers slanging to each other in their language of mime, mouthing silently to back up this writing on the air. From here – The Milfort Weaving and Finishing Works – I'd walk on down Clonard Street on my way home from school, turn down Odessa Street and Sevastapol Street, to emerge at the impressive sandstone façade of the Falls Road branch of the Andrew Carnegie Library.

Now I remember that 'library', in some households, was a euphemism for once-euphemisms like loo and water-closet: contemplating that last antique compound, I'd see water wobbling in the opened mirror door, and I'd step right through its trembling mercury to emerge reversed on the other side, like some ghost from the future who hover-glides invisibly through empty childhood streets just after dawn, following the jiggled tinkle of the milk-cart, or a postman coming home from night-shift, disembodied from his job of sorting letters into pigeon-holes. You could float on board a tram and *doppelgänger* its lone pilot as he exercised his minimal control of stops and starts within the pre-determined iron parallels of time. In the still gaslit thoroughfare, fruitmongers were up early, with long poles already drawing out their awnings to shade their produce fresh and cool from that morning's market.

It has occurred to me, in these dreams, to visit my parents before I was born (meeting a younger self seemed too improbable), but the dream mechanism always manages to subvert this outcome, and I find myself, instead, back where I started, listening to my father in the dark of the 'library' of 100 Raglan Street. And as I write, in 12 Glandore Avenue, my toilet *is* a library: some years ago, I put up three mahogany-stained pine shelves on its back wall, and filled them with second-hand books that might have once resided in a public library:

The Mason Wasps by J.H. Fabre
British Ferns and their Allies by Thomas Moore
Pharos the Egyptian by Guy Boothby
Rovering to Success (Life-Sport for Young Men) by Lord Baden-Powell
Kai Lung's Golden Hours by Ernest Bramah
The Life of the Fly by J.H. Fabre
With Stanley on the Congo by M. Douglas
Laughter and Wisdom by Stephen Leacock
Biggles Flies West by Capt. W.E. Johns
The Romance of Fish Life by W.A. Hunter
I Said Oddly, Diddle I by Paul Jennings

Electricians and their Marvels by Walter Jarrold
More Hunting Wasps by J.H. Fabre

— books chosen for a variety of reasons: for their titles or design; for their illustrations; for nostalgia; sometimes for their content. Sitting on the *faux*-Edwardian commode seat, the occupant is inclined to reach back for a volume, open it, and sniff it, thus releasing dormant pheromones of yellow-glued bindings and foxed paper. Sometimes a pressed flower flutters out, as if emerging from a pupa, and one imagines the nature rambles of long Victorian evenings, presided over by a Lewis Carroll figure; or recently, in the pages of the *Complete Poetical Works of Robert Service*, beautifully produced by Barse & Co., of New York, NY and Newark, NJ, I came across the visiting card of one The Reverend K.N.J. Loveless, complete with a coat-of-arms which bears a remarkable resemblance to that of Belfast, with his two rampant sea-horses to Belfast's one. I can hear my father reciting Service's 'The Shooting of Dan McGrew' in the whispery dark of the outhouse:

> *A bunch of the boys were whooping it up in the Malamute saloon;*
> *The kid that handles the music-box was hitting a jag-time tune;*
> *Back of the bar, in a solo game, sat Dangerous Dan McGrew,*
> *And watching his luck was his light-o'-love, the lady that's known*
>   *as Lou.*

And, as I sniff again, the book hits me with a rush of brown lino smells that appertain to libraries and doctors' surgeries, where you might see a print of Millet's *The Angelus* hung above the waiting-room mantelpiece, and the dim bronze gongs of St Peter's waft across the intervening time. I see its soot-encrusted twin spires, and all the other neo-Gothic campaniles of Belfast, ubiquitous as factories or barracks. Unbearably tall mill chimneys teetered against the Atlantic-grey sky, churning out thick ropes of smoke like fleets of armed destroyers.

They bring me back to my mini-library, where, above the books, I've put a framed reproduction for Wills' Woodbine cigarettes, featuring, 'In the Dardanelles, the five-funnelled Russian destroyer, *Askold*, commonly known as the packet of Woodbines'. It reminds me that my father, when he wasn't smoking Park Drive, would smoke Woodbines, which came in leaf-green art nouveau packets of five, ten or twenty. My father stopped smoking some years ago, but still carries, it seems to me, an aura of crumbled tobacco-dust. These days, when he comes to visit, he spends good half-hours in the library, browsing through its relics of an Empire. Sometimes he comes down with a book under his arm; often, it is the Belfast Street Directory of 1948, the year that I was born.

FROM ABBEY ROAD TO
ZETLAND STREET

Pondering the tome of the Street Directory, I am reminded of the cabalistic or magical implications of the alphabet, which manifest themselves in a word like 'abraxas': according to *Chambers Dictionary*, 'a mystic word, or a gem engraved therewith, often bearing a mystical figure of combined human and animal form, used as a charm . . . said to have been coined by the 2nd-cent. Egyptian Gnostic Basilides to express 365 by addition of the numerical values of the Greek letters'. A version, it would seem, but perhaps invented independently, of abracadabra, 'a magic word, written in amulets . . . found in a 2nd-cent. poem by Q. Serenus Sammonicus'. Remembering chanting the alphabet by rote as a child, I visualize the names carved into the school desks, one on top of another, till they're nearly indecipherable; I smell the colour blue in the speckled delph ink-wells, and hear the cursive scratch of a steel nib as I learn to write between the ruled lines of a copybook.

As I look up my first Alma Mater, St Gall's Public Elementary School, under Waterville Street (no. 2), I am reminded how the arbitrary power of the alphabet juxtaposes impossibly remote locations, as in the preceding entry, Waterproof Street, which runs from Fairfax Street to Byron Street, in East Belfast, some three miles away; then we have Watson Street, off Railway Street – slightly nearer, in the Sandy Row district, in the vicinity of Murray, Sons, & Co., tobacco and snuff manufacturers, whose heady aura could be detected sometimes in the school yard of St Gall's, given a western breeze, like the way we could hear the roar of the crowd at an international fixture in far-off Windsor Park.

Similarly, streets named after places form exotic junctures not to be found on the map of the Empire: Balkan and Ballarat, Cambrai and Cambridge, Carlisle and Carlow, Lisbon and Lisburn, and so on, through Madras and Madrid, till we eventually arrive, by way of Yukon, at the isles of Zetland, whereupon we fall off the margins of the city.

I am trying to think of myself as a bookworm, ruminating through the one thousand, five hundred and ninety-six pages of the Directory in teredo mode, following my non-linear dictates, as I make chambered spirals in my universe, performing parabolas by browsing letters and the blanks between them. I have never seen a bookworm, but I have often glimpsed a tiny lenticular blip of near-transparent yellow, which scuttles from the fold between two suddenly opened pages: this, possibly, is the booklouse, described in Macmillan's *Encyclopedia* as 'a soft-bodied wingless insect, also called the dustlouse, belonging to the order Pscoptera (about 1600 species). Booklice inhabit buildings, often feeding on old books, papers, and entomological collections.'

The Directory, indeed, has been much distressed by my metaphorical bookworm expeditions into it over many years. I've repaired its cracked spine and rubbed edges with green carpet tape that in its turn is beginning to come apart. Nevertheless, it remains an impressive piece of book-production, measuring nine by five by three inches, and bearing embossed advertisements on its 4 mm thick boards. Even the page-edges of the closed volume carry ads; wondering how the concave surface was managed, I imagine teams of printer's devils wielding big, convex rubber stamps with doorknob handles.

One of these notices is for 'John Ross & Co., Largest Auction Rooms in Ireland', reminding me that I bought the Directory itself in the said Rooms, in a job lot consisting of some bric-à-brac, a Brownie box camera, and a sheaf of old postcards, two of which I am looking at right now, and whose juxtaposition, when I bought them, seemed to form some mysterious alliance. The first is postmarked 'Belfast 3.30 p.m., SP 3, 13', and bears the address '22 Raby St, Ormeau Rd., Belfast'. Its front is an elaborate colour production whose centrepiece is a retouched photograph of a man and a woman embracing, cheek by jowl, within a floral border; in the top left corner, a picture of an ocean liner, and in the top right, a steam train, both vehicles surmounted by shamrocks; below the couple, two disembodied hands – one wrist is lace-fringed, the other shirt-cuffed – emerge from bouquets to squeeze each other gently. At the tail of the card, a verse:

9

Until We Meet Again

> *Parting darkens our sky — alas!*
> *But every cloud has a silver lining —*
> *Love will brighten the days, as they pass,*
> *And hope of re-union forbid our repining.*

The message on the back is written in a fine-nibbed, delicate hand:

Dear Jim,

How are you living the life on *The Ocean Wave*, have you any vacancy's for a Galley Slave, if so I will go, how would you like that, (I Don't Think) Mrs A Gourlays' address is 66 Castlereagh Street, Mount Pottinger. Did you have time to see any of Russia at all what do you think of it, is it any better than Belfast. Mr W. Yeates took a Photo of mine, which I intended to send to you, so you can write and ask him for it, as he won't give it to me, it is not a very good one, but it will do until I get a better one. (Was you ever out in a wee Boat or were you ever in Larne), lovely weather for Brown's Bay, what do you say, we all rise in the morning to go for a Swim. This is all now Thanking you for PC's received from Falkirk & Russia, Write soon, with Kind Regards, Gertie. (*Please Excuse Card*)

I am somewhat flummoxed as to how this card reached its destination, since the Raby Street address appears to be that of the sender, and can only surmise that Jim — on *The Ocean Wave* — is in the navy, and that the card was forwarded by some special Forces mail. The second card bears neither stamp, date, nor address, but the evidence would suggest that it has been sent by someone serving in the Great War. The front is a conventional landscape scene in an oval frame; the back is printed 'Luxographie A. Noyer, Paris No. 55 – Fabrication Francaise' and bears the following message, written in indelible pencil:

> *My dearest Gertie*
> No letter today either but I dont think its your fault. I seen in the paper today that P. Barron and McManus of Ballyshannon were both wounded. When is it all going to end I get tired more & more every day I think its thinking of you what makes it worse. I hope that you wont be angry at getting a P.C. but onestly it holds more than I have to write Imagine this few lines to my own pet I cant think what else to write about Im sure pet all my letters must be just the same over & over again I cant help myself every day is the same old thing over again including Sunday I really dont know Sunday from any other day I often think is it going to last for ever This & you my little darling is all I can think of night & day I hope for your sake that when you get this . . . *[here the 'indelible' pencil has been heavily rubbed, and is illegible]* . . . mother I was asking for her with all my love from your very own Friend x x x children x x x

It is difficult to imagine two messages more different in tone. Can these two Gerties be one and the same? I think it's possible, but unlikely; nevertheless, their coinciding in the heterogenous jumble of an auction room gives me an eerie feeling, as if, in retrospect, they had been predestined to meet. It reminds us of the poignancy of auction rooms, of vacancy and death, as the contents of a house are held in limbo until sold in disparate lots, and the domiciled relationship they had is broken up: if furniture could speak, what tales might it not tell, when the whatnot is divested of its aspidistra, and the overmantel mirror loses the reflection of its parlour? For every stick and bit implies a narrative, and we ascribe their provenances.

So the story goes, as the auctioneer, like a dominie or cleric, climbs into his box to open a new chapter. As a newcomer to auctions, I was fascinated by the skewed incremental scale of bidding: 'Eighty? Sixty? Forty? I have thirty. Thirty-two. Thirty-five. Forty. Forty-two. Forty-five. Forty-seven. Fifty. Fifty-five. Sixty . . .', going up in fives until it hit the eighty, and then proceeding in tens; and I admired the accuracy with which the porters could predict, if asked, at what time in the sale a certain lot would come up, and its going price. I am reminded of the importance of numbers in the Street Directory – 'The Numbering of Tenements in the Streets of Belfast is not consecutive but alternative: one side is marked with ODD figures, 1, 3, 5, and so on; and the opposite with EVENS, as 2, 4, 6, etc.', as a head-note has it; and now I remember the boy I once knew, who collected house numbers.

Not for him the logistical and temporal complications of trainspotting, nor even the mindlessly simple pursuit of writing down automobile licence plate numbers, which I did myself for a while; a favourite venue was the front seat on the top deck of a trolley-bus, where one could simultaneously pretend to drive and note the passing of the desultory, mostly black traffic. This boy, Master X, had reduced male pre-adolescent hobby-mania to its essence, which is number, variety, and set: in this case, numbers are inherently variable, and any list of them will form a set; yet, presuming his numbers were set under street-names, apparently similar numbers were not identical, since 2 Waterproof Street, say, is manifestly not 2 Waterville Street; so, every number was coloured by its geographical location. Perhaps, in his book, numbers became things.

Cigarette cards, bubble-gum wrappers, barbed wire, spark-plugs, hock, anything in the shape of a pig, gold ingots, pewter, traffic cones, beer cans, hypodermic syringes, clocks, rugs, rubber bands, dogs, Lagondas, penny-farthing bicycles, pennies, farthings, golf-balls, billiard-cues, Ming, stones, marbles, mirrors, Constables, accordions, pocket-watches, Dinky toys, Meccano, rope, tobacco tins, hotel-room sewing-kits, airline sick-bags, tulips, train-tickets, electric torches, books of matches, postcards, phonographs, ball-point pens, piranhas, dictionaries, hand-bells, thimbles, cameos, transistor radios, pressed flowers, Christmas cards, mangles, window-glass, initialled handkerchiefs, tiles, bricks, autographs, celluloid film-stock, movie stills, paper, ink-wells, swords, pistols, anchors, fishing-rods, carp: all these, and many more things beyond my ken, have been collected.

Having defined his set of operations, the apprentice collector, after some experience, will find that many sub-sets exist within the set; and if he is to continue his hobby with any seriousness, he must specialize. Within the vast realm of postage stamps, for example, one might make a thematic collection, like the simple concept of a 'stamp menagerie', which could include the Cod of Newfoundland, the Tapir of the State of North Borneo, the Gom-Pauw of South West Africa, and the Pigmy Hippo of Liberia; and one can see how a collector of barbed wire could spend a lifetime in the pursuit of deviant strands caused by a hitch or a snag in the production line; the tobacco-tin collector might confine himself to a particular company, or cut (twist, plug, shag and bird's-eye come to mind). In this context, Master X's operations had the virtue of clearly definable sub-sets, i.e., streets, though I do not know how far he set his limits within the city; and I do not believe that he possessed a map, so the whole process must have been one of constant exploration, as his notebook became a street directory devoid of residents.

Returning to the Street Directory and Ross's Auction Rooms, I note the various objects in the room where I am writing, which were purchased in auction rooms: the oak desk, the overmantel, the big deal table, the fire-screen, the Hohner melodeon, the anonymous ukelele, the daguerreotype of Brothers Water and Place Fell, the glazed chessboard set in a heavy moulded frame, the Lloyd Loom chair, the pair of cobra-shaped brass candlesticks, the mahogany-framed Edwardian sofa; and the model aeroplane of heavy brazed aluminium, which looks as if it might be an apprentice piece from Short Bros. aircraft factory, whose nose is the face of a clock. It is twin-engined, so that the hands of the clock are like a third, skewed prop, and it ticks away – ticks over – as, adjusting my rough scrawled holograph draft, I tick these words into the micro-chip self-justifying memory of my Sharp FW-560 Fontwriter Personal Wordprocessor, thinking of the boy-next-door who had so much pocket-money he could afford to burn his model aeroplanes.

THE MODEL SHOP

Sometimes the city is an exploded diagram of itself, along the lines of a vastly complicated interactive model aircraft kit whose components are connected by sprued plastic latitudes and longitudes.

At the same time it mutates like a virus, its programme undergoing daily shifts of emphasis and detail. Its parallels are bent by interior temperatures; engine nacelles become gun pods; sometimes, a whole wing takes on a different slant. Everything is redolent of glue – scorpion-tailed tubes of it are scattered everywhere – and I almost drowsed in its unguent aroma, till I felt my vision being clarified and heightened. Now that I can see the city's microscopic bits transfixed by my attention, I wonder how I might assemble them, for there is no instruction leaflet; I must write it.

Remembering making model aeroplanes, I am absorbed by various degrees of difficulty. First World War aircraft presented little problem beyond the interconnective biplane struts; Second World War represented a more complicated technology, as in the case of the Wellington bomber, with its revolving gun-turrets and elaborate undercarriage. If I trembled but one millimetre, the Perspex windscreen would be smeared indelibly with excess glue, and my alter ego pilot, whose anal stub I'd just stuck into its cockpit matrix, would be blinded by a fingerprinted cataract.

For I was no expert, compared to that sodality of boffins who, like entomologists or taxidermists, explored realms of minutiae unknown to the layman. They were adept at sanding down the tiny plastic nipples on the edges of detached components; or, not liking the cut of some particular jib or aileron, they would cannibalize similar items from a family variant and file them to the right proportions; in other cases, bits were custom-made from melted-down, remoulded waste.

Masters of *trompe-l'œil*, they would contemplate the spectra of commercial colour charts and manufacture new hybrid tints from them: Tree-frog Green, Khaki Storm, Salamander Blue. They studied the chameleon in Belfast Zoo, since the whole enterprise was camouflage: in this respect, *faux* waterline stains were made, by subtle use of masking-tape and spray-gun, on the hulls of flying-boats and amphibians. Some distressed their fighter planes by drilling bullet-holes in them with Lilliputian drill-bits. Others, in their noble struggle for veracity, would 'press the wheels on to a heated surface, in order to obtain flats to simulate the aircraft's weight',* therefore sacrificing the craft's ability to 'fly', since flats would look wrong in the air, unless, of course, the wheels were really 'flat'; but then, how would it get off the ground? No. Flight must not have been intended, and 'Whispering Death'

---

*'Whispering Death' – 'Robert Humphreys models an "Aussie" Mk. 21 Beaufighter in 1:72 scale,' *Scale Models International*, April 1996.

remains eternally in stasis, grounded, an exhibit of an earthbound plane of reality.

And yet, as an object to be contemplated, it is like an aircraft in a real museum, retired from the war theatre to better inhabit the culmination of a drama. There is a narrative behind it, and there are wheels within its wheels. We learn, for instance, that the Beaufighter's construction resembled the cannibal techniques of model-makers:

> Derived from the Beaufort torpedo bomber, the Beaufighter made use of numerous Beaufort parts, enabling production to be switched from one type to another without significant disruption to the production line. Major common parts were the outer wings, tail unit and undercarriage, the fuselage being modified to accept a reduction in the number of the crew being carried from four to two . . . the new aircraft was powered by the powerful Hercules radial engines . . . Naturally, changes were made to the Beaufighter during its development life, e.g. the original undercarriage was changed for a Lockheed designed unit, and the Beaufighter Mk. II was powered by Merlin engines. On later marks, the long dorsal fin became standard.

And its nickname? 'A combination of the unique whistling sound which was produced by the Beaufighter's sleeve-valved radial engines, along with the tremendous punch it carried, earned the aircraft the nickname of "Whispering Death" from the Japanese.'

So, you imagine Mr Humphreys, whistling as he recreates the past, and you realize that the model's flattened tyres bear witness to the weight of history: 'In all, the RAAF received 583 Beaufighters from various sources, and it was one of these, a Mk.

21, A8-50, which I decided to build. This particular aircraft, coded DU-H, served with No. 22 Sqn. RAAF, and was based in Sanga Sanga airstrip in the Philippines in 1944.'

I admire such true believers in mimesis, even when approaching me with tremulous, blabby lips, emitting the cacophony of Messerschmitts and Hurricanes, their arms spreadeagled as they hold opposing forces in their hands and make dog-fights with them in hospital corridors. They are in a parallel reality. As we try to make contact, they gaze through us with the terrible clarity of angels, then float past into history on extended wings.

It reminds me that, from time to time throughout the Troubles, especially after incidents more atrocious than usual, there would be crazes of religious mimesis. Typically, they were witnessed in damp patches on the many-layered wallpapers of terrace houses, or in their tiled fire surrounds, which, if you believed the sporadic reports, bore images of a Turin Shroud Christ. Never a Virgin Mary, as I remember it,* which struck me as strange, since I surmised, like other iconographers, that these phenomena were a Northern response to the 'moving statue' syndrome which was wont to break out in the South in summers darkened by incessant rain, in which the brightest things were the daffodil-yellow anoraks of German tourists.

---

*However, some time after writing this, I came across the following: '**Mexican Virgin "makes divine appearance"** in metro puddle – Every hour, about 2,000 people pay their respects to a dried-up puddle in a Mexico City underground station, in which they believe the Virgin of Guadaloupe has manifested herself.

The "Subway Virgin" appears in a stain, about 10 inches long, left on Sunday after the water had evaporated.

"I believe, yes, that it is the miraculous appearance of the Virgin of Guadaloupe," said

Apparently, as you passed a roadside shrine, a blue-robed Madonna would wink at you from Her white-washed stone canopy. Others would see the image of Her hand beckon, or She would nod Her plaster head ambiguously. For, since these statues were dumb, their limited vocabulary of gesture could convey any message whatsoever to the eye of the convinced beholder. Some interpreters were inclined to think that these signals expressed regret at the demise of the Family Rosary; others saw them as a warning of impending Armageddon. Abortion and divorce were frequently discussed.

A contemporary photograph in the *Irish News* shows an elderly housewife in a print apron pointing to and alleged Christ's face in the fireplace, like an angel standing over the abandoned sepulchre. As I remember squinting at the badly reproduced image, it seems arrested at the opaque spawny embryonic stage of a Polaroid, not quite coalesced: it is neither one thing nor the other; but it is just possible to believe you see a bifurcated beard, the skewed bracket of an eyebrow; here, half an ear, there an unblinking cataracted eye.

The image would inevitably fade from public notice. Yet the ephemera bore witness to the power of icons, and the almost

---

Amanda Soliz, a supermarket worker who had joined the queue of thousands waiting to leave floral and monetary offerings and to light candles near the stain they say bears a resemblance to Mexico's dark-skinned manifestation of the Virgin Mary.

The Mexican archbishop's office doubted yesterday that the image was a true miracle, saying it failed to rank with the divine appearances in Guadaloupe in 1531, Lourdes in 1854, and Fatima in 1917.

"There are no theological elements that lead us to consider this a divine presence through these lines that have formed due to a water leak," it said.' (Guardian, 6 June 1997)

Russian Orthodoxy of the Tridentine Rite comes back to me in incense mingled with damp overcoats smelling of tobacco, and many candle-flames are wavered by the dim bronze gongs. I hear the clunk of a copper penny dropped through the slot of a money-box as payment for a candle. It brings to mind the candle auctions of the sixteenth century, where an item would be offered for sale as long as the candle burned, and the bid on the instant of expiry would be successful; from whence, I imagine, the expression, 'the game is not worth the candle', as the disappointed punter finds himself the custodian of an exorbitant set of objects, such as ten Venetian glass candlesticks.

So, your wavering orison dwindles to a smoking wisp-wick. How much more efficient are the Tibetan prayer-windmills, whose mantras are propelled by every breath and zephyr of the heavens! Even the votive offerings at Irish shrines have a longer shelf-life: the little pile of ball-point pens (signifying litigation), the hearing-aids, the walking-sticks, the rags tied to branches (signifying God knows what; the request was of a private nature, though a guardian angel might be party to it).

And, in those troubled times, from time to time, angels could be witnessed with their long wing-cases trailing behind them, crawling up the neo-Gothic blackened spires of St Peter's Pro-Cathedral like translucent locusts, or materializing on the airy girders of unfinished office blocks. The Bishop of Down and Connor denounced them as demonic visions; nevertheless, they continued to prosper in corners of the eye, lurking in alleyways like winos, never fully revealing themselves. As we passed, we could hear the rustle of their carapaces.

MOORELAND

On the 1st of November 1950, the Assumption of the Blessed Virgin Mary was declared a dogma* of the Church. Until then, as explained by the *Catholic Encyclopaedic Dictionary* of 1931, it had been merely a traditional belief:

ASSUMPTION, The. i. It is the teaching of the Church that at the death of the blessed Virgin Mary her body was preserved from corruption and that shortly afterwards it was assumed (Lat., *assumere*, to take to) into Heaven and reunited to her soul. This belief is not an article of faith; nevertheless Pope Benedict XIV declared it to be a probable opinion, the denial of which

---

*DOGMA (Gr., ordinance) A truth directly proposed by the Church for our belief as an article of divine revelation. The vulgar notion of a dogma, as an arbitrary doctrine imposed nobody quite knows why, is thus seen to be at fault; the content of a dogma is truth revealed by God and thus must be believed: it is not assumed to be true because many believe it.

would be impious and blasphemous. The doctrine is universally held throughout the Church, and appears to be more or less explicitly believed by all dissident Eastern churches. No direct reference to this corporal assumption is made in the office of the feast itself, but it has been a subject of explicit belief for at least 1,500 years, being stated by St Juvenal of Jerusalem at the Council of Chalcedon in 451 and the feast was already celebrated in the East in that century . . .

ii. The feast of the Assumption is kept throughout the Church on Aug. 15 as a holiday of obligation (*q.v.*) . . . it is also observed by the Orthodox and other dissident Eastern churches under the title of the Falling Asleep of the All-holy Mother of God . . .

We used to light bonfires (or bonefires, as we more correctly called them in our Belfast accent) on the 15th of August, ostensibly to celebrate this feast; but I suspect a pagan occasion has been assumed here, since the Church explicitly sought to absorb local customs into its liturgical calendar. As Pope St Gregory the Great indicated to St Augustine:

> The temples of the idols in that nation (of the English) ought not to be destroyed but let the idols that are in them be cast down; let water be blessed and sprinkled in the said temples and let altars be built and relics placed therein. For if those temples be well built, it is meet that they be converted from the worship of devils to the service of the true God. And because they are used to slaying many oxen in that worship, some solemnity must be provided in exchange . . . For without doubt it is impossible to cut off everything at once from their rude natures.

> (Bede, *Eccl. Hist*. i, 30)

In Irish, August is *Lughnasa*, the month of Lugh, the Celtic god of light and genius, equated by Julius Caesar with Mercury; traditionally, his name was attached to the harvest festival held on the 1st of August (Lammas); perhaps the 15th is an extension or reiteration of this feast?

At any rate, the bonfire would be built in the left-over patch of land at the back of Mooreland. We would begin scavenging for its constituent elements towards the end of July. We would go in gangs across the hinterland of fields to climb trees and mutilate them with blunt hatchets. We'd scout building-sites for planks, wooden shuttering and cable-spools. We'd knock on doors and ask for old furniture, for August was a kind of Spring, when old suites would be thrown out, and new ones bought. Gradually, the bonfire would start to take shape, with its bits of stuff purloined from skips; its rustling, drooping willow branches forming a tepee; the broken sofa at its heart, where boy sentinels reclined in rota, lest the bonfire should be stolen, or set alight by marauding Protestants, or rival Catholics. There was also a crow's-nest armchair at the apex, where one could be ensconced in Pharaonic isolation, to survey the realm of the neighbourhood.

Trying to remember if we had a Billy effigy, in the manner of Protestants burning the Pope on the Twelfth, I've just phoned my brother Pat for corroboration. No, he says, but do you remember the year we tied up S— M— -, and put him in the bonfire before lighting it, and didn't drag him out until the last possible moment? I don't, perhaps because the guy in question was my brother's age, three years younger than me, and thus belonged to a different generation; at that age, three years is a generation. I remember S— as a big-boned, strong, dark-haired boy – awkward, perhaps, but not a candidate for bullying. Pat, being a teacher of pupils with 'learning difficulties',* and thus something of a pragmatic psychologist, attributes S—'s scapegoat status to his being beaten up or whipped by his father, for whatever misdemeanour, on a regular basis; I do remember this, but not his tormented status as a living effigy.

It reminds me of the boy we used to bribe to eat still-warm cow's dung, although the circumstances were less dramatic: the boy, after all, made a profit; and the herbivorous aroma of cow's dung is not unpleasant, unlike dog-shit. (Similarly, horses' droppings have a wholesome smell, like processed hay.) Come to think of it, I was such a boy myself: once, I was bet a thrupenny bit that I wouldn't eat a matchboxful of live earthworms (boys, in those days, habitually carried such accessories in their pockets). At any rate, I emptied the contents on to my palm and mouthed their writhing vermicelli before gulping them into me. Thrupence was a substantial sum then – it could buy you six half-penny chews, for instance, or one bar of Cowans' implacable Highland Toffee, which lasted for hours. It seemed a fair deal; and I could imagine myself, for some seconds, to be a Kalahari Bushman, before entering the cornucopia of the sweet-shop.

O three-dee bit, twelve-sided paradigm of the duodecimal system! Small, thick, brass coin, mysterious as those obols pierced with holes that emanated from the Far East, where they

---

*Perhaps this is no longer the correct expression for what used to be the official syndrome 'educationally subnormal', or ESN.

were threaded into necklaces and bangles of currency! I am almost tempted to go tomorrow to the antique stalls of Donegall Pass, where, last Saturday, I saw a glass salad-bowlful of them being sold at a 4000% inflationary rate of 50p each. I'd buy about £4 worth, to see if I could still manage the house-of-cards trembling-fingered balancing trick of standing them on edge one on top of another, till, trying to place an optimistic seventh or eighth, the expensive column teetered, fell and clattered in bits across the scratched mahogany veneer of the table; sometimes, one would roll off the edge of the piazza to hit the brown lino way below with a dint and trickle off under the sofa into oblivion.

The body of the sofa was itself a time-capsule, a *corpus* packed with small objects that had crept from hands or pockets into interstitial areas between upholstery and frame: a repository of coins, hair-clips, pencil-sharpeners, broken crayons, holy medals, pencil-stubs and curtain-rings. We discovered one such involuntary cache one August in the fifties, when we threw out our old horsehair-stuffed, hide-covered sofa, and half-dismantled it with a hatchet before dragging it off to the place of immolation where, on the Fifteenth Night, it would be assumed as smoke into the heavens, its ashes wafting over the fields and chimney-pots, its skeleton carbonized into the scorched, brick-like earth, where bits of twisted metal were still hot to the touch for days. Years later, I will remember the burned barricades of other Augusts: the crooked collapsed frames and chassis of Belfast Corporation buses; oil-drums; globs of smouldering rubber; heaps of broken brick; anthracite-black cobblestones; roadways frosted with the smashed glass of milk-bottle petrol-bombs.

I wrote that yesterday, and now, another August has occurred to me. About four hours ago, I was in the city centre. A benefactor had given me £60 worth of Waterstone's book-tokens, so I went to their shop in Royal Avenue and exchanged my tokens for these books:

Roland Barthes by Roland Barthes :
Selected Writings, Vol. 1: 1913–1926 by Walter Benjamin
Encyclopaedia Acephalia by Georges Bataille, Michel Leris, Marcel Griaule, Carl Einstein, Robert Desnos, and writers associated with the Acéphale and Surrealist groups, and
A Nostalgic Look at Belfast Trams since 1945 by Mike Maybin

I'm browsing through the latter volume when all of a sudden my eye is caught by a photograph of Castle Place, in August 1952; as the caption notes 'there are a lot of pedestrians about, probably doing their shopping'.

What arrests me is the figure in the middle right foreground, who, unlike all the other pedestrians, is walking in the roadway, slightly to the left of the pavement. Although his back is turned towards the camera, I strongly suspect, from his postman's uniform, his cap tilted to the back of his head, the strap of the bag slung on his right shoulder, his dumpy personage and jaunty midstride, that this is my father. I suffer from progressive myopia, so I take off my glasses and peer more closely into the photograph to corroborate my initial vision, which might have been too good to be true; but yes, I recognize his dapper little feet, the way he walks with his hands held rather stiffly, and I'm told that I too have a stiff-handed walk, though I'd deny it. His general demeanour convinces me. The circumstances, too, are right: the art deco clock above Samuel's the Jewellers shows five past twelve, which time, I imagine, would coincide with the second delivery of the day, and my father must have just come from the GPO round the corner with a fresh batch of correspondence; and I know that for some years my father's beat, or 'walk' as it was called, included Cornmarket and its environs, towards which he is obviously headed, as he passes Swears & Wells the furriers, whose window is being gazed into by several elegant-looking ladies (illegible posters suggest a sale is going on).

I say I am convinced that this is my father; but, to be sure, I phone my brother Pat, who lives not far off; indeed, his presence is one of the reasons I came to live here in the first place. He arrives two or three minutes later. Looks at the photograph for a minute or two, pondering. He is 90 per cent certain; but he will check it out with my father, since he is going up to see him tomorrow (Sunday, January 1997) in Cushendun, some forty miles away, where he lives with my sister Caitlin.

If indeed it is my father, it is appropriate that he should be pho-tographed in the company of trams, for he always loved trams, and his happiest early memories are of being taken on the tram by his father to the various termini of Ligoniel, Dundonald, Castlereagh, Greencastle . . . The trams had a romance and a magic unlike any other vehicle, and when he travelled on the last tram to Ardoyne Depot he felt exiled from his past. Yet he saw the trams again, in his dreams: shortly after this, his father died suddenly; he had woken my father up for work one morning, and when he got home that afternoon, my father's father was dead; he had no time to say good-bye to him.

From that day, almost every night for twenty years, my father had the same dream: he is standing on the corner of Clonard Street and the Falls waiting for a trolleybus; but lo and behold, an old tram comes clattering down the road instead, and he is filled with joy. He is about to step on, but the tram will not stop for him, alas; it vanishes, city-bound into a smog. Wondering what this dream might mean, my father eventually plucked up courage to approach a doctor friend who had some acquaintance with psychology. 'In your subconscious mind', the doctor advised, 'there is a connection between your father and the trams. The tram represents your dead father; and you will never board that tram as long as you live, no matter how many times you dream about it.'

In the 1952 photograph, the two trams have an indomitable, upright presence, like Mississippi steamboats sailing nobly past each other, or vehicles invented by Jules Verne. I visualize the dark blue of their livery, the blue of many fathoms deep; and get the leather perfume of upholstered seats which let out a small gasp as you sat on them; and I remember my father taking me on the tram, on one of its last routes, to Ligoniel, where we would climb Wolfhill,* and gaze down like guardian angels across the city we had temporarily flown. Then we'd take the tram back home.

Eventually, my father did get to board the dream-tram. One St

---

*So-called because it was one of many places where the last wolf in Ireland had been killed.

Patrick's Day, egged on by my younger brothers Breandán and Liam, he fulfilled a long-standing promise to take them to the Transport Museum in Witham Street. When he entered, he had no time for the water-carts, the vintage cars and the steam loco-motives: he had eyes only for the tram, and when he climbed on board and ventured on to the open upper deck and sat down, he closed his eyes; for a while he was a boy again, voyaging to Greencastle, not the father of a family, but a father's son. When he opened his eyes they were filled with tears. And he never dreamt about the trams again.

Now, 'tomorrow' has become 'today', and my father's verdict on the photograph has come *via* Pat. He feels the postman is not him: although the circumstances seem to fit, there is one flaw in the proof: he wore his bag on his *left* shoulder, not his right.

The more I peer into the reproduction of the photograph, the more it disappears, as it becomes all dots and chiaroscuro, as I read narratives where there are none, ignorant of all the teeming others, and their names and destinations.

THE GENERAL POST OFFICE

Being the son of a postman, I was perhaps naturally inclined to become a stamp-collector, later attaining the status of a philatelist of sorts. Philately (there is a muddled etymology to this word, which I do not propose to go into) implies study, the classification and taxonomy of minutiae, of variations in dies, fonts, paper, watermarks and perforations; in this Lilliputian world, flaws and errors are as eagerly sought after as genetic mutations by microbiologists, or quarks by physicists. It was my still-implicit interest in stamps that led me to buy the Benjamin volume mentioned in the last chapter, because I'd serendipitously opened it at this passage, as I browsed the book in the shop:

> To someone looking through piles of old letters, a stamp that has long been out of circulation on a torn envelope often says more than a reading of dozens of pages . . . Stamps bristle with tiny

numbers, minute letters, diminutive leaves and eyes, They are graphic cellular tissue. All this swarms about and, like lower animals, lives on even when mutilated. This is why such powerful pictures can be made of pieces of stamps stuck together. But in them, life always bears a hint of corruption to signify that it is composed of dead matter. Their portraits and obscene groups are littered with bones and riddled with worms.

Of course, such acts of découpage would be anathema to the philatelist, though not that far removed from the practice of the tyro collector, who would glue stamps willy-nilly into school exercise-books, thus rendering them useless for exchange or study; but in time, those who persisted with their hobby would get to know the delicacy of hinges and protective mounts, the power of magnifying glasses, and the serried order of the perforation gauge.

In my early teens, having progressed thus far, I bought a spring-back loose-leaf album (the F.G. Kent, manufactured by Frank Godden Ltd., 111–112 The Strand, London WC2) with 'leaves of heavy paper, cream-tinted, groove-fluted and printed with feint quadrille'; also, an Osmiroid fountain-pen with interchangeable nibs; and *How to Arrange and Write-up a Stamp Collection*, by Stanley Phillips & C.P. Rang,* published by Stanley Gibbons Ltd., the Vatican of the philatelic world, who still maintain a premises at 391 The Strand. I practised for hours, and learned a passable block roundhand which still serves a purpose on occasions, as

---

*I still love this name: one can, of course, read it as the past tense of a verb; more interestingly 'rang' is Irish for 'class', cognate, no doubt, with 'rung' (as in a ladder) and 'rank'.

when I recently inscribed the date, and the names of the bride and groom in my sister in law's wedding album. 'Leo van Es, Oonagh Shannon, 23 August 1996'.

I was initially drawn to collect, sort, mount, and annotate the stamps of the British Empire, for I admired their sober, typographical designs and regal, defunct profiles, their inks of pale rose, carmine, lilac, slate, bistre, cobalt and vermilion; but this was a vast pandemic field, in which the minor Indian States alone – Chamba, Gwalior, Nabha, Faridkot, Sirmoor, Rajpipla, Travancore and Cochin, to name a few – took up some seventy pages of the Gibbons catalogue. Gradually, I began to specialize in Great Britain and Ireland; then, moved, perhaps, by a latent republicanism, I confined myself to Ireland alone.

> Until the creation of the Irish Free State in 1921, Ireland had always used our British stamps, but then fresh arrangements had to be made. At first the British stamps were simply overprinted with the words 'Saorstat Eireann', but in 1922 a newly designed issue came into use. Some of these bore a map of the whole of Ireland – and that, of course, is hardly correct, since the six Northern counties are not in the Free State at all, but remain part of the United Kingdom. It is now many years since those stamps were issued, but the error has not yet been put right.
>
> T. Todd, *Stamps of the Empire*, London, 1938

This is not entirely accurate: in fact, the first Irish stamps were the current GB issues, overprinted in 'Gaelic'* type with the

---

*Commissioned, I believe, by Elizabeth I, for the first Irish translation of the Bible, by William Bedel, in 1681–85.

words 'Rialtas Sealadach na hÉireann' (Provisional Government of Ireland). These appeared on 17 February 1922; the 'Saorstát Éireann' (Irish Free State) overprints came later, on 6 December. Their ephemeral and contingent nature is manifest in the plethora of minor varieties which exist: broken type, missing or reversed accents, a spectrum of inks, fine distinctions in alignments and spacings.

> When the overprinted stamps first appeared they unfortunately received undue attention from speculators, which caused excessive inflation of prices, followed by the inevitable slump. Now that they are obtainable at reasonable prices, however, they offer very wide scope for philatelic study and should rank with other dominions in the regard of philatelists. The uncertain political tendencies also make surprises always possible.
>
> *The Regent Priced Catalogue of the Postage Stamps of the British Commonwealth of Nations*, London, 1934

One could quite easily, I imagine, devote a lifetime's study to these early cancellations of the Empire and their typographical minutiae: I was overawed by the immensity of the task, which could be almost infinitely extended if one also took into consideration what Benjamin calls 'the occult part of the stamp: the postmark', the sometimes indecipherable demography of hours, dates, and names of places. I collected a few nominal examples of the Provisionals before moving on to the Definitive Series.

The first Definitive Issue, of 6 December 1922, with twelve values, from the ½d bright green to the 1s bright blue, uses four designs: the Sword of Light, the Map of Ireland (including the Six

Counties, and without a political border), the Arms of Ireland (all four provinces) and the Celtic Cross, another icon of completeness and eternal status. The Commemorative Issues, beginning in 1929 with Daniel O'Connell (Catholic Emancipation Centenary), are equally propagandist; they include the Shannon Barrage Completion of Shannon Hydro Electricity Scheme, 1930), the Adoration of the Cross (International Eucharistic Congress, 1932), a Hurler (Golden Jubilee of the Gaelic Athletic Association, 1934), and Ireland and the New Constitution (Constitution Day, 29 December 1937), which shows an art nouveau female figure resting her left hand on a harp, her right on a partly opened scroll which reads 'In Ainm na Trionóide Ró-Naomhtha' (In the Name of the Most Holy Trinity).

The commemoratives of 1941, the 25th anniversary of the Easter Rising, provide an interesting ideological detour.

Easter was very late that year. Monday, 24 April 1916, was a mild sunny day in Dublin, which was virtually deserted, huge crowds (including most of the officers and men from the British Garrison) making their way out of the city in the early morning to the Fairy House race-course for the first big meeting of the season. Apart from a few bystanders the only people to be seen in the city streets were members of the Irish Volunteer Force and the Irish Citizen Army, but, since Sir Edward (later Lord) Carson had founded the Ulster Volunteers in Belfast three years earlier, in a blatant attempt to resist any move by the British Government to grant Home Rule to Ireland, the spectacle of armed men drilling openly was quite commonplace.

James A. Mackay, *Eire: The Story of Eire and her Stamps*, London, 1968

The first Easter Rising commemoratives, which appeared on 12 April 1941, are defined by Gibbons' British Empire catalogue as 'provisional issues': these were the standard 2d map of Ireland and the 3d Celtic Cross, in new colours, orange and blue, overprinted with '1941 I GCUIMHNE AISÉIRGHE 1916' (in memory of the *resurrection* of 1916 – the Rising, after all, was conceived as a liturgical event) – an ironic reference, surely, to the first overprints, suggesting that the Republic is laying retrospective claim to its pre-1922 past, as well as to disputed territory. The definitive commemorative did not appear until 27 October. Why did it take so long? Was the committee split over the appropriateness of celebrating armed rebellion? Mackay continues

Shortly before noon on 24th April a body of about sixty irregulars . . . (now welded together to form the Army of the Irish Republic) passed down Sackville Street and halted outside the General Post Office. The man in command of them, James Connolly, Commandant-General of the IRA, gave the order to charge. Swiftly they entered the building, disarmed the constable of the Dublin Metropolitan Police on duty, and summarily ejected the counter clerks and their customers. The windows on the ground floor were smashed and hastily barricaded, and sentries posted. At the rear of the building the Telegraph Instrument Room contained its normal complement of girl telegraphists under the supervision of Miss Gordon, the Assistant Superintendent. A sergeant and three privates were also on duty. Troops had been posted to guard the Instrument Room since the outbreak of war but only a few weeks before Easter 1916 their ammunition was suddenly withdrawn, so that on the fateful morning they were virtually unarmed. When they heard shots being fired at the front of the building they barricaded the door in the corridor connecting the public office with the Instrument Room, but by this time the rebels had entered by the back door and sprung into the room. This party was led by The O'Rahilly, who shot the sergeant when he made to resist.

The 2½d blue-black definitive commemorative of 1941 is known as the Gunman: it depicts a Gulliver-sized Volunteer armed with a bayoneted rifle, poised at his post above a Lilliputian GPO; the stamp has a sombre border like a death notice. Although the GPO looks to be in pristine condition, and not the bombed shell it became after the Rising, it is interesting to note that the four main varieties of the Gunman stamp are known as 'Broken Statue', 'Broken Pillar', 'Damaged Capital' and 'Broken Windows'; but these are minor flaws, detectable only to the magnifying-glass-armed keen-eyed philatelist comparative dimensions of Volunteer and GPO imply that the individual is more powerful than established authority, that his authority comes from the barrel of a gun, or is assumed by him in the name of those powerless to speak, for the stamp also bears the first words of Padraic Pearse's Proclamation: 'In ainm Dé agus in ainm na nglún d'imigh romhainn . . .' (In the name of God and of the generations that have gone before us . . .)

Banal, pious, badly drawn, next to worthless in monetary terms, the Gunman is not a beautiful stamp, but it fascinates me. I love the blue-black ink that seems to have a tint of bottle-green in it, so that it summons up the dull enamelled frames of Royal Ulster Constabulary bicycles armed with upright handlebars, three-speed Sturmey-Archer thumbswitch gears, stirrup brakes and faltering hub-dynamo lamps; the colour of gunpowder, broken slates or magnets; the ooze-blue clay of the Lagan at low tide; coke-smoke from the Gasworks; livid, live-lobster blue; rubber bullets, purple cobblestones, a smear of rotting blackberries; cinder-paths at dusk, when no one walks on them; the black arm-band of the temporary postal worker.

The Gunman stamp is both post script and prescription. In its subversion of authority, it installs a new authority. The taking of the Post Office was a symbolic act, for nowhere was the Crown as near ubiquitous as on postage stamps, these little emblems of the temporal realm that drop daily through your letter-box, representing complicated fiscal arrangements and mechanisms for their delivery. Sheets of stamps, books of stamps, coils of stamps unscrolling from antiquated cast-iron slot machines: one could make an epic documentary of one day's issue, salivated on by thousands of tongues, vast spectral demographies of deoxyribonucleic acid chromosomed into the sticky backs of stamps, thumbprinted on to envelopes, or impressed by one delicate trembling fingertip, the aura of gum still lingering like a retroactive kiss on the tongue. All of this takes place in boudoirs, public houses, studies, cafés, libraries, ports, railway stations, hotels, aerodromes, schools, surgeries, pleasure gardens, post offices, garages, on piers and esplanades, on board trains and boats and planes; correspondences seethe everywhere in steel and gold-nibbed copperplate and roundhand, in the braille of manual typescripts, in violet indelible pencil scrawls, in purple carbon slips, and ransom demands made up from cut-up newspaper headlines; declarations, proposals, deferments, invitations, assignations, refusals, bills, threats, promises, applications, accounts, submissions. The President of the Provisional Government of Ireland understood that in these documents the spirit of a nation resides.

> When Pearse summoned Cuchulainn to his side,
> What stalked through the Post Office? What intellect?
> What calculation, number, measurement replied?
>
> W.B. Yeats, 'The Statues'

It was said that Pearse had a cast in his right eye, and insisted on his photograph being taken in left profile: I remember one such black-and-white icon, hung on the kitchen wall of 100 Raglan Street, like a President Kennedy – the same upward-gazing, youthful aspiration – or the depiction of Edward VIII on the stamps of his short-lived British reign of 1936, all conferring in the ancient power of profile, like those on Roman coins, establishing their vast Caesarean dominions with obverse images of chariots, hooves of the Pegasus Express, streaming out like hyphened light from a Vatican radio beacon.

The cordon of steel gradually grew tighter and tighter around the Post Office, the heart of the rebel position. From all sides shells rained down on the once proud building and the end was inevitable. The Post Office, with its maze of basement corridors and stout walls, was well constructed to withstand bombardment and at one stage the military considered using poison gas to eliminate the rebel stronghold. Happily, this was not used, but a combination of high explosive and incendiary shells turned Sackville Street and Lower Abbey Street into a holocaust in which it seemed no one and nothing could survive. Under cover of the blaze the troops closed in, but it was not till Saturday morning that the final shelling and the capture of the Post Office took place. The majority of the rebels, in the meantime, succeeded in tunnelling their way out of the burning building. The rearguard, led by The O'Rahilly, was mown down by machine-guns in the closing encounter. Pearse, Connolly and a few others actually escaped through the main doorway under the noses of the besiegers and took refuge in a nearby grocer's shop. At 3.30 p.m. Padraic Pearse surrendered his sword to Brigadier General Lowe, who treated him with great courtesy.

James A. Mackay, *Eire: The Story of Eire and her Stamps*, London, 1968

And Pearse's profile puts me in mind of that of a Catholic priest, in bas-relief on a tomb in Milltown cemetery. The Revd Domhnall Ó Tuathail, a renowned Gaelic scholar, died in the pulpit on 3 December 1922, three days before the issue of the first 'Saorstát' overprinted stamps. His epitaph is taken from *Íosagán* (Little Jesus), a work of saccharine religiosity by Padraic Pearse: 'IS IOGHANTACH AN GRÁDH BHÍ AIGE DO'N NÍDH IS ÁILNE 'S IS GLAINE DÁR CHRUTHAIGH DIA: ANAM GLÉGHEAL AN PHÁISTE' (He had a wonderful love for the most beautiful and cleanest thing ever created by God: the shining soul of a child). The Reverend's left eye has been used by the faithful as a holy touchstone, and through time it has been worn into a polished black monocular socket. When I went back yesterday to check these details, I decided to have a look at the Republican plot as well. As I stood before its granite Ogham plinths, brows-ing the lapidary columns of names from 1798 on, I realized a British Army patrol had infiltrated Milltown from the Bog Meadows. I bowed my head as the soldiers filed slowly past me, cradling their guns like babies, scanning the regions of the living and the dead.

MILLTOWN CEMETERY

When British special forces shot dead an IRA team in Gibraltar in March 1988, the three bodies were brought to Belfast for martyrs' funerals. On 16 March at Milltown Cemetery, a lone Loyalist, Michael Stone, fired shots and threw grenades at the crowd, killing three people.

Jonathan Bardon and David Burnett, Belfast: A Pocket History, 1996

According to folklore, Michael Stone, when challenged, gained entrance to the heavily stewarded cemetery by uttering the Sinn Féin graffiti slogan, *Tiocfaidh ár lá* (our day will come). Apocryphal or not, the phrase is riddled with historical and linguistic ambiguity. Strictly speaking, *tiocfaidh ár lá* is bad Irish, based on an English subtext; in Irish, one cannot own a day (ownership being a hazy concept in that language) nor can a day have active volition. Accordingly, an alternative expression, *beidh an lá linn* is sometimes seen inscribed on gable walls – literally, the day will be with us, or in English, the day will be ours. This, it seems to me, is a reflection, conscious or not, of 'Lillibulero', 'the famous ballad in mockery of the Irish Catholics, which sung James II out three kingdoms', according to Chambers, 'from the meaningless refrain'. However, it is generally agreed, at least in Ireland, that the refrain (*lillibulero bullenala*, in full) is a corruption of the Irish, (*an*) *lile ba léir é, ba linn an lá*, that is, 'the lily was plain to be seen, and the day was ours'. A further irony: 'Lillibulero' was the theme tune of the old BBC World Service.*

The name Michael Stone carries a double reverberation: Michael is more usually associated with Catholics (hence the term 'Mickies'), who regard St Michael the Archangel as the conductor of the souls of the dead; and stone images of this angel are posted at some of the graves in Milltown Cemetery. An apologist for nominal predestination, à la Tristram Shandy, could make much of this case; or a psychiatrist might interpret Stone's act as one of revenge against his name. There are other twists – St Michael's was the principal voice heard by the French royalist, or loyalist, Joan of Arc; and the Archangel's role in leading a successful military campaign against the rebel forces of Lucifer might well have occurred to Stone. The word-bubble ambiguities of 'Michael Stone' rub up against each other like pebbles, accidentally contiguous on a huge beach.

---

*After writing this I consulted the traditional singer Brian Mullen, who has a new twist to the derivation: the Gaelic scholar Breandan Ó Buachalla has a most plausible theory that *Lile* refers to the astrologer William Lilly (1602–81), who made accurate prognostications about the outcome of the Jacobite wars.

Sometimes I am in religious awe of the power of names. Milltown is a banal enough example, but it carries for me a recollection of the tiny mill-village adjacent to the cemetery, which you approached by a steeply descending chalk-and-dirt loaney that took you off the broad thoroughfare of the Falls Road into a time-warped zone of half-occupied ancient staggered dwellings and a derelict mill that had once been powered by one of the many streams that emanated from Black Mountain, flowing beyond the mill into the misty fen of the Bog Meadows. There was a disused sandstone quarry nearby, carved out by artifice and weathering into a microcosmic Grand Canyon, which I used to explore in detail in my early teens, imagining brick-kilns, tunnels, chambered galleries and mausoleums within its compass. Then, St Gall's Gaelic Athletic Club maintained its HQ in the rear of the moribund Milltown Industrial School, a grim-looking building which might formerly have been the mill-owner's residence, and was taken over by the De la Salle Brothers who managed St Gall's Public Elementary School. I am a past pupil of the school, and an erstwhile member of the club, which acquired some ground on the verge of the Bog Meadows and was made, by dint of some voluntary and moonlighted labour, into a hurling and football field. In my day, it was rough, slanted and bumpy, with baldy patches in it; now, when I perceive it, driving on the M1 through the remnants of the Meadows, it has been ironed out into a broad green flat sward; and there, just beside it, is the tiny red pit of the quarry.

It was on the former pitch that my left retina was detached

when I jumped to catch a high ball and the *sliotar** was deflected by my fingertips against my open eye, and I became instantly half-blind. The remedy for this injury, in my case, was to lie in a hospital bed for a week without moving my head, in order to allow the retina to regenerate its contact with the vitreous humour. This inordinately boring operation was indeed a success, but I attribute some of my steadily progressive myopia to that accidental, or mishandled ricochet. It requires me to look closer into things.

Driving on the M1 at night south of Milltown, you can observe a curious optical phenomenon, as the headlights of the passing traffic bounce off the gravestones and the blank stone eyes of archangels in an orchestra of random constellated Morse, like the flash outbursts of Olympian photography in colossal stadiums, and you feel the dead are signalling to you.

The stream that powered the mill was the same that gushed from a rocky orifice on Black Mountain and gurgled down the Mountain Loaney, a steep winding limestone path which was both river-bed and road, and in summer it was great to walk barefoot up it with your shoes tied around your neck, relishing the ache of your palpable soles against the pebbles, and the bracelets of cold water chilling around your ankles. When you'd made it to the spring, you'd put your mouth to its forceful gout and gulp it breathlessly and thankfully, as it spattered your face and hair and rinsed away, with a glacial

---

*'A good quantity, as of food at a meal, a hurley-ball' – Revd Patrick S. Dinneen, *An Irish–English Dictionary*, 1927.

shock to the brain, all thoughts of tiredness. Then it was time to turn around, and look back and down at the city you had come from.

Here and there, scattered throughout the maze of factories, mills, barracks, schools, the filing-systems of terraced houses, are glints and gleams of water: mill-dams, reservoirs, ponds, sinks, and sluices, all fed by the little rivers springing from the Antrim Hills: the Forth River, the Mile Water, the Clowney Water, the Falls Water. Without this water, there would be no Belfast as we know it, since its industries were impossible without it. Wandering at ground level within the dense urban fabric of brick walls, in the valleys of shadow cast by the tall factories with their blanked-out windows, it was beautiful to get, through the iron rails of a locked factory gate, a glimpse of a wind-rippled mill-dam on which drifted a flotilla of swans. All of Belfast murmurs with innumerable rills, subterranean and otherwise, like the Farset River that ran below the yard of St Gall's School in Waterville Street.

Without the Farset, the name of Belfast would not be.

The late Deirdre Flanagan, in her authoritative study, *Béal Feirste agus Áitainmneacha Laistigh** (*Topothesia*, Galway, 1982), notes that the 'educated' accent on the first syllable, Bélfast, has been prevalent for at least three generations, preceding the admittedly powerful influence of the British Broadcasting Corporation; but many of the working class pronounce it Belfást, as do most country people, and practically all of my father's generation

---

*'Belfast, and place names within it'.

(those few who survive), since the Irish *Béal Feirste*, from whence it derives, is weighted on the last syllable. What the name means is another thing:

> The utmost obscurity and perplexity, however, attend the derivation of the name . . . the name of Bealafarsad, which means, according to some, hurdleford town,* while others have translated it, the mouth of the pool. Either of these explanations might receive some corroboration from local facts, but as it is a matter of complete hypothesis, there seems to be further room for further speculation.

So wrote the exasperated George Benn, in 1823. Dubourdieu, writing some years earlier, claims that Belfast 'is supposed to have derived its name from Bela Fearsad, which signifies a town at the mouth of a river, expressive of the circumstances, in which it stands'. Ward, Lock's *Guide to Northern Ireland* (no date, but it looks like a 1950s job) has yet another version: 'While the bell in Belfast's civic coat-of-arms is a feeble pun, the word "fast" refers to the "farset", or sandbank (also the now-covered-in High Street river "Bel" in Celtic means "ford", i.e. Bel-feirste, the "bel", or "ord" of the "farset")'.

Here is Deirdre Flanagan (in my inadequate translation):

> Despite authoritative glosses by scholars on the appellation 'Belfast' since the times of Joyce,† its etymology remains largely

---

*Interestingly, the Irish for Dublin, *Baile Átha Cliath*, means precisely 'hurdleford town'.

†Patrick Weston Joyce, social historian, musician, linguist and geographer, 1827–1914.

misunderstood, especially by the general public – the notion that
it means the mouth of the river called the 'Farset'.

She then draws our attention to numerous sources which corroborate her assertion that the name of Belfast derives from the
ford or sand-bank in the River Lagan. *En route*, she quotes some
interesting sixteenth-century English mutations: 'Belferside,
Bealefarst (an old castle standing on a ford), Bellfarst, Kellefarst
(sic), Bellfarste, Bellfaste, Belfaste, Belferst, Belfirst, Belfyrst,
Belfarst, Befersyth, Beserstt, Belfast', and I imagine these
Shakespearians in doublets mangling the Irish language with their
tongues as they strut on the bridge across the River Farset, or the
Town River, conducting important business.

The first reference to anything resembling Belfast is in the
Annals of Ulster, '*Bellum Fertsi inter Ultu & Cruitne, 668 AD*', a piv-
otal battle resembling a mirror of the Battle of the Boyne in 1690,
and glossed on by Jonathan Bardon in his magisterial *Belfast: An
Illustrated History* as a battle between 'the Ulaid, a warrior caste of
the Erinn' and 'the mysterious Cruithin, a people closely connected with the Picts of Northern Britain.' Bardon gives the date
as 666 AD, an altogether more apocalyptic number, being the one
of the marks of the Beast which appears before the end of the
world in the Bible. It is not my role to establish which of these
dates is right, but their disagreement accords with the slippery
metathesis of *fertas* – the earliest record of the word – into *fearsad*.
Patrick Dinneen in his 1927 edition of *An Irish–English Dictionary*
glosses it as a shaft, a spindle, the ulna of the arm, a club, the
spindle of an axle, a bar or bank of sand at low water, a deep

narrow channel on a strand at low tide, a pit or pool of water, a verse, a poem. In keeping with all of this, my father tells me that the Axis forces in the Second World War were known in Irish as *Lucht na Feirste*, the Axle People, as if they had recently invented the wheel; or you can see the word as the snub hub of a Stuka's propeller blades.

Serendipitously, the Farset is an axis between the Catholic Falls and the Protestant Shankill, as its power source was responsible for a string of mills in which both denominations were employed, with separate entrances for Prods and Taigs from North and South of the divide, notwithstanding the same terrible conditions, producing linen which they could never afford to buy. Instead, the women who wrought in the mills made underwear for their children out of flour-bags.

The most satisfactory translation of Belfast, according to Deirdre Flanagan, is 'approach to ford'. I register this meaning tentatively, remembering or peering at the Farset, though I didn't know its name then, between the rusted bars of the iron railing of the entry at the back of St Gall's Public Elementary School in Waterville Street, gazing down at its dark exhausted water, my cheeks pressed against the cold iron. I did not know its name, then, but was mesmerized by its rubbish: a bottomless bucket, the undercarriage of a pram, and the rusted springs sticking out of the wreck of a sunk abandoned sofa.

THE BUNAGLOW

The three-piece suite, comprising a chesterfield and two companion armchairs, was traditionally focused around the hearth so as to form a winter stockade, beyond which was Arctic lino; within was a warm snug, where the fire threw flickering patterns over the bit of mesmerizing Persian carpet. On the mantelpiece, besides the dead-centred analogue clock and the two mute china dogs, there'd be a brass letter-rack in the shape of a turf-cutter's donkey and cart (a souvenir of Galway) crammed with buff envelopes; a tin of Rinstead pastilles; a snowstorm featuring the Eiffel tower; a pewter mug half-filled with loose buttons, foreign coins and pencil-stubs, etcetera. In lieu of television, we stared into the burning coals, dimly aware of the disembodied static voice of the bakelite sun-burst-grilled art deco radio, sometimes making our own sporadic conversation, or listening to my father repeat a story for the third time that week. At Family Rosary time, these circumstances would be overturned, as we knelt down and dug our faces into the dulled velveteen cushions, trying to contemplate the Mysteries without deviation, exploring the mental darkness in the interstices of the chesterfield, feeling the posterior heat; decades slipped through our fingers, as the quarter-hour of mantra dragged towards its terminus.

Some years ago, I inherited a nearly identical piece, its scuffed hide beginning to fray and split into hyphens between its regimented sentences of brass tacks: I was about to say 'carbon-copy', with its implication of shirt-button-keyed manual typewriters; but the flimsy sheet itself, that left blue smooches on your fingertips, is wrong on this occasion. The chesterfield came from Sans Souci Park, where I had shared a house with three peers;* when we split up, as is the inevitable wont of four unmarried heterosexual male cohabitees, the furniture went different ways. I still have the utility oak bed, dressing-table and wardrobe with its mirror Narnia door, a suite that I bought in a defunct auction rooms whose name I can't remember, but whose premises lay where the old Dublin Road Toll House in Bradbury Place used to be. Its one low storey was flanked by tall Victorian buildings, making it look like a tea-cosy cottage; its threshold lay below pavement level, its lintel below head height, so that, stooping into the imaginary room beyond, one could visualize the slow metronome of a pendulum clock, and a kitchen dresser with its orchestra of Delft placated by the light of a Vermeer interior. The

---

*One of them was the artist, John Kindness, whose 'Belfast Frescoes' are discussed in the chapter 'Electric Street'.

same calm brightness falls across the crinkles of a wall-map, or pours like cream from the blue jug, as it dots the bodice buttons of the girl who is reading a letter: gazing at this reproduction of a painting, we eavesdrop on its silent narrative, whose full story we will never know, since its rendering, in salient places, is deliberately illegible. What seem like pearls weighed on a minim scale are weightless blips of light.

In my childish circumstances, the scroll-armed chesterfield would sometimes become a flying-machine, a hybrid of Verne's Clipper of the Clouds and Andersen's Flying Trunk. Crewed by three or four children (though one could manage it with ease) it made remarkable expeditions for such an ostensibly floor-bound item. We often flew to Turkey in it and back in the space of a day, or less. We would always remember the sherbet fountains, the elaborate hubble-bubble pipes and refractory camels, the scent of kif and kumquats drowsing through the alleyways and cool arcades; when night came, suddenly as brushed mascara, we knew that it was time to leave. After describing some Immelmann turns and loop-the-loops, we'd return the vehicle safely to home base, gliding through the immaterial walls, hovering for an instant above the four cardinal points of its castor-dents in the lino, before settling into them, as if programmed.

At any rate, the Sans Souci chesterfield – no, 'settee' is what it had become by then – became part of the furniture of 'The Bunaglow', where my wife Deirdre and I lived for seven years. The Bunaglow is the gardener's cottage attached to Riddel Hall, formerly , according to the 1948 Directory, a 'Residence for Women Students at Queen's University: Miss Power Steel,

Resident Wdn., Miss Boyd, matron; Richard Chamberlain, gardener', and latterly, the headquarters of the Arts Council of Northern Ireland, where, at the time of writing, I have worked for twenty-one years. In 1948, neither Hall nor cottage were numbered; some thirty years on, the Post Office designated the Hall as '181a Stranmillis Road', and the cottage as The Bungalow opposite 198 Stranmillis Road' (occupied, in 1948, by Miss V. Jolly); but the metathetic computer of the Northern Ireland Electricity Service addressed its bills to 'The Bunaglow', and it is still called that by us, in spite of a recent rationalization whereby the Arts Council is 185 and the cottage 187.

'Bunaglow', in English, sounds like a brand of coal or anthracite; more interestingly, if accented on the last syllable, it can be exactly transliterated into Irish as *'bun na gcló'*, a phrase redolent with ambiguity, but almost impossible to translate. 'Bottom of the shapes' is a possible interpretation, but not entirely satisfactory. 'Bun' is a base, a bottom, foundation; but it can be extended in many ways, as elucidated by the Revd Patrick S. Dinneen, in a full column of his marvellous *Irish-English Dictionary* (new edition, 1927). To take some instances: *'ar bun'*, established; *'tá an teanga ar bun'*, the language is alive; *'an madadh rua i mbun na gcearc'*, the fox guarding the hens; *'téim 'na bhun'*, I set about doing it; *'bun an urláir'*, the floor furthest from the fire, three tricks at cards; *'bun ribe'*, a carbuncle or excrescence. *'Cló'* is a stamp, type, print, impression, as in the expressions *'ar a shon gan a bheith ann acht a chló, d'aithneochtha gur tarbh a b'eadh é'*, though it was only the embryo you could see it was a bull-calf; *'cuireadh 'na cló chum póige'*, the expression of her face inviting a kiss; '*ba thaitneamhach cló*', who was of entrancing beauty; '*an cló*', the printing press; and '*cló*' is also the act of conquering, subjugation, destruction, defeat; variety, change. So, depending on context, '*bun na gcló*' can mean the origin of species, the establishment of stamps, the bottom line, a fount of images, an authority of peers, the arbiter of fashion, Commander of the Echelons, a bank of type, a metronome, the basics of taxonomy, the founder of a dynasty or sect, monotype, the genesis of embryos, Platonic forms, the inspiration for a memoir, Master of the Rolls, the original cliché, an impersonator or inventor, a minutebook, the *primum mobile*, the foot of tributaries, the General Post Office, where they all hang out, an ABC, a catalogue, a tramline terminus, party lines, 'the cynosure of all eyes', the Royal Mint, 'render unto Caesar what is Caesar's', where the buck stops, a tinder-box, Aladdin's lamp, a veritable Tower of Babel; in other words, a jungle.

The Bunaglow lies within a unique suburban precinct of half-wild woodland and parkland made up of the grounds of the Arts Council, Stranmillis College, Queen's Elms Halls of Residence, and Lennoxvale House, formerly the residence of the Vice-Chancellor of Queen's University: comprising, perhaps, about seventeen acres, give or take a few; but its microcosmic ecosystem is immeasurable. Here are badgers, foxes, rabbits, field mice, owls; glades packed with bluebells, entanglements of wild roses, rhododendrons, hawthorns; a little espaliered crab-apple orchard; arbours, formal lawns, a derelict tennis court, two large ornamental ponds (formerly a principal source of water for the town of Belfast); mazy mossy pathways, gravel walks and cobbled courtyards. There is one ancient knobbly oak, a survivor of the aboriginal forest of the Lagan Valley. Plunging off the track into the remnant woods, you get a whiff of what it must have been, as your feet slide into the soft mulch and the fungal dead-leaf aroma is cut by the diuretic tang of stinging-nettles; the place is dense with whispering of insects and the noise of the leaves as they strive towards the light; dryads murmur from within the trees, and moths flit through the dappled moonshine, trembled by a zephyr. If you listen closely, you can hear the occasional swash of a car, far away on a dark suburban road. And for an instant, in a migraine flicker, you imagine yourself in the motor's cockpit, manipulating the big Mercedes emblem of the steering wheel, absorbing the luminous blips of its console, as you drive full-beam into the tunnel of the calibrated dark, observing the insignia of street-names momentarily as you pass them, knowing the assignation will be met, or not. Then with a rush you're back alone in the woods, where a night-owl hoots like a muted car-horn.

Years passed in a wing-beat. I shivered, and decided to go back to where the Bunaglow lay in its Hansel-and-Gretel dell at the end of a sylvan tunnel. I knew there'd still be a low glow in the fire; I imagined a man slumped in an armchair before it, thoughtfully smoking a pipe, and rehearsing the story he'd tell me when I got in.

THE *TITANIC*

There are many stories told about the *Titanic*: labyrinthine anecdotes, moral tales, recovered memories, retrospective omens.
Here is a small sample of them:

For months and months in that monstrous iron enclosure there
was nothing that had the faintest likeness to a ship; only something that might have been the iron scaffolding for the naves of
half-a-dozen cathedrals laid end to end . . . at last the skeleton
within the scaffolding began to take shape, at the sight of which
men held their breaths. It was the shape of a ship, a ship as monstrous and unthinkable that it towered there over the buildings
and dwarfed the very mountains by the water . . . A rudder as big
as a giant elm tree, bosses and bearings of propellers the size of
windmills — everything was on a nightmare scale; and underneath the iron foundations of the cathedral floor men were laying,
on concrete beds, pavements of oak and great cradles of timber
and iron and sliding ways of pitch pine to support the bulk of the

monster when she was moved, every square inch of the pavement surface bearing a weight of more than two tons. Twenty tons of tallow were spread upon the ways, and hydraulic rams and triggers built and fixed against the bulk of the ship, so that, when the moment came, the waters she was to conquer should thrust her finally from the earth.

Wyn Craig Wade, *The Titanic: End of a Dream*, 1979

The R.M.S. *Titanic* was built by Messrs. Harland & Wolff at their well-known shipbuilding works at Queen's Island, Belfast, side by side with her sister ship the *Olympic*. The twin vessels marked such an increase in size that specially laid-out joiner and builder ships were prepared to aid in their construction, and the space usually taken up by three building slips was given up to them. The keel of the *Titanic* was laid on March 31, 1909, and she was launched on May 31, 1911; she passed her trials before Board of Trade officials on March 31, 1912, at Belfast, arrived at Southampton on April 4th, and sailed the following Wednesday, April 10th, with 2,208 passengers and crew, on her maiden voyage to New York. She called at Cherbourg the same day, Queenstown Thursday, and left for New York in the afternoon, expecting to arrive the following Wednesday morning. But the voyage was never completed. She collided with an iceberg on Sunday at 11.45 p.m. in Lat. 41° 46′ N. and Long. 50° 14′ W., and sank two hours and a half later; 815 of her passengers and 688 of her crew were drowned and 705 rescued by the *Carpathia*.

Lawrence Beesley, *The Loss of the Titanic*, 1912

A floating palace sailed from Southampton in 1898 on her maiden voyage. She was the biggest and grandest liner ever built, and rich passengers savoured her luxury as they journeyed to

America. But the ship never reached her destination: her hull was ripped open by an iceberg and she sank with heavy loss of life.

That liner existed only on paper, in the imagination of a novelist called Morgan Robertson. The name he gave to his fictional ship was *Titan*, and the book's title was *Futility*.

Both the fiction and the futility were to turn into terrifying fact. Fourteen years later a real luxury liner set out on a similar maiden voyage. She too was laden with rich passengers. She too rammed an iceberg and sank; and, as in Robertson's novel, the loss of life was fearful because there were not enough lifeboats. It was the night of April 14, 1912. The ship was the R.M.S. *Titanic*.

Passenger's preview of doom

In many other ways than the similarity of their names the *Titan* of Robertson's novel was a near duplicate of the real *Titanic*. They were roughly the same size, had the same speed and the same carrying capacity of about 3000 people. Both were 'unsinkable'. And both sank in exactly the same spot in the North Atlantic.

But the strange coincidences do not end there. The famous journalist W.T. Stead published, in 1892, a short story which proved to be an uncanny preview of the *Titanic* disaster. Stead was a spiritualist: he was also one of the 1513 people who died when the *Titanic* went down.

Backward recollection

Neither Robertson's horror novel nor Stead's prophetic story served as a warning to *Titanic*'s captain in 1912. But a backward recollection of that appalling tragedy did save another ship in similar circumstances 23 years later.

A young seaman called William Reeves was standing watch in the bow of a tramp steamer, Canada-bound from Tyneside in

1935. It was April – the month of the iceberg disasters, real and fictional – and young Reeves had brooded deeply on them. His watch was due to end at midnight. This, he knew, was the time the *Titanic* had hit the iceberg. Then, as now, the sea had been calm.

These thoughts took shape and swelled into omens in the seaman's mind as he stood his lonely watch. His tired, bloodshot eyes strained ahead for any sign of danger, but there was nothing to be seen; nothing but a horizonless, impenetrable gloom. He was scared to shout an alarm, fearing his shipmates' ridicule. He was scared not to.

Then suddenly he remembered the exact date the *Titanic* went down – April 14, 1912. The coincidence was terrifying: it was the day he had been born.* Reeves' mounting sense of doom flared into panic-stricken certainty. He shouted out a danger warning, and the helmsman rang the signal: engines full astern. The ship churned to a halt – just yards from a huge iceberg that towered menacingly out of the blackness of the night.

More deadly icebergs crowded in around the tramp steamer, and it took nine days for Newfoundland icebreakers to smash a way clear.

The name of the little ship that came so near to sharing the *Titanic*'s fate? She was called the *Titanian*.

The Reader's Digest Book of Strange Stories, Amazing Facts, London, 1975

I regret I omitted in my last year's Ephemeris to record the death of my old friend and correspondent, Mr. R.H. Penny, better known as 'Neptune'. I have known him for about 40 years. He was a most honest and conscientious man, and the late Mr James Burns, Editor of the *Medium and Daybreak*, told me

---

*My father, William Carson, was born on 14 April 1916.

personally that he (Mr. Penny) was the most conscientious man he had ever met.

Mr. Penny was also very friendly with the late Mr. W.T. Stead, the editor and proprietor of the *Review of Reviews*, and did all he could to persuade that gentleman from undertaking that fatal journey to America. As many of my readers will recollect, he was drowned with hundreds of others in the *Titanic*, which struck an iceberg and was totally lost. I have often thought it strange that Mr. Stead's familiar Spirit *Julia* did not warn him of the impending disaster. He had unbounded faith in this entity, and her admonition might have saved him from a premature death.

Incidentally, I may remark that Mr. Stead was a friend to Astrologers.

Mr. Penny was also fond of Spiritualism and the Occult sciences generally. He was a clever Astrologer, and I miss his correspondence very much.

Raphael's Astronomical Ephemeris of the Planets' Places for 1922

The night was one of the most beautiful I have ever seen: the sky without a single cloud to mar the perfect brilliance of the stars, clustered so thickly together that in places there seemed almost more dazzling points of light set in the black sky than background of sky itself; and each star seemed, in the keen atmosphere, free from any haze, to have increased its brilliance tenfold and to twinkle and glitter with a staccato flash that made the sky seem nothing but a setting made for them in which to display their wonder. They seemed so near, and their light so much more intense than ever before, that fancy suggested they saw this beautiful ship in dire distress below and all their energies had awakened to flash messages across the black dome of the sky to each other, telling and warning of the calamity happening in the world beneath . . .

I had often wanted to see her from some distance away, and only a few hours before, in conversation at lunch with a fellow passenger, I had registered a vow to get a proper view of her lines and dimensions when we landed at New York: to stand some distance away to take in a full view of her beautiful proportions, which the narrow approach to the dock at Southampton made impossible. Little did I think that the opportunity was to be found so quickly and so dramatically. The background, too, was a different one from what I had planned for her: the black outline of her profile against the sky was bordered all round by stars studded in the sky: her bulk was seen where the stars were blotted out. And one other thing was different from expectation: the thing that ripped away from us instantly, as we saw it, all sense of the beauty of the night, the beauty of the ship's lines, and the beauty of her lights – and all these taken in themselves were intensely beautiful – that thing was the awful angle made by the level of the sea with the rows of porthole lights along her side in dotted lines, row above row. The sea-level and the rows of light should have been parallel – should never have met – and now they met at an angle inside the black hull of the ship.

Lawrence Beesley, *The Loss of the Titanic*, 1912.

My edition of *The Loss of the Titanic* was published by Philip Allan & Co. in their 'Nautilus Library' series, reminding me of Jules Verne's Nemo, of underwater exploration, and my own dreams about the *Titanic*, where I am a disembodied robotic eye, gliding like a wayward star through the adits of its wrecked Atlantean cathedral, or through a porthole oculus, taking account of tilted apses and saloons, wandering their marble stairs and passageways.

THE STAR FACTORY I

The Star Factory had been long since demolished, but bits of its structure still lay at the back of my mind. Floating through its corridors, ascending its resounding Piranesi iron staircases, or wading through a flooded loading-bay, I realized that for some time I had confused the Factory with other establishments, or other purposes, and its dimensions had expanded. Exterior adjuncts of itself lay scattered on the landscape like relics of a bombed city. Other images ran parallel to it: the asbestos-roofed outbuildings on the margins of abandoned airfields, or the skull-and-crossbones signs on electricity pylons and perimeter fences; sometimes I could hear the clicking of defunct railway signals and the solitary parps of car horns; more often than not – on at least two or three occasions – I found myself re-entering the turnstiles of the Falls Road Baths with my hired bathing trunks and towel, experiencing its warm chlorine atmosphere almost instantly. Then I felt a discovered-cupboard memory of putting on a gas-mask from the nearly recent war, of my face being absorbed by its aromatic black rubber interior and taint of antique fear.

Or, according to another narrative, the Factory contained a great secret. Beneath the ankle-deep oily water that covered the terrazzo floor of one particularly murky corridor, discarded or lost objects could be detected shimmering: keys, watches, gold rings, a salamander brooch, watches, gold rings, fountain pens, the porcelain arm of a doll, like things scattered on the sea-bed from some titanic wreck. These must have been the votive offerings of pilgrims, metaphors for past lives or the lives they wished to follow, like the pennies we throw into wishing-wells or the shallow depths of public fountains. Many employed stratagems of augury before they came; but their observation of the avian paths afforded them no insight, for their futures would be altered by the very fact of entering the Factory.

Hence, there were dynasties of paths and destinations. Each family would tend towards certain entrances or adits, and the abstract space within was riddled with the swarming wormholes of their past and present; they moved, indeed, like slow illiterate teredos who might absorb the ink of letters oblivious to their freight of meaning, who browse on commas and full stops, and then enjoy a colon, inhabiting a sentence without digesting it. They had no thread of Ariadne. Of necessity, the story they had entered comprised many stories, yet their diverse personal narratives and many-layered time-scales evinced glimpses of an underlying structure, like a traffic flow-chart with its arteries and veins and capillaries.

They called this the Zone. The Zone was not the Factory, though it was of the Factory and bore its aura. It was an interactive blueprint; not virtual, but narrative reality. It was called the Zone in order to distinguish it from all the other enclaves into which the previous city had been long divided; these were proper nouns with lineages of real names and topography behind them – Shankill, Falls, Ardoyne, Rosetta – and their nomenclators were maintained in high esteem. It was they who had been first consulted when the Zone appeared.

Period eye-witness accounts are notoriously unreliable, though it is retrospectively agreed that something happened. Some saw it as a tremor of the atmosphere, a visible shivering as if some new colour had been added to the spectrum; others felt the city bodily lifted up and set down again in slow motion. Crucifixes were reported to have fallen off bedroom walls at the exact time. Some others, in hindsight, swore blind that they had been in times and places where they'd never been; someone heard a cock crow thrice in the unlikely vicinity of the Clock Bar, where, it was rumoured, the minute hand had jumped back ten minutes, thus restoring it to that oxymoron, legal bar-time. There were many sightings of angels, some of whom bore swords of light. Dogs howled unaccountably, as they would at the sound of an ice-cream vendor's chimes or the vibrations of a red accordion.

One observer described, with great reluctance, how a Brobdingnagian space vehicle had materialized above the city, its Argus multitudes of portholes blinking in an alien Morse. Pods had then evolved in lifeboat mode from the womb of the mother ship, drifting and descending like a dandelion propaganda drop of tiny Zeppelins. Meanwhile, he perceived its great dark broad Polaroid VDU windscreen glance down at him with split-second infinite incomprehension before it turned its gaze to the more important ship-building and tobacco manufactory quarters. Then it vanished, as if 'was' had never been.

Such were the stories my father would tell me, gleaned or reinvented, I suppose, from early speculative fiction cinema and obscure Esperanto novels, which language he had learned in order to subvert the world dominance of English. He corresponded with fellow Esperantists in the Soviet Union, China, Holland, the Vatican City, and Springfield, Massachusetts. Just after the war, one of his agents in a remote province of the eastern Union had imparted, through their long-established book-code, the news of some great cataclysm in the forested interior, whose epicentre was a disused salt-mine. These details tallied with his recollections of the sudden demise of the Star Factory.

As he told it, I could visualize the mine's Darwinian interior, fossil-strewn, honeycombed with snow-crystal-starred vaulted caverns lighted flickeringly by antiquated flambeaux. Hoary workers, beards and eyebrows rimed with salt like polar explorers, struggled doggedly among its veins and seams and lodes and nodes of rare commodity. Gangs of metronomic hod-carriers moved in insect single file on regiments of scaffolding and ladders, as if reconstructing Babel underground; their whispered echo-chambered conversations sounded like white noise.

This, in turn, might lead to the story of why the sea is salt, or we might ponder the meaning of the phrase 'to salt a mine' – 'to introduce pieces of ore, etc. into the workings so as to delude prospective purchasers or share-holders into the idea that a worthless mine is in reality a profitable investment', and my father would then recall that Judas Iscariot is identified in Leonardo's *Last Supper* by the salt-cellar knocked over accidentally by his arm. Salt of baptism, salt of preservation, salt of salary, salt of the earth: in its ritual duplicities and confirmations, a grain of salt could be an emblem of the Star Factory, and it was likely that the Grail which lay at the Factory's heart was saline. Those who sought the starry rock did so out of many motives – selfish, altruistic – and their findings were ambiguous, since what they found, invariably, was not what they were looking for. Some were disappointed by this narrative device; others were illuminated; none could relate what they had seen, since this too was a precondition of the story – that its unexpected obstacles, its twists of character and plot, remain unsharable.

In other versions, the Grail would take the form of an Aztec crystal skull, where the explorer was required to plunge his thumbs into its empty eye-sockets, with dazzling effect. We saw liana-tangled cities of the recently discovered lost Americas; jungle-torn pyramids and pylons soared through tattered wraiths of cloud; unknown, multicoloured birds arrayed the spars of a galleon stranded in the tree-tops; and recumbent idols gazed at us with baleful eyes and lips. Following with difficulty the time-worn sketch-map, we would fall through trap-doors in the forest floor, or were caught in sudden snares that left us dangling by one leg in mid-air; we encountered snakepits, blowpipe ambushes, and secret passageways that ended in a blank Inca stone wall.

Nevertheless, such parables – for parables they were, each with its internal moralistic tract – contained a whole array of escapologists' routines. These confirmed the usefulness of cliché, as in 'with one bound Jack was free', the supposed opening sentence of a chapter of the serial, where its antecedent ended with your man manacled and shackled in a dungeon. Such was the muscular force of Christianity, which lay close to miracle. Sudden leaps of logic, intermedial dénouements and deviations from the beaten track were typical, as in the Celtic Twilight Zone where 'Gospel truth' met 'myth'. St Patrick has a dream wherein he hears the voices of the pagan Irish cry out for salvation. Oisín, coming back from *Tír na n-Óg* (The land of youth), falls off his magic steed and is transformed into an ancient. Patrick, eventually baptizing him, accidentally sticks his crozier into Oisín's foot; the old warrior grins and bears it, thinking it to be an element of *rite de passage*. Patrick banishes the serpents.

The serial mode allowed ample scope for such scenarios, whose iconic details might be mirrored over many episodes, in different shifts of emphasis or context. At such points, my father's voice would elevate and quicken, since remembering the narrative depended on these rhythmic clusters or motifs. Compressed mnemonic musical devices, each contained within itself the implications of its past and future, like a Baroque phrase which undergoes conversion and inversion as the tune proceeds in constant renegotiation. They were *aides-mémoire* for both audience and teller.

It has been suggested that the mind of the storyteller is

inhabited by constellations of such crucial points, whose stars are transformed or regurgitated into patterns of the everyday. A kitchen interior, for example, is a suitable location, wherein its panoply of objects – soup tureens, check tablecloth, an icon of the Sacred Heart, a kettle steaming on the hob, the cast-iron mincer clamped to the deal table, its drawer crammed with ranks of jostling cutlery – become hooks on which to hang the items of the story; the room becomes a virtual embodiment of many stories. That plume of steam, for instance, could be the bugle of an army, or the imminent arrival of an unpunctual local train: both are equally important in their contexts. A sod of turf becomes a parable of poverty or labour. The votive lamp beneath the Sacred Heart reminds one of the power of electricity or the skull-and-crossbones of a pirate ship. The hands of the grandmother clock can smile or frown.

As more and more stuff, and its constituent warps and woofs, are tacked to the contents of the memory theatre, there is still room for more. The edeitic storyteller will develop spatial knacks and tricks, such as placing seven ornamental eggs, each with its proper daily function, within the delph hen, which utters different spakes according to your angle of approach.

The dresser, which in 'real' life is a family repository, is an important focal point within the system. We need not, here, consider the elaborations of its ornamental plate display, nor the obvious mugs; let us concentrate, instead, on the contents of a drawer filled with bits of string, a bunched red fist of rubber gloves, empty cotton reels, an elastic-bound, dog-eared deck of cards, a two-point electric plug, a measuring tape, two brass door-knobs, three mouth-organs, and a solitary knitting-needle – these are but some of the objects I retrieved just now, perusing one adjacent drawer of the table under the machine on which I'm typing. How many hands of cards were dealt, how many conformations? How many skirts were hemmed, how many buttonholes? What wild tunes were played, how many dirges? What squeaking cleanliness of dinner plates? How long is a piece of string? Everything you open seethes with memory.

Within one alcove of the dresser, you are sure to find a chocolate-tin button-box – Quality Street springs to mind, with its Dickensian vignettes of ladies in white muffs, and their top-hatted consorts – that made a Tannoy backwash as your wrist sagged beneath its weight of shifting jostling contents: shingly mock tortoiseshell and mother-of-pearl, clouded amber plastic, beads of jet and jade, squeaky plaited leather mushrooms, the synthetic horn of a duffel-coat toggle, a spiky thistle brooch with a broken catch. Each of these were implicated, for each could tell its tale of dangling by a thread before it teetered off into a narrative abyss.

There are other alcoves, other niches, each a cornucopia of past associations, so that when the storyteller leaves this present world and enters the domain of recitation, he is faced with a dilemma: if he is to use the dresser as a storyboard, with its strategically memorized *loci*, he must either wipe out their implications in his own life, or acknowledge them.

The erasers adopt a variety of expedients. A popular method is to take the various thingmajigs and place them in a vast imaginary Belfast sink, and wash them, leaving them to dry on a mental rack before they are replaced; another is to chalk their cartoon outlines on a mind's eye blackboard, before you wipe them off with a yellow duster. Some masters of the genre hold post-cerebellum public auctions, complete with expensive admission-price catalogues, whereby they sell off the entire contents of the house, and then return to each purchaser, buying the object back at an invariably higher price; but this is no odds, since making money is an act of will.

The eraser mode is necessarily self-abnegative. In the rare instances where the story is narrated in the first person, the audience will assume it to be code for third person; so, the storyteller becomes someone else in their ears, and all they know of his identity is what he tells them. Yet, he might reveal a detail of himself unwittingly, or show himself to be naive about the implications of his story. The story had been made by others who preceded him, who understood the contradictions of omniscient narration. The eraser contemplates an idiom whereby he becomes invisible, a mere conduit for the ornamental flourishes received from generations past, yet mitigated by the grain and circumstances of his voice, his presence into the literal room. In this way, he becomes himself.

The acknowledgers of personal mnemonic must have different strategies. That brown glazed mixing-bowl, for instance, in a Giant story, is where he imprisons humans with a delph plate; it also summons up the whole of a sunlit, oven-warm kitchen where the embryonic storyteller remembers his mother's churning air in or bubbles out with a wooden spoon, his licking off the thick buttery glop, then scouring the white of the bowl with fingertips; and this skim or residue must leak into the story, or be incorporated into it. This terrain is honeycombed with oxymoron and diversion, and the tiny ancillary moments of your life assume an almost legendary status. There are holes within holes, and the main protagonists are wont to disappear at any time, as in my father's story, which follows:

THE *FRONTIER SENTINEL*

Johnny McQueen and Agnes Reed were married during the war, and at that time houses were difficult to rent; and the couple couldn't afford to buy one. At the time of the story, they were living in two cramped upstairs rooms in Newry town. They had none of the modern amenities that newly married couples expect now: all they had was a gas ring for cooking, and access to an outside loo. Times were hard for them.

The McQueens would have liked nothing better than a house of their own, and they devoted many prayers to this intention. One morning, as he read the paper, Johnny spotted an ad for a cottage that was up for rent in Mullaghbawn, with half an acre attached. 'I'll go to Mullaghbawn today,' says he to Agnes, 'and by the grace of God, perhaps we'll be in luck.' Away he went, and to cut a long story short, he got the house. The pair wasted no time, and the next day they were installed in their own little house in Mullaghbawn.

Before, Johnny would have gone out for the odd jar, and was into sport too, going to soccer on a Saturday and Gaelic on the Sunday; but now, he never went out at all. He was too busy painting doors and walls and windows; but the time came when there was nothing left for him to do, and the house was like a little palace.

One night, when he was sitting by the fire, contentedly smoking his pipe, Agnes says to him 'Johnny dear, you've nothing to do tonight. Why don't you take yourself off to the pub, or you could go to the big match in McArdle Park; I believe Crossmaglen Rangers are playing tonight.'

'Do you know, Agnes,' says Johnny, 'I don't seem to have any interest in that kind of thing any more. I think I'll go into Newry town tomorrow and see if I can buy a spade and a shovel or whatever, and maybe I can do something with that half-acre out the back, for it's in pretty bad shape, and I'd be better off doing that than watching football.'

The next day, Johnny was up at the scrake of dawn. He went into Newry town on the bus and bought what he needed. He was no sooner home than he went out the back and started to dig. After a while, Agnes calls out to him:

'Johnny, your breakfast's ready!'

'I'll be in in a while,' says Johnny, and goes on digging.

After another while Agnes looks out. Johnny had a big hole dug, with two big heaps of soil on either side of it.

'Johnny,' she calls out, 'your breakfast's getting cold!'

'Sure I can warm it up myself when I'm finished,' says he, and he digs on.

A couple of hours went by and Agnes looked out again. She couldn't see Johnny at all; he was down in this great hole, digging for all he was worth. So out she goes, and says:

'What in God's name are you at, at all?

Johnny emerges from the hole and stands looking at it proudly.

'By God,' says he, 'isn't that a beautiful hole? What do you think, yourself?'

'Think?' says she. 'Are you telling me that you've been out all day digging a hole? What use is it? What can you do with it?'

'I know what I can do with it,' says Johnny, 'I can put it in the paper and sell it, that's what I'll do.'

The next day Paddy Murphy was eating his breakfast and reading the *Frontier Sentinel* in his house in Newry town.

'Listen to this, Kathleen,' he says to his wife, 'here's the most peculiar ad I've seen in a long while: SUPERLATIVE HOLE FOR SALE; ALL ENQUIRIES TO "FOUR WINDS", MUL-LAGHBAWN, CO. ARMAGH. I think I'll take a run over there right now, and see what it's all about.'

Paddy got the bus to Mullaghbawn, asked for directions, and it wasn't long till he stood outside McQueen's. He knocked on the door and Johnny came out.

'Are you the man that has the hole?' says Paddy.

'I am,' says McQueen, 'are you interested?'

'I am,' says Murphy, 'but I'd like to view before I buy.'

'This way,' says McQueen, 'it's out the back. It's a bloody great hole. Satisfaction guaranteed.'

He took Paddy out and showed him the hole.

'That's her,' says he. 'What do you think?'

Paddy looked into the hole.

'By God,' he says, 'I never saw such a hole in my life. She must be thirty foot deep.'

'She is,' says Johnny, 'and maybe more. Are you for buying?'

'I am, surely,' says Paddy, 'how much are you looking?'

'Well,' says Johnny, 'she's worth twenty pound, for she took me the guts of a whole day digging her, but seeing I'm a Newry man myself, I'll let her go for ten.'

'Fair enough,' says Murphy, 'it's a deal.' He hands McQueen a tenner. Then he began to think.

'I'm living in Newry,' he says, 'and this hole's in Mullaghbawn. How am I to get her from one place to the other?'

'Well,' says Johnny, 'there's always the Ulster Transport Authority.'

'Right enough,' says Paddy, 'I'll go there straight away. Good luck to you, sir, and thanks for the deal.'

Paddy landed at the UTA depot in Newry, and he said to the clerk: 'I'm just after buying this hole beyond in Mullaghbawn. She's a beautiful hole; she must be forty foot deep and broad to boot, and I'd like to hire a lorry and six men to bring her back to Newry.'

He gave the clerk the particulars about the current location of the hole, and where he wanted it to be deposited.

'That's all in order,' says the clerk, 'I'll have a lorry and a gang of men out there in no time, and you should have the hole some time tomorrow afternoon.'

Murphy thanked the clerk and went straight home, and said to his wife: 'Do you mind that hole I saw in the paper? Well, I've bought it, and it should be here tomorrow afternoon.'

Paddy spent the whole afternoon pacing the floor, waiting for the hole to arrive. Night came, and there was no word of the hole. At last he had to go to bed, but he didn't sleep a wink, thinking of the hole that never came.

He got up at the scrake of dawn, and as soon as the UTA office had opened, he went in and demanded to see the manager.

'Good morning, sir,' says the manager, 'and what can I do for you?'

'It's like this,' says Murphy, 'I bought a hole beyond in Mullaghbawn. You never saw the equal of this hole: as near fifty foot deep as makes no odds, and broad to boot, and I was looking forward to having her installed in the back garden, and I hired a lorry and six men in this very office for the job, and damn the hole have I seen yet. What kind of service do you call that?'

'You're right,' says the manager, 'this won't do at all. Who did you give the order to?'

'That wee red-haired man over there,' says Murphy.

The manager called over the wee red-haired man. 'Mr Green,' says he, 'this gentleman is telling me that he bought a hole yesterday in Mullaghbawn. This hole was sixty foot deep, and broad to boot; and moreover, the honourable gentleman tells me that he hired a lorry and six men — and that it was yourself who dispatched the order — to take this hole to his place, and that the hole hasn't arrived yet. Have you any explanation?'

'Oh,' says Green, 'are you the man that bought the hole? Well, I sent out a lorry and a gang of men to Mullaghbawn, and after struggling with this hole for seven hours, they eventually succeeded in placing her on the back of the vehicle; but there's a wild steep incline between Mullaghbawn and Newry, and the hole fell off the back of the lorry. The men were trying their level best to get the hole back on, when the lorry fell into the hole. The men then tried to haul the lorry out of the hole, but fell in themselves, and we haven't seen sight nor hair of them since!'

THE NEW OXFORD
BILLIARD HALLS

I translated that story from my father's recounting of it (I heard it many times as a child) in his slim compendium of anecdote and memoir, '*Seo, Siúd, agus Siúd Eile*',* which might be rendered as 'Here, There, and There Again', or 'This, That, and The Other'; or, simply, perhaps, 'Miscellanae'. Translation seems implicit in the title, not least in the sense of moving a thing from one place to another. Its rambling ambiguity appeals to me, since it's pretty close to what I'm doing now, as I beat about the bush of this book, hedging my bets, dodging the issue within a woolly discourse, while trying to snag a thread which might be spun into a yarn.

It is instructive to watch a master storyteller in action as he manipulates his various latitudes of anecdote and parable, and

---

*Coiséin, Béal Feirste, 1986.

suits them to contemporary circumstances, bending the previous rules of the story a little to make it fit whatever conversation in whatever venue; and the room becomes a geodesic dome in which he moves through longitudes of time, incapable of being here and now without remembering the previous narrative zones he's passed through. Sometimes, at grand soirées or ceilidhs, you might get three or four such characters, each vying to get his spake or spoke in, within the tricky, poker-faced etiquette demanded by such verbal jousting, each winding the others up with improbable logic and loopy propositions.

So the globe spins on its tilted axis, and the supper interval arrives in a lull. Tea is handed round in cupfuls chinking on their saucers, and a plethora of sandwiches — thick-cut ham and mustard, cheese and Branston pickle, salmon, chicken, egg and onion, 'salad' (lettuce, scallions and tomato lathered with Crosse & Blackwell's salad cream), tuna — appears from nowhere, packed in triangle flotillas on willow-pattern plates, so that as they're deliberated over and picked off, details of the underlying blue legend are revealed. I should also mention the bite-sized sausage rolls, the little plump cocktail sausages, and the pearl onions, the cubes of yellow cheese and chunks of pineapple threaded on to cocktail sticks (a perverse trio taste explosion), not forgetting the barmbrack slices with their odd sultanas glistening through smotherings of butter, the split-open fruit scones likewise, the sultana loaf itself, the wodges of currant soda bread, the radially dissected apple pie, the butterfly buns, and the final sophistication of assorted biscuits out of a tin.

By this time, the animated flow of the solo story has been

taken over by cross-currents of talk, as the audience evolves into a company. Different nodes and knots of atmospherics crack about the room, as people shift their chairs a bit to rearrange the conversational domain, some leaning over backwards with one ear cocked, or hunched forward, concentratedly twiddling their thumbs in trying to catch the drift of a private elaborate joke; all this while the multitude is being fed, and parts of speech are syncopated by the noise of munch and slurp and sup and glug. Big freckle-fisted young men balance cups of tea on their broad thighs and grab sandwiches in threes or fours, one hand stuffing their faces while the other deposits a stash on paper-napkin-covered paper plates (those ones with the calibrated edges) for future reference. Then there's a not-too-covert mineral bottle of poteen going the underhand rounds, poured in modicums into cups of tea to fortify them, or brimmed into the improvised miniature shot-glass of the screw-top, held delicately between finger and thumb, and knocked back with a subsequent appreciative gasp.

The ample repast I describe is a rural one, but might, on a reduced scale, be applied to Belfast. Here, the kitchen of the terraced 'kitchen' house performed a similar function to that of its more expansive country cousin, occupying most of the ground-floor plan. 'Kitchen', so-called, for, although most of the cooking happened in a wardrobe-sized scullery, the word still retained its social dimensions and gestures of hospitality, and lent itself to the main living space of the house. On the occasion of a wake, room could be made for the many mourners and the people paying their respects, sometimes in a relay, rosary fashion, as decades of the populace filed in and out. The staircase would become an omnibus, where a dozen or a score might be accommodated, cheek by jowl; but this involved a difficulty, since the corpse was invariably laid out on a double bed in the grander of the two minuscule upstairs rooms, and to view it, you had to climb a throng of passengers, stumbling over shoes and thighs and ankles. Arriving at the top, you stepped into the tiny chamber made big by the flames of two beeswax candles at either side of the bed, and saw the body stretched, trembling in the candlelight as if hovering above the coverlet it lay upon. Dusty yellow light fell through the drawn blind of the one window.

When the coffin came, sometimes the stairs would be so narrow that the undertakers had to take the window out. Otherwise the coffin might get stuck in an indecorous angle. So they lifted the empty coffin in through the glassless embrasure, and lowered it back on to the street. When the time came for the funeral procession to congregate, an Angel of Death would arrive to supervise the proceedings, the same Angel who was first on your doorstep with news of the decease. Typically, these were little shabby-dapper gregarious men who'd started off as bookies' runners, and now survived on a mysterious series of moonlighting enterprises. They smelled of billiard chalk. They had the gift of the gab and sometimes acted as assistant managers of parish Gaelic football teams. They were partial to the odd bottle, and were often propped at bar counters in between jobs. Some were married, and some were not, but every family seemed to extend to one.

At funerals, their mild social nuisance value was transformed into a virtue, as they nominated quartets of coffin-carriers from the cortège and synchronized the 'lift' from one team to the next. After the burial, they'd make courageous attempts to buy rounds in the nearby Gravediggers' Arms, before generously allowing themselves to be forestalled. Then they would embark on a panegyric of great football players of the past, as exemplified by the deceased's second cousin, who could drop a fifty-yard ball at a perfectly weighted angle to his team-mate's tangential run, and sprint up from behind mid-field in about two-point-something seconds to collect the return pass, after which he waltzed round two defenders before burying the ball in the top right corner; the Angel could see the net bulging still, as the seated shirt-sleeved crowd behind the goal rose up in a simultaneous wave to applaud the beautiful move, which he would demonstrate in slo-mo on a bar table, with matchboxes proxying for forwards, and cigarette-packets for backs.

Other examples followed from the teeming archive of his inward eye: how the chalk-marks on a snooker table illustrated, if pored over through a magnifying glass, the manifold screws and skids of the balls colliding and ricocheting, how each stroke left a dot of chalk on the cue-ball, which in turn deposited a microscopic track across the baize or, more especially, against the nap of it. So, one could reconstruct an epic frame from an examination of the empty green arena, until its supervisor, with a wide brush, wiped away the evidence.

Meanwhile, a choreography of trundles, clicks and clunks unreeled from the tape-recorder of his mind, eliciting the occasional shudder of a mis-cue, or the dead noise of a 'kick'. Then the conjuror's white-gloved referee would place a transparent device adjacent to the guilty ball, which he'd pick up and gnarl as if washing his hands of it; sacerdotally, he'd replace it on its invisible spot, and vanish the device back into the pocket of his black tux. During this lull the congregation would take the opportunity to clear their throats; the challenger thoughtfully chalked the tips of his cue and blew on its tip, before returning to the table with renewed, unbroken concentration and aplomb to make an unprecedented safety shot that came to rest in the jaws of a baulk pocket. From that point on, the snookered champion had no come-back, and the aisles of The Crucible were littered with beaten dockets.

THE GREAT NORTHERN
RAILWAY

A 'beaten docket' is Belfast parlance for a betting-slip that has passed its sell-by date; so it is appropriate that a public house not two doors away from a bookmaker's (Crown Turf Accountants) should be so called. The Beaten Docket is on a corner of Amelia Street and Great Victoria Street, directly opposite the Crown Liquor Saloon on the other; both face the allegedly most-bombed hotel in the world, The Europa, which occupies the site of the former Great Northern Railway Station, demolished in 1967, the first terminus of the Ulster Railway, whose train service from Lisburn to Belfast opened in August 1839.

Inside the station, overlooked by the big Roman-numeralled public clock, were several devices which enabled you to spend waiting-time, and money: a six-foot scale working model of a steam-engine in a glass case; an immense red unreliable cast-iron scales, whose needle trembled between calibrations as you stood on its steelyard platform and tried to make yourself heavier by exerting hand-pressure on the bezel of its clock-face; a similarly shaped item, whose calibrations were the alphabet, and which embossed the slogan or name of your choice on an aluminium strip; another glass case, containing watches and soft toys which invariably slipped from the grasp of the mechanical grab you had paid a penny to operate; then there was a whole array of smaller slot-machines that looked like miniature monocular traffic-lights and which dispensed multi-coloured gobstoppers, fortune-cookie-type plastic eggs which broke open at their equators to reveal the tiny components of your lucky dip, and dimpled golf-ball globes of chewing-gum. Hence, the whole concourse had the air of an amusement arcade, anticipating gregarious, day-trip holiday excursions, and sea-breeze posters advertised the virtues of comparatively far-off resorts. Yet, the gender-segregated waiting-rooms implied a more formal etiquette, where men and women slumbered apart in out-of-date upholstery. If you were lucky, you could sometimes see the stationmaster emerge from his office to check his watch against the public clock, flipping open its engraved lid with his thumbnail, looking at the time, winding its milled silver knob, then holding its back to his ear to hear its innards tick, dangling it momentarily on its pendulum fob before throwing it into the slit of his waistcoat pocket, after which he disappeared into his sanctum, and smoked another eighteen-minute pipe of Passing Clouds tobacco.

In 1959, queuing at the ticket booth, I am impressed by this routine. At the iron gate, another uniformed official takes my ticket and, in one deft movement, docks it with an empty star and hands it back to me. I tuck it into the breast pocket of my jacket. As I step on to the platform, under the neo-Gothic, cast-iron-ribbed glass roof – that ocean-bottom greenish rippled glass, that bends the world a bit as you look through it, and the wisps of steam this side of it resemble the passing April clouds outside above it – the waiting engine huffs impatiently, and white plumes escape from its stilled pistons.

I am taking the short two-stop trip to Balmoral. Enclosed alone in a compartment that smells of tobacco and autumnal-coloured moiré cut-moquette upholstery, I try to anticipate the momentary dislocation which occurs when you think your train is moving off backwards, until you realize a parallel train has moved forward, and yours is stationary. Eventually, you do move off for real, accelerating slowly past marshalling yards, where goods trains have been shunted in linear alphabets of flat-bed trucks, closed wooden wagons and cabooses, cylindrical gas and chemical containers, cattle-carts, and brake-carts. The whole elaborate system of junctions, sidings and crossovers is corroborated by interlinks of rods and levers, wires plumbed into black tubings snaking parallel to the tracks, under intervallic staves of telegraph wires strung out between high poles, as the sleepers below exude oil and creosote, and the heraldic armatures of railway signals click their intermittent semaphores, trying to orchestrate the movements. There is a burned-out cindery feel to the landscape, and the air is full of grit and glitter. The skewed angles of the deep cuttings resemble those of an exhausted open-cast coal-mine, whose zig-zag downward gradients culminate in a black tarn. Derelict, scummed mill-ponds flash with brackish, desultory April light, as runnels and sluices sink into culverts under the water-towers and coal-depots and engine-sheds. High brick walls of overlooking factories advertise their wares of vitriol and linen in fading white-painted letters, and the gable end of a gospel hall commands us to prepare to meet our God.

Then, to the southwest, the rows of terraced houses, backyards teetering with crazy DIY pigeon-lofts of all shapes and sizes, weekly wash fluttering, back doors giving on to a cinder track behind the perimeter fence of wired-together railway sleepers. To the high northwest, clouds scud across Black Mountain; lower down, they are reflected in the meres and bayous of the Bog Meadows, a place abounding in waders, coots, dippers, grebes, swans, and other birds whose names I do not know. The broad acres of the Bog Meadows, where land and water are ambivalent, formed a natural buffer-zone between the Protestant Lisburn Road and the Catholic Falls: I knew that even then, at the age of eleven.

Now I remember making expeditions to the Bog Meadows with two or three peers, armed with catapults, setting out from the new estate of Mooreland into winding Stockman's Lane, finding a gap in its blackthorn hedge just above the Blackstaff bridge, to plunge into a rural field knee-deep in damp grass, buttercups and rushes, that sloped away from another recent Avenue of houses still smelling of new plaster, pine and brick; tumbled over behind a back garden, an abandoned cement-mixer was beginning to be overgrown with bindweed. Beating a path in single file through the long grass, we would negotiate a jersey-snagging, straggly barbed-wire fence, to emerge on the edge of the

Meadows proper, where you had to jump a five-foot-wide ditch to enter the other realm.

Sometimes we would step the slippery stepping-stones across the Blackstaff into the margins of enemy territory, which we approached with the same trepidation felt by Robert Harbinson, coming from the other side, in his 1960 memoir of a Belfast childhood, *No Surrender*:

> But the rows of houses did not go on forever. Beyond them lay the Bog Meadows' marshy steppes where refuse heaps broke the flatness, and the narrow, shallow Blackstaff River meandered, colourless and unmusical . . . God ordained that even the Bog Meadows should end and had set a great hill at their limit, which we called the Mickeys' Mountain. Among a knot of trees half-way up the flank a small cottage sheltered, and near by two fields were cultivated. Seen from the Bog Meadows they stood out amongst the bracken and heather like a giant hatchet. In terms of miles the mountain was not far, and I always longed to explore it. Somewhere, or in the hidden hills beyond, lay the boot stuffed with gold pieces buried by Neeshy Haughan, who once upon a time robbed the rich to help the poor, kindnesses repaid by a hanging at Carrickfergus. What things might be bought with the highwayman's long boot of gold! But the mountain was inaccessible because to reach it we had to cross territory held by the Mickeys. Being children of the staunch Protestant quarter, to go near the Catholic idolaters was more than we dared, for fear of having one of our members cut off.

I've just shown this passage to my brother Pat, who is making his traditional Thursday night visit, and he comes up with a story that

I hadn't heard before, that the occupant of the cottage in the Hatchet Field was so stuck for company that he used to post letters to himself, so as he could ask the postman in for a cup of tea and a chat; this sounds slightly apocryphal to me, but then the Hatchet Field seemed to attract stories, and the cottage, when it fell vacant, gained the reputation of being haunted, maybe by the ghost of the same waylaid postman. In my dreams, the cottage has spawned many, more elaborate versions of itself, so that the area is like a scarped and anticlined Italian hill town, with terraced zucchini gardens and stepped passageways in between the houses set at odd angles to each other: an independent, self-sufficient state, remote from the business of the city which sprawls below it. I am disappointed when, in waking life, I look up and see that it is not there: even the cottage has gone, and not a stone has been left on a stone. But the faint outline of the Hatchet Field* remains.

Imagining myself standing within it, I look down across Milltown Cemetery, across the Bog Meadows, to the Great Northern Railway line, to where I am disembarking, aged eleven, from the local train. It was here, at Balmoral Halt, that I used to go trainspotting, walking the mile or so down Stockman's Lane armed with an indelible pencil stub and a police notebook. Sometimes I would take a detour into Musgrave Park, which bounded one side of the Lane, to explore the Islands of the Lake, as they were grandly known. In truth, the lake was a stagnant shallow pond, but to a boy it formed an exotic ecosystem teeming

---

*So called for its shape, and not for any sinister design.

with insect and aquatic life: gnats, beetles, dragonflies and mayflies, newts, frogs, snails and leeches. It was a pleasure to stand barefoot in the Lake, wriggling one's toes in the cool muck and appreciating the near-warm knee-bracelet of the surface water, as the intermittent June sun – huge gold-rimmed clouds sailing overhead – cast shafts of light into the cloudy weedy underwater thoroughfares and grottoes, the whole Everglades shimmering and buzzing with activity. The three low islands within it were named, in diminishing order of size, but not necessarily of importance, as the First, Second and Third Islands. The First Island was also the one usually entered first, since it was accessible by a series of stepping-stones which brought you the five yards from the mainland into its tangled wilderness of willow, poplar, blackberry and ivy. Within it was the mysterious ruin of a small brick hut with a tiny, tea-chest-sized cellar in it, covered by a rusted iron trapdoor, which inspired speculation that this was a sealed-off portal to a maze of subterranean and subaqueous passages linking the Islands in a cipher of the recently antique Maquis war, *maquis* being a dense anti-Nazi undergrowth of shrubs, which was very appropriate to the Islands' flora. To get to the Second Island from the First necessitated wading in Wellington boots or bare feet, until a gang of us undertook a major engineering project and built a causeway over to it using the bricks of the ruined hut, thus occupying a whole summer.

I liked the Second Island because it contained an especially climbable tall poplar tree, in whose uppermost branches one could sway for empty summer hours, gazing out across the Bog

Meadows to where the verdigris-green dome of the City Hall dominated the skyline of the city centre. As for the Third Island, it was relatively inaccessible and featureless, and we did not visit it much; but it was necessary to the dimensional configuration of the archipelago.

After this detour, I would reach my destination, and would stand at the end of the gravel-covered platform, staring down the long shining curve of the track, anticipating the approximate arrival of the Belfast-to-Dublin Enterprise Express. I am reminded, now, that I was less than efficient as a trainspotter: I didn't own a watch, and was fazed by the multiple columns of train timetables; so I contented myself by listing engine numbers, wheel configurations, and amount of carriages (especially mind-numbing, when applied to long slow goods-trains, which could run to a hundred and something modules of giant linear script). Nevertheless time was witnessed by the unreliable hands of the King's Hall clock, a giant thirties modernistic affair with minimalist blips instead of numerals, which overlooked the Halt: I have just corroborated this by consulting the free Fortwilliam Pharmacy (our local chemist's) calendar, whose months are illustrated by archival photographs of Belfast; the King's Hall is May, which is appropriate, since this was the time of the Balmoral show, when the rural population of Ulster would cram the Exhibition Grounds behind the Hall to watch displays of plants and livestock, and the place was cacophonous with bleats, whinnies, cackles, and the glottal stops of country voices; the warm May air was redolent with sweet hay and dung.

The other months have other resonances.

JANUARY. *Castle Place*: this is the exact same image as that described on p.26, Castle Place and High Street, looking east, early 1880s. I cannot think why this photograph of high summer stands for January, but this print is a bit bleached, and the white awnings seem to carry a perceptible dip of snow.

FEBRUARY. *Botanic Gardens*:

'The most striking and interesting feature of Belfast Botanic Gardens is the Palm House, with its two wings flanking a bold elliptical dome. One cannot but applaud the determination of the men who directed the Garden in its early days and who, without outside financial help, built a curvilinear glass house before Kew or Glasnevin had one . . . Originally the conservatories were heated by two brick flues, but in 1862 hot water pipes fed from Cockey's Patent Boiler were installed by Musgrave Brothers for £95. The new system was not entirely satisfactory and in very cold weather the old brick flues had to be lit to supplement the water pipes. During severe frost it was thus possible to keep an indoor temperature of 32°F in the cool house and 45° in the stove house. New boilers were installed in 1871 and they were supplemented in 1881 by large terminal-end Saddle Boilers capable of heating 3,500 cubic feet of water. The work of installation was carried out by Wimmington Co., who also removed the pipes of the smoke flues. Further changes in its heating were made in 1892 when the Saddle Boiler was taken out and John Hall of Queen Street put in two Red Rose boilers.'

(*The Palm House and Botanic Garden, Belfast*, by Eileen McCracken, Belfast, 1971)

MARCH. *Victoria Street Station*: there is no Victoria Street Station, and this photograph shows the concourse of Great Victoria Street

Station described at the start of this chapter, albeit from a rather spare perspective. The hands of the four-faced turret clock above the big Gothic double-fronted kiosk show fourteen minutes past eleven; the place is practically deserted, so it must be a Sunday.

APRIL. *Linenhall Library*: it is April as I write, and I am aiming to have this book written by May; it is good to have a deadline, as it concentrates the mind. I feel a twinge of guilt when I swing my telescope to gaze into the beautiful book-lined constellation of this library, which is the most important repository of Belfast knowledge; I often think I should have consulted it more, as groundwork for the writing. But I have not the temperament for such research: trawling through catalogues; filling in the buff requisition slips; drumming my fingers on the desk while the library assistant disappears into an annex to search for one's requests; being disappointed when a promisingly titled book turns out to yield nothing in the way of interesting facts, or does not exist on the shelves, having been stolen, lost, or loaned. Or perhaps you do come across a mildly emblematic historical reference, and feel obliged to use it because of the time spent in discovering it, and you contort your text to make it fit. At any rate, I have fond memories of the library's reading-room, whose big sash windows overlook the busy throng of Donegall Square; and I think of dust-motes drifting down through prisms of light that end on the magnified, open pages of books drowsed over by scholars and fanatics. The focus of the photo is a wall-clock, but I can't make out the time from this reproduction of it.

JUNE. *Queen's University*: here, the image is badly blurred, and it looks like the Oxford College pastiche façade of the building is in the process of materializing from another dimension, an effect reinforced by the ghostly absence of people on the extensive foreground of lawns; other period views show white-clothed tennis players caught in mid-flit. I was an ostensible student at Queen's, between 1967 and 1971; looking at its central tower, I remember the winding stair within it, which led to a superior turret from which you could spy on aspects of a darkened Belfast; having discovered the hidden entrance to this eyrie, I used to bring girl-friends up here on nocturnal expeditions. Similarly, we used to scale the fence to wander the grounds of the Vice-Chancellor's gardens, a mysterious moonlit space of lakes and arbours between Stranmillis and Malone. Above its dark remove, the stars were swayed by moving clouds and branches.

JULY. *Belfast College of Technology*:

'1900–07, by Samuel Stevenson: Symmetrical baroque building of five storeys in Portland stone; central staircase with rusticated columns set on a frontispiece whose quoins run up to a moulded cornice; Gibbsian columns support a segmental entablature enclosing Belfast coat of arms over door opening with wrought iron gates; arcades of giant order attached columns at second and third floors support main cornice, above which an additional storey was added in the course of construction; circular corner bays rise to double-storey lanterns with copper domes.'

(Marcus Patton, *Central Belfast: An Historical Gazeteer*, Belfast, 1993)

*

AUGUST. *The Hippodrome*: at the time of writing, the site of this once ornate building is a car-park, pending future development. Previously, it was a theatre, then a cinema, and latterly a bingo hall. Patton notes that in 1993 it contained 'interesting stage machinery, with ropes drawn down to the control deck, like some terrestial *Marie Celeste*'. It was refaced with metal cladding c. 1960, and until recently it was believed that much of the original façade remained intact. However, when the cladding was torn off in 1997, it was discovered that a majority of the architectural detail had been obliterated; and it was demolished, amid much preservationist controversy.

SEPTEMBER. *Plaza Ballroom*: I remember the big resounding sweaty space of the Plaza from my schooldays, c. 1965–6, when it held lunch-time 'hops', where we used to go to drink warm Coca-Cola and watch schoolgirls and typists and mods and rockers demonstrate the latest dance craze. The three black motor cars parked outside the Plaza come from the twenties or thirties.

OCTOBER. Queen's Bridge: this is a great photograph, looking east to where the tall chimneys of glassworks, ropeworks and foundries punctuate the skyline of the County Down side of the Lagan. The bridge carries a complicated traffic of trams, drays, hand-carts, and pedestrians. Sailing-ships, barges and pontoons are tied up at the adjacent docks, and below the bridge is a dark reflection of itself in the tidal water. This used to be a regular venue for suicides, but this focus has long shifted elsewhere.

*

NOVEMBER. *Belfast Free Library, Royal Avenue*: this, too, is referred to, as the Central Library, on p.178 of *The Star Factory*. I've only just noticed the blurred – but legible – detail in the right-hand bottom corner, to the northwest of the Library, where the words 'Brown Horse Billiard Tables' are painted on a gable wall. This would be the defunct Brown Horse bar; trying to visualize what replaced it, I can only get a featureless blur. Annoyed by this lapse of memory, I jump into the car and drive down to where it was. The city is deserted at this time, eight of the clock on a beautiful spring evening, and the setting sun casts a long light down the unpeopled streets. I'm back at the desk in ten minutes. It turns out that the building is indeed featureless: new brick, some eight storeys high – I forgot to count them – this must be a storage annnex of the Library, a useful change of function; even more useful is the recent change I marked as I drove down the Antrim Road, where, on the corner of the Limestone, a bank has been replaced by a bar, done up in a pastiche Victorian style, with a wooden interior in which glass-fronted cupboards display old packs of cards and matchboxes. As I drove past, two police-men were interviewing three youths outside it, reminding me that further down the Limestone Road other changes have taken place in the past few days. Catholics have been intimidated from their houses, part of an ongoing head-counting territorial dispute in North Belfast, where many huddles of opposing loyalties rub up against each other in frictions, factions and fractions, a subject too labyrinthine to be entered into here. But I should note in passing that my eleven-year-old boy was beaten up – split lip, black eye, bruised ribs – a few weeks ago, as he walked past

Tiger's Bay, in his first major excursion from home without telling his parents, and that is another story in itself, of loss of innocence, and gain of education. A different version of the same story happened to me when I was nine, when a classmate and I took the out-of-bounds short-cut home down Cupar Street from St Gall's Public Elementary School.

A long time ago, back in the Brown Horse, I see myself in a whiskey mirror, ordering a drink in it, as the light of a gold, blurred afternoon stolen from school falls through an etched window, and time is momentarily arrested as you lift the glass to your underage drinker's lips, and sip. Later, I would go and join the smoke-break idlers – schoolgirls, schoolboys like myself – on the Library steps, where lights were proffered in cupped hands, or transferred from one cigarette end to another, and you registered the almost inaudible smooch as they touched.

DECEMBER. *Royal Belfast Hospital For Sick Children*: The 'Royal'* has a great reputation and is much loved by members of both communities. Here are neat rows of iron cots; sunlight falls through the generous casement windows on to the polished floorboards, and shimmers in the chambered ceiling; the sick children peer into the lens above and between the bars of their cots, attended by four Nightingales in starched uniforms.

When I was about nine or ten, I was in the Royal for a few days, for a minor adenoids operation. Here I fell in love for the

---

*Whose foyer is graced by the bronze presence of a twice-life-sized enthroned Queen Victoria bearing an orb and sceptre.

first time in my life, barring maiden aunts. Being fit, and not sick, I was allowed to wander the other wards. In one of them I met an older,* ailing boy called Noel, who was in for some long-term, unspecified illness, and who could barely walk. I struck up a friendship with him and used to carry him on my back on our travels around the many corridors, wards, offices and annexes of the hospital, conducting a conversation with him behind my back, as he instructed me, from his higher perch, to go this way, or that, and he saw things I didn't. I thought he was brilliant and wise, and it was my privilege to serve him, and to be his steed. We seemed to be able to talk about anything, and invented many interests in common, pretending an extensive knowledge of stamps or model aeroplanes to each other, as we inhaled imaginary fumes of Airfix glue and the Humbrol enamel paints that came in little dinky Lilliputian tins of a bigger scale than the aircraft you were building, for if you put one against the other, the smaller-than-cotton-spool-sized tin looked positively Brobdingnagian. Then we would enter the realms of Laputa. When the time came for me to leave this perfect companion, I was devastated. I moped around the back-yard of 3 Mooreland Drive for days, crying to myself. After many days, the pain subsided – though I remember it yet – and I was free to wander the fields of the Owenvarragh.

---

*At that age, 'older' might have been a few months.

OWENVARRAGH

At the back of Mooreland Drive was a plot of undeveloped land that would become Owenvarragh* Drive; beyond that, fields of grass and buttercups dotted with cows' clap, that I remember harvesting with a coal shovel and a tin bucket as manure for our back garden. The undeveloped half-acre was, for us children, a foyer or rehearsal space for that rural hinterland beyond us, containing its essential elements in miniature: here, a small tributary of the Owenvarragh River ran between blackthorn hedges, where we built tree-parlours. Ensconced in them, invisible to adult eyes, we made up secrets for ourselves, which remain

---

*From *abhainn bharrach*, barred river, the bars being stakes or staves; and the Owenvarragh, in its lower reaches, from Stockman's Lane to where it joins the Lagan, becomes the Blackstaff. *Barra* can also mean a sand-bar, or *fearsad*; so these waters – Blackstaff, Owenvarragh, Farset – form an etymological confluence.

untold, and so intricate as to be untellable. We dug fist-sized cat-acombs in the clay banks of the stream, and installed in them the bodies of frogs, mice and birds, returning to them years or weeks later to disinter their clean white skeletons.

The small stream was enormous in its details of meander, its microscopic reefs and deeps and sandbars, the purl of its current round an imposing stone; sometimes, flood-borne minor Mississippi rafts of twigs would form a log-jam and a rippling dam of water became pent behind it, where we would launch paper-boat flotillas and bomb them with clay pellets.

Beyond this adjunct of our new estate lay the Cows' Field,* its boundary marked by a tall electric pylon protected by storeys of barbed wire and skull-and-crossbones signs. When it rained, the pylon buzzed with intimations of mortality and suicide, and the cows would low and moan as they staggered up off their knees in an almost-integrated body to find uncontaminated pastures on the margins of the force-field. Years later, people would claim compensation for the cancers allegedly induced by these Eiffel Towers.

South of the Cows' Field lay the Jungle, demarcated on one side by the Owenvarragh, and on the other by the railings of Musgrave Park Hospital, which occupied a low plateau above the river, looking like a derelict RAF aerodrome with its rows of isolated Nissen huts, each one of which was a hospital ward. Making our way through the Jungle, we were subliminally aware of this near-necropolis above us, and its empty gravel

---

*So-called because it was invariably inhabited by cows.

walks whose order contradicted our meanderings. Although
the Jungle was a mere strip of river bank some ten or fifteen
yards across and some four hundred long – a bonzai zone of low,
implicated scrub and thorn – we kept finding *terra incognita* in
its labyrinth; or, exploring different routes between known
places, we saw them from a new perspective. Here were tiny
glades carpeted with moss and microcosmic galaxies of flowers;
pools in them, sometimes, flickering with embryonic fish and
water-bugs; dense undergrowths of ferns; rank columns of
umbellifers, and phalanxes of bulrushes. One loop of the river
was almost completely ceilinged by over-arching trees: this was
a secret place of mine, where I would sit alone for hours on a
minor sand-bank, studying the compass-needle flickerings of
dragonflies, entranced by the languid fish; once, I saw a king-
fisher dive like a blue bolt through the clerestory of branches
and break the surface water in an eye-blink, before coming up,
almost instantaneously, with a struggling silver flash in its
beak. It was easy to imagine dim organ-music in this miniature
cathedral, where leafy bifurcations met and whispered in confessionals, allowing tremolos of light to penetrate its shades.

I knew then that if ever I was on the run – an IRA man, say –
I could retreat here, to the heart of the Jungle; here would be my
final See, or siege. Here I'd be absorbed and camouflaged, protected by its genius, with whom I'd long communed.
Incorporated by its teeming ecosystem, I'd become a detail of its
verdurous glooms and winding mossy ways, whose divarications,
and the routes and tributaries between them, were innumerable.

Yet, others must have had the same idea: scouting the territory, we would come across small clearings dotted by the charcoal interims of camp-fires, where important pow-wows had occurred throughout the long campaign of summer. Some of these we recognized as our own residue; around others, still warm to the touch, we found scattered cigarette-butts, evidence that others, older than us, had been here previously; and we felt a Crusoe wobble of fear, like when he saw a footstep on the sand of his supposed desert island. For we knew that the Jungle was an intermediate ground, that it contained a demarcation between Catholic and Protestant territory, though where precisely this border might be, or where we might infract it, no one was prepared to say. No map delineated it. We were given no specific caveats against it by our parents, since, after all, they only knew the Jungle by our non-committal reports; yet, we got osmotic rumours of the broader picture, where the Protestant majority might view our new estate as the tip of the iceberg of the Falls Road minority community, expanding under demographic pressure westwards into lush farmlands and the ornamental parks of planters' houses.

Making our way westwards through the Jungle, we felt the force-field of home gradually diminish, till, its signal imperceptible, we were exposed like aliens on the margins of our known world. This point was marked by the hospital rubbish tip, which spilled down from its elevation in a cornucopia of dead flowers, bloodied bandages, Roman-toga tumbling drapes of bed-linen, disgorged orange rubber tubing and discarded hypodermics. Staggering up its scree, we were archaeologists of the avalanche, finding dead Ever-Ready batteries, rusted scalpels, odd shoes, crutches, Bakelite plugs; once, we disinterred a practically intact radio. We dreaded to imagine the hospital activity that lay behind this waste, the Frankenstein interiors of morgues and incubators palpitating with galvanic zig-zag sparks.

Contemplating these inner dimensions, we were also implicated in the wider landscape, finding new bearings and perspectives as the skyline of Black Mountain, a long mile or so to the North, shifted to accommodate our purposeful meanderings, whose river-source lay in the mountain. The sky seemed bigger here; unbalanced by it, we would get a dizzy, pleasurable tremor of agoraphobia. After a repast of camp-fire carbonized potatoes and scorched woodsmoke-perfumed toast, we would sprawl on our backs and gaze into the hemisphere above, seeing pictures in its lagooned archipelagos of moving cumulus and jigsaw-puzzle sky. On rare cloudless days, it almost hurt to look into the huge blue levels, where the diamond point of a jet scored a silent white line miles long, and amethyst became forget-me-not.

A blue, small-petalled flower grew abundantly in the nearby 'Seven Sisters' meadow – so-called, I presume, from that salient number of sally-rod* trees in its march hedges – and we used to gather bouquets to decorate the altar of the Virgin Mary, whose plaster statue would be brought down on the First of May from the landing window-sill it usually occupied, to be placed on a special doily on top of the parlour sideboard, and

---

*It occurs to me that 'sally-rod' is Ulster rhyming slang to 'Prod', i.e. Protestant.

flanked by two ice-cream sundae glasses filled with these blue mayflowers. This recalls the Belfast street tradition of the May Queen where, as David Hammond writes in his *Songs of Belfast*,

> . . . squads of children, dressed up in women's dresses, high-heeled shoes and old lace curtains, escort their own May Queen through the streets, flanked by two guards. They are furnished with a brush-pole for the Queen's acrobatics and a tin can for collecting money. The encounters with rival Queens are always exciting and vituperative. Modesty and restraint are not predominant features of the occasion.

Indeed not. I remember the said child Queens parading in their finery, and it would seem that their deportment and vocabulary owed much to the army of female linen-workers — doffers, weavers, winders, tenters, rovers, spinners, drawers, peelers — who occupied the Lower Falls then, and whose rude formidable presence scared me, as they'd march out from the factories at fog-horn closing-time in linked-armed, chanting phalanxes, taking up the width of the road, and the desultory traffic of the time — trolleybuses, coal-carts, breadvans — would have to draw to an important halt for them.

Hearing the chant of their songs, I am brought back to David Hammond, who used to front a BBC Northern Ireland Home Service schools programme, *Singing Together*; and I was convinced I could remember listening in to it, until I consulted my wife Deirdre, who tells me that she was listening to it when she was about ten, in 1965, when I was seventeen and well outside the aegis of such recreational education, and hadn't met her yet, and wouldn't for quite some time.

So, trying to think myself back into a room in St Gall's Public Elementary School, I can see myself – my eye of memory hovering like a fly – at a scarred initialled desk in Junior or Senior Infants, as Primary One and Two were known then. It is 1954, the centenary of the proclamation of the doctrine of the Immaculate Conception,* and the May altar is especially elaborate this year, starred with many blue and white flowers. The big valve wireless with its confessional brass grille has just been switched on, and it makes a hum as it warms up in preparation for the coming programme. Putting my ear to it over the intervening decades, I can make out snatches of English folk songs through the temporal crackle and blips of passing Morse, rendered in a jolly rumbustious fashion. *As I went down by Strawberry Fair, SINGING, SINGING buttercups and daisies! As I went down by Strawberry Fair, FOL-DE-ROL!.* And I would trip merrily along the gutter on my way home from school in time to it, not knowing, as I do now, that it was a sanitized bawdy ditty collected by notebook-wielding classical composers from beery Lincolnshire farm-labourers, and really had no place in an Irish Catholic Public Elementary school. I do not think that we were allowed to listen to the radio very much, since the school was founded by the Frenchman Jean-Baptiste De la Salle, and controlled by the De la Salle Brothers, who were maintaining a discreet but effective profile in Ireland, would have been rightly suspicious of its Received Pronunciation anglophone Imperial ideals. But there was an ambiguous entropic time-bomb of irony implicit in their calculations, since one of

---

*And of the apparition of the Virgin at Lourdes.

the main aims of Catholic working-class education of that British welfare state era was to teach us to be – if not priests or brothers, or schoolteachers – potential employees of the Imperial Civil Service, because knowledge was power, and if enough of us infiltrated the system, the system might change in our favour; and it is said by some that the Northern Ireland Education Act of 1947, which guaranteed free secondary education for all denominations, was responsible for the onset of the current Troubles, as the educated Catholic students of the sixties took to the streets to demand civil rights for all, and we all know what happened after that. Another pundit declared that the Act had made potentially good carpenters and plumbers into bad poets.

I still love the radio and the comfort of its disembodied voice. Often, insomniac during the writing of this book, scribbling memoranda to myself, I've tuned into the BBC World Service to overhear its missives to abroad, recalling an era when London, more importantly than Rome, was the hub of the universe, emanating authoritative spokes to its dominions. I hear it murmur as I write, and feel complicit with its now-declining realm.

RADIO ULSTER

In the fifties, 'radio' was a medium, as in 'Home Service'; it was not the receiving mechanism, which was called a wireless, referring to non-telegraphic Marconi transmission, as the air-waves, beamed out from radio beacons, became an ambient wallpaper pattern in the home, a background sometimes listened to, or not. As adults talked over it, I would think of tall Empire State Building masts emitting invisible zig-zag lightning-pulses of communication. I would press my ear against the big warm humming Bakelite body, and mentally shrink myself to walk about inside its Toltec labyrinth of valves and tubes and crystals, sometimes encountering giant dust-beetles who would scan me momentarily with alien antennae, and then go about their scarab business of managing the dark interior. There are many sanctuaries within it, many aisles and transepts, dimly lit by the red glow of votive lamps. A sacristan with a broken insect leg sometimes appears to tend the candles, trimming them with an enormous scissors, or snuffing them out with a minuscule bishop's hat on a long stalk. The veins on the back of his hands are rivulets of congealed wax. Sometimes, I encounter creatures like myself, but cannot speak to them, since each of us are rapt or lost in private explorations, murmuring before the shrines, or behind the closed doors of confessionals, where one whispers to the priest through a wire grille which smells of brass, nicotine, aftershave, and cassocks.

These sanctuaries remind me of the BBC Radio Ulster programme, *Tearmann*, which is Irish for sanctuary, with its other connotations of glebe, refuge and asylum; it's a kind of Irish language *Desert Island Discs*, where a featured person is asked to talk about his or her ideal sanctuary or home ground. Interestingly, my father, who appeared on the programme a few weeks ago, chose the language itself as a sanctuary: '*Ba ghnath liom mé féin a chur i bhfolach innti*', as he said, 'I used to hide myself within her', and I see him burrowing down into it, the way I used to, as a child, stick my head into his postman's bag, relishing its enormous gloomy smell of canvas, twine, and faded correspondences. I see him making the language into a book-lined room which has false-shelved secret passageways that lead to glimmering Atlantic beaches and the smell of turf-smoke dwindling upwards from the chimneys of the white-washed cottages scattered about the landscape, intervened by stretches of bog-cotton and little cobalt-blue loughs. I, too, hide in language, within this book; in this respect, at least, I am my father's ilk, or *macasamhla*, as it is in Irish, literally, 'a son of resemblance', hence copy or type, as in *mac leabhair*, a copy of a book. So we have the expression, '*gurab leis gach leabhar a mhac'*, 'to every book belongs its copy', a version of the pronouncement made in one of the first recorded copyright disputes, an account of which I cannot resist quoting here; this is from Patricia Lynch's anthology of the lives of some early Irish saints, *Knights of God*. which my father gave me when I was about ten or eleven:

The Precious Book

A young student staying at Columcille's college, on his way to the West, declared that among St. Finnian's collection of manuscripts was one of the finest he had ever seen.

'It's far better than anything you have here!' he told Columcille.

'St. Finnian!' cried Columcille. 'You mean St. Finnian of Clonard?'

'I do, indeed!' said the student. 'Isn't it a pity you haven't a copy of the book here?'

Columcille laughed.

'That's easily arranged. I will copy it myself! I was at school under St. Finnian. He loves books almost as much as I do and he'll be only too pleased for another copy to be made!'

He set out at once for Clonard. There weren't trains, or buses or motor-cars in Ireland then, but Irish people were always travelling, in chariots, on horses, and, if they had neither chariot nor horse, they went on foot. There were sailing boats and currachs in every port and on every river.

St. Finnian was proud of his old pupil and welcomed him to Clonard. They sat talking about old times, what had happened to the other boys who were at school with Columcille and the terrible state of the world outside Ireland.

Columcille told how he had heard of St. Finnian's precious book.

'I'd be very glad to have a copy of it in my own library!' said Columcille.

The old man leaned back in his chair and shook his head.

'You can read it while you are here and I hope you will stay a very long time. You can study the manuscript, but you must not copy it,' said St. Finnian.

'But——' began Columcille. Then he stopped. He remembered that St. Finnian never changed his mind. He was clever, generous, but obstinate.

Columcille was obstinate too.

'There should be more books!' he thought indignantly. 'There can't be too many and St. Finnian knows as well as I do that the only way to increase the number of books is to copy them. All over Ireland people are learning to read and they need books!'

Late into the night he strode up and down the cell where he was lodged, trying to think of some way of persuading Finnian to let him copy the manuscript.

'I'll give him anything I have. I'll make two copies if he'll let me have one!' he muttered. 'But I must have that one!'

The next day St. Finnian showed Columcille the new buildings, the fine stone wall, and then he showed him his library.

There were far more manuscripts in it than Columcille ever hoped to possess, St. Finnian was so friendly that Columcille could not believe he would still refuse, so he asked him again.

'Copy anything else you wish and do not hurry over the work. Stay till you can stay no longer, but do not ask what has already been refused!' St. Finnian told him.

Like all the O'Neills, Columcille was very proud. He was ashamed that he had asked twice. Leaving St. Finnian without a word, he went back to his cell, determined to leave Clonard at once.

But he could not go without a copy of that precious book.

'Why should he refuse?' he asked himself. 'It isn't to be understood. 'Tis true that Finnian is old and he always was unreasonable, but he does love learning, and all I ask is that where there is one book I shall make two.'

He sat in his cell until all around him the monks and students were asleep. He stared out from the door towards the building where Finnian kept his manuscripts. The night was dark. There was no moon. Not a light shone in the whole place. Far off a dog barked and answering cries came from the forest.

Slowly Columcille walked across the enclosure. A leather satchel swung from a strap over his shoulder. In it he kept his parchments, pens and inks, his paints and a flint for striking a light; a good, thick candle too, made of mixed beef and mutton fat.

The great oak door of the library was latched but not chained. There were no thieves inside the monastery walls.

Yet, like a thief, Columcille noiselessly opened the door, entered and closed it behind him. He struck a light, fixed his candle on a stone slab and took down the manuscript he had determined to copy.

It was a wonderful piece of work. Each capital letter was in colour, with tiny drawings in the curves and loops. Columcille laid it on a desk and turned the pages.

'An artist who loved God made this book!' he said aloud.

He settled to his task.

All night he worked. His hand was stiff with grasping the pen; his head ached; his eyes were closing with weariness when he heard the crowing of a cock.

Starting up he saw that darkness was fading. A pale light was coming into the sky. Dawn was breaking. Soon everyone in Clonard would be up, washing, cleaning, cooking and all praying as they worked. The boys in the school would be yawning and stretching, pleading for another ten minutes, then rushing out into the chill morning air.

The candle wick, the tiny scrap that was still unburned, sank sideways in the melted grease and spluttered out. Columcille scraped it off the stone and, dropping it on the floor, ground what was left of the candle into the rushes strewn on the earth. He replaced the manuscript, gathered up his parchments, his brushes, pens and ink, and went swiftly out. As he reached his cell the great bell rang. Another moment and he would have been discovered.

'I must not work so long,' he decided. 'There are some who rise before dawn to pray. The risk is too great!'

The next night, the following night and the night after that, Columcille wrote and painted, drawing with such care and skill that he knew his copy would be far better than the original book.

During the day he taught in the school, made poems, studied, and slept all he could. Like the other monasteries of Ireland, Clonard had many guests and no one wondered that Columcille should stay so long.

The night came when Columcille copied the last page, the last line. Where there had been one book there were now two. He laid down his pen and leaned back, happy that he had worked so well.

His candle was burning clearly and the tiny light shone out into the night. A shepherd, returning from the fold, saw the gleam and, fearing that robbers were stealing St. Finnian's precious books, crept close up and peeped in.

He could see a monk sitting at a desk with two books before him. He remembered that the famous Psalter was kept there and that the Abbot had forbidden anyone to copy it.

'Why should a man work secretly at night unless he is doing something forbidden?' thought the shepherd. 'St. Finnian is my master. I will not have him wronged!'

He was about to cry out and raise the alarm. Changing his mind he slipped away and beat on Finnian's door.

Finnian heard the story in silence, but he was furious.

'Bring Columcille before me!' he ordered.

Columcille came, marching like a soldier, his head thrown back, his grey eyes flashing.

'You asked if you might make a copy of the Psalter of Clonard!' said Finnian.

'I did!' agreed Columcille.

'And I refused!' declared Finnian. 'You have disobeyed me, but since the work is done I demand the copy.'

'The copy is mine!' cried Columcille. 'I have made the world richer. Other copies shall be made and the sacred learning will spread through Ireland.'

'I will appeal to the King!' said Finnian. 'He shall decide between us!'

All the priests, nobles and poets of Ireland who could reach Tara were assembled there when Diarmuid, the King, was to decide between Finnian and Columcille.

St. Finnian spoke first. He was old and his voice trembled, yet anger made it clear and piercing.

'The book is mine!' he said. 'I had it written. 'Twas my money paid for the smoothest parchments, the clearest ink and the finest ground paints that should make it beautiful. The leather for the cover came from my tannery, the binding was done in my workshop. The book is one of the glories of Clonard! Students and scholars from the most distant parts of Europe have come to study in my library. I made them welcome. I made Columcille welcome. He was my pupil. I was proud of him. When he asked permission to copy my Book of Psalms and I refused, I could not believe he would disobey me. Columcille has betrayed my hospitality! The book is mine. It was copied against my wish. Therefore the copy is mine too!'

'Finnian is right!' cried so many it seemed that everyone in that great hall agreed with him. Yet there were some who shook their heads.

'We will listen to Columcille!' they murmured.

Columcille stood up taller than the men around him, and so straight and fierce amid all these learned men that they remembered he might have been a soldier or even king.

'I have built churches!' cried Columcille. 'They are the monuments of our faith. But without the words and teaching of the Church what meaning would they have for us? It is the written books that matter, and we have so few. All over Ireland men and women are crying out for learning. We have saints and scholars, but we could have more! Where I have found a book, I have always copied it, so that always I was bringing more books into the world. St. Finnian's book is precious. I did not rob him of it. I did not harm it. Only now there are two. I am willing that my book shall belong to Ireland! Any man or woman who can read shall have that copy laid open to study freely. But I will not give it up to Finnian! No! I will not give the toil of nights to Finnian who refused his consent. I will not!'

His keen eyes flashed round on that crowded hall and shouts and cries answered him—

'The copy is yours, Columcille! The copy is yours!'

The noise ceased. All looked at Diarmuid, who sat on his throne, troubled and anxious.

It was a long time before he spoke.

'Here is my judgement – the book was Finnian's. He had the right to refuse or to consent. He refused. Therefore the copy is his. I follow the law – to every cow its calf. That is my judgement, Columcille, and you must abide by it. Give the copy to Finnian!'

Columcille then goes to war over this decision, and the Lynch book has a great illustration by Alfred Kerr of the ringletted and bearded cloaked saint clutching the book in his left hand, and directing the war-traffic behind his back with his right hand, where lancers prance their Clydesdales, and the chain-mailed moustachioed infantry are grim-lipped; and Columcille's one visible eye stares off the margins of the page, anticipating his self-exile, when, after the battle, he vows never to see Ireland again.

I have no doubt that one of the reasons for my father giving me the book in which this story appears is because its first section is devoted to 'Saint Ciaran – the First of Them All'. This is Ciaran of Clear Island, one of the many Ciarans (diminutive of Old Irish, *ciar*, dark-haired) which abound in Irish hagiography; perhaps he wanted me to follow in his footsteps, though the path of the Clear Ciaran is straighter than the one I'm taking through this book:

Patrick took a bell from under his cloak and put it into Ciaran's hands.

'This bell will guide you. It will not make a sound before you come to the well at Fuaran. Then it will ring with a clear note. Be silent as the bell. Do not speak to anyone until the bell rings. Remember – it may be a long time, but I will come!'

Here, our hero gets a ship from Rome to Ireland. Then:

The Bell Rings

Ciaran found a road and followed it. Before evening he came to a well. The water was cold and clear, with a sparkle in it. He drank and washed himself, but there was never sound from the bell.

The road kept near the coast. Sometimes it was a fine highway where two chariots could pass. Then it would grow rough and narrow so that only those who walked could use it.

Ciaran met other roads but did not look at them.

'Time enough to go exploring when the bell rings,' he thought.

When he had been among foreigners, unless they knew Latin, he could not speak with them. Now he was among those who spoke his own language and it was hard to keep silent. People on their way to fairs walked beside him, talking of the price of grain and mead and of the long distances on bad roads. Drivers, liking the look of him, slowed up to offer a lift. Women tending fires, or washing clothes in a stream, called out, wishing Ciaran a safe journey, and he could only smile at them.

Ballad-singers and story-tellers were the best companions. They didn't want him to talk, only to listen, and Ciaran was a good listener.

When the road went round a bay he was glad to cross in a boat. If it went inland along the bank of a river to a bridge, he watched out for a ford.

'Isn't the straight way the best when a man is in a hurry?' he asked himself.

The road went through a thick wood and night was coming on. Ciaran walked in darkness yet he could see sunlight beyond the trees. He went slowly, wondering where he could find shelter.

Eventually, the bell rings. Ciaran finds the well, and builds an oratory. He befriends boars, foxes and badgers, and preaches to them; people coming to the well for water stay to listen. Then, one day, after a sleepless night,

Ciaran stood up and went out of the hut. Dawn was coming over the wood. The tops of the trees were touched with gold. He could hear the crackling of dried leaves and twigs. Strangers were coming.

He climbed the hill which rose above his oratory . . .

At the horizon, clouds piled against the sky.

'Are they clouds?' wondered Ciaran. Turrets, golden and rose coloured, stood beyond the waves. Towers, white or palest blue, rose from glowing roofs. Dawn came, through windows shaped like flowers and stars.

Ciaran had heard stories of Falias, Gorias, Finias, Murias – ancient magic cities of the Danaans who lived in Ireland before the days of history. They were built in a single night, each with its special treasure.

'Can this be one of those cities?'

Then seven hills rose beyond the glittering roofs and Ciaran gazed once more upon the glories of Rome, while the bell of St. Patrick rang from the oratory . . .

I can remember, or imagine my father telling me a story like this, as I hear his voice by way of the disembodied medium of radio;

and I visualize him ensconced in an armchair in my sister's kitchen in Cushendun, where he lives now, looking like a hatless Toby jug with his hands clasped on his pot belly. As he talks, he reveals some aspects of himself that I hadn't picked up on before: for instance, he used to compose poetry in the toilet of the General Post Office where he worked, 'losing himself in the language', escaping clocked time, and I momentarily think of jail journals being written on that semi-opaque thin parsimonious post-War bog-roll (but it would be difficult to write on today's absorbent luxury) and wonder why such documents are never called diaries; 'journal', perhaps, has more implications for posterity and reflection, as the prisoner ponders the world beyond his cell, and justifies the crooked path that led him inside, escaping into language, as he renegotiates his memory to make a story of his life, finding a pattern within it he wouldn't have thought possible, until the words took over, and made hitherto disparate trains of thought connect, as if building an instant underground tunnel between two railway lines; and prisoners often do escape by way of trains, especially when shackled in pairs to each other in forties American films, clambering aboard through the conveniently open door of an empty cattle-car, after they had disengaged themselves by lying parallel on the track so as the wheels of the train would cut their fetters into clichés. And tunnels, were, of course, especially popular, in which the biggest logistical problem was the disposal of dirt, as men walked stiff-legged in the compound with bags of it inside their regulation thick khaki trousers; recently, a Republican tunnel was discovered emanating from an H-block in the Maze Prison, whose name I am sure has nothing to do with the English for labyrinth – more likely, it is a corruption of the Irish for buttock, *más*. I can't remember the waste-disposal details of this plot, but bits of bedstead heads had been used to shore up the walls; the guys had installed an electrical lighting system; later, it was alleged that the authorities knew about the attempt all along, but had maintained a fictional ignorance of it, in order to let the prisoners usefully divert their energies.

Which brings me back to my father, who had spent some days inside, having been mistakenly interned, during the Second World War, in lieu of my Uncle Pat, his brother, who was rumoured to have been in the IRA. This was a minor confraternity of dedicated men who wore slouch hats and trench coats, and conducted manoeuvres on the back-roads of the Antrim hills above Belfast, like distant Irish deputies of Legs Diamond, transported by their one motor-car, which had two rusted pistols and a ceremonial sword concealed beneath its gaping floor-boards; I now remember a corroborating photograph of my Uncle Pat with one foot on the running-board of such a vehicle, grinning like an innocent gangster from under his brim, surrounded by four comrades; and I feel again the tremble of loyalty I felt for his cause when I first set eyes on this snap in my teens. Outside of such photo-calls, IRA men were practically invisible at the time, seeming to exist by rumour or osmosis in a narrative dimension largely inaccessible to the overwhelmingly non-combatant Catholic population. I used to think of them secretly meeting in minuscule cells built into cavity walls, or lying parallel in threes beneath the floorboards of a 'safe house', munching the triangular slices of buttered soda farl provided for them by a spinster sympathizer; I was sure they knew the sewer system of the city inside-out, where they were wont to flit like wills-o'-the-wisp from manholes, into culverts, into niches where they'd stand like statues as the dark police passed underneath unwittingly.

Their underground status was a kind of voluntary imprisonment; indeed, many of them wanted to get caught so as to achieve temporary martyrdom. I used to have fantasies myself of being committed for some idealistic crime or other, and would dream of spending my undistracted time inside quite pleasurably, writing The Great Book, like a monk in his cell, describing Celtic loops and spirals. Coincidentally, in the course of writing this book you are reading, I was sent some entries for a children's Hallowe'en story competition, the 'Spooker Prize', based in Derry. This story by Chris McCauley seems appropriate in the context. It is called:

Star Factory

Star Factory,
Foyle Road,
Derry. Friday 13th October

There is a huge half-crumbling derelict building on Foyle Road. It is called the Star Factory. It has five storeys but I have a far more interesting story to tell you, one you have never heard and one you will never forget.

It was a dark, chilly and completely boring October night. I sneaked out of the house and called round for some friends. We decided to sneak into the school grounds to have a game of football. Climbing over the gate in Bishop Street, we stealthily slipped over to the building beside the PE hall. I looked to see if anyone had seen us. Nobody was there, so we crept cautiously down to the pitch.

The game was going well and nobody had seen us. It was almost impossible to score against Kevin 'Schmeichel' Ryan or tackle Andrew 'Striker' McIvor and Seamus 'good pass' O'Reilly. But then ghosting through the middle I hit a shot fiercely. It ricocheted off Seamus's head and into the Star Factory. I wasn't going to let my new ball sit there for long so I was after it like Michael Schumaker on a Sunday evening.

Over the wires I went, I rummaged through the rubbish. I searched everywhere but there was no sign of my ball. Then I noticed a door I had never seen before. It was a solid wooden door with metal studs and rusting hinges. The paint was cracked and peeling. Surprisingly, the door showed no signs of being burnt, although the walls were scorched a dark ash-black from the fire which had destroyed the building. There was an old rusty handle which strange to say turned quite easily. I should have known then that something weird was going to happen, but I could never have guessed.

The door swung open to reveal a chamber . . . (*here, the photocopied typescript must have got a dog-eared bottom edge, and some words are missing*) . . . to get that ball if it was the last thing I did (it was a foolish mistake).

I marched straight into the room. Just at that moment, all along one wall there was a haze which simmered for a moment, then turned into people. They were women all working at sewing machines making shirts. They seemed to hover above the ground and the shirts floated into piles on their own. I began to walk forward. I couldn't stop myself. It was as if my body had been taken over by some strange power. The apparitions didn't seem to see me, but then an old woman beckoned me to her. Something told me there was nothing to be afraid of, so I slowly walked towards her.

'You should get out of here,' she whispered. 'Because if you stay here for over half an hour you will become a ghost like them, and you will only be allowed to be human for half an hour a year. You don't want to end up like them.' She pointed to some ghostly boys who had come looking for their footballs when they went in the Star Factory and beside them a cabinet which just . . (*a word or two is missing in the original*) . . . above the bottom of the cabinet with an eerie glow. These were the lost footballs. At that moment the college clock began to strike twelve. I ran towards the door as fast as I could. Just as I was about to reach for the handle the bell struck twelve and the door slammed shut. I went to grab the handle but my hand went straight through it. Too late!

I am now a ghost, trapped in the Star Factory, for the exception of half an hour, when I am able to leave the ghost world and enter the human world. I have taken this year's time to write this story to you in the hope that people will know the real danger of the Star Factory but I am already running out of energy. I must go.

Yours phantomly,
Chris McCauley

This beautifully constructed story, this missive from the Underworld, still gives me a serendipitous* *frisson*, and I am

---

* I confess I never knew the derivation of this word, until I looked it up, just now serendipitously, in *Chambers' Dictionary*. **Serendipity**, the faculty of making happy chance finds (*Serendip*, a former name for Sri Lanka. Horace Walpole coined the word (1754) from the title of the fairy tale 'The Three Princes of Serendip', whose heroes 'were always making discoveries, by accidents and sagacity, of things they were not in quest of'.)

grateful to Chris McCauley for allowing me to reproduce it here.

The two Star Factories suggest that there might have been a minor chain or constellation of them, but in a way I prefer just the two: I would say that the Derry Star would have been the first, Derry having been famous for shirt-making, and the Belfast Star an offspring, which gives an interesting twist to the Derry *versus* Belfast rivalry, whereby the Derry people imagine themselves to be superior beings, more talented with anecdote and wit than we taciturn Belfastians; and while they inhabit a Northwest Athens, we endure an industrial slum. Also, they are great singers in Derry, as evidenced by local girl Dana's having won the Eurovision song contest in 1970.

I think now of the Belfast to Derry railway, which once occupied the track of the Great Northern line south of the Bog Meadows, and the strung-out corresponding static march of electricity pylons some hundreds of yards to its north. At that time, pylons were wont to be blown up by the IRA, as if they were not already dangerous enough, with their skull-and-crossbones signs and barbed wire looped around the perimeter of their first stages. When it drizzled, they sounded like badly tuned field radios, and sent shivers down your spine as you crossed their force-field. One such armatured Eiffel Tower occupied a salient position just behind Mooreland; on rainy nights, drifting off to sleep, I imagined its sigmatic noises to be interference from the stars.

BALACLAVA STREET

I still dream about the half-acre behind Mooreland, and its various stages of field, leftover landscape, vacant ground, plot, building-site, half-built houses, and completed semi-detacheds. Here, there is a network of small paths between the privet and convolvulus demarcations of back gardens, where it sometimes rains cherry-blossom, or the overpowering odour of sweet-pea stains the air with tinctures of pale lilac, purple, yellow-pepper-yellow, ruby, celadon, and dazzling apple-white. Starch-white sheets billow on clothes lines, washed in Surf or Tide. Little picket gates and hedgy archways provide interesting access points to the gardens and their crazy paving winding among small lawns, rose arrays and vegetable patches. One such creaking gate leads to the stepping-stones of the stream. There is a small beach of gravel here, where I can hunker for unknown hours and watch the current burl and bump across the pebbles.

Stepping across to the other side, I plunge into the era of the building-site: an aura of raftered pine and brick, wood-shavings and cement-dust.

It was a world of half-finished structures, whose exo-skeletons of scaffolding were connected, Babel-wise, in gangways, hoists, ladders, platforms, ropes and planks. It had the presence of a great interminable siege, as we stalked its storeyed parapets and battlements and gazed down across its blasted landscape of earth-works and ziggurats of brick, and churned mud where cement-mixers were embedded like mortars. Discarded hods and buckets lay scattered everywhere, like details in a documentary of Breughel building techniques.

Before the building-site proper existed, deep trenches were dug in the back field. Roofed with corrugated iron and floored with bits of cast-off carpet, they made admirable suburban HQs, where our wish to be invisible could be realized, as it was in wardrobes, hedges, under stairs or attic roofs, in peek-a-boo routines of out-of-sight and out-of-mind.

Games of pursuit were thus inevitable – Cowboys and Indians, hide-and-seek, of course, but also the many variants of tag, or tig,* as we called it. In Rally-o, the person tigged had to remain rooted to the spot, but could be freed if a peer spat over his head and shouted 'Rally-o!' at the same time. In ground-tig, the players who were not 'it' could be out-of-bounds by being above

---

*I am pleased that *Chambers 20th Century Dictionary* gives 'tag' as 'the game of tig'; 'tig' is defined as a touch, a twitch, a game on which one who is 'it' attempts to touch another.

street-level, however infinitisimally: one would perch on garden walls and swing on gates, or clutch at hedges and lamp-posts with all fours, discovering new latitudes of elevation. This was a game for taunts and bluff, where a player could cock a snook by advancing to an almost-tiggable position from the refuge of a dustbin, like a runner trying to steal a base in baseball, which can be thought of as an elaborate game of tag.

Kick-the-tin, a hybrid of tig and hide-and-seek, employed an empty tin can as a release-mechanism, which, if kicked away from its central location, allowed players time to find new hiding-places while 'it' retrieved the can and replaced it on its spot. Thus the can was a kind of clock with differential radii, depending on the angle and length of the kick: it recalls the vatic tin-can ghost of the Lower Falls, which was heard tripping down the gutter, but never seen, any time there might be trouble in the offing. It was first heard in the twenties, when a policeman was shot dead outside the National Bank on the corner of Balaclava Street; since its habitat has been demolished, it has not been heard, but its memory lives on, even within the minds of those who'd never heard it, since it had acquired the status of a story.

Now, when I lie awake on a windy night and hear the vacillating roulette trickle of a tin can, I feel a shiver of impending doom, as Glandore blurs into Balaclava, the can resounding off the street in fits and starts – melismatic, rallentando phrases, broken by lulls and false denouements – till at last it ticks to a stop, or I fall asleep. Then I am prompted to step out of my body, to glide at second-storey level through the dark streets in a Wee Willie Winkie nightgown, making sure that everyone is safe in bed –

Rapping at the windows, crying through the lock,
Are the children in their beds? Now it's eight o'clock —

which reminds me, that in my father's and mother's time, men
were hired to walk the streets with long poles in the dawn to
knock on bedroom windows, like antonyms of lamplighters,
waking people up for work, before the advent of alarm-clocks. A
broken Westclox alarm-clock with luminous numerals and hands
was a fixture in one of the tin-roofed catacombs of Mooreland,
providing the hastily conscripted crew with an important focus of
radium power; on other occasions, it could be a compass, or a
depth-gauge, as our dug-out-turned-submarine escaped the
enemy above by sinking to hitherto unfathomable depths. The
needle descends the dial; the riveted steel panels start to creak
and give at the seams as the sea spits and boils through them; and
the whole craft threatens to break up under the unprecedented
pressure, till it settles, with a slow, musical bass clank, on an
angle of the sea-bed. At this stage in the story, the sweating crew
heaves a collective sigh of relief, except the captain, who has
seen it all before and knows there's more to come.

We placed the clock in a tabernacle niche gouged out from the
clay wall of the trench. There were other votive cavities, containing an array of minor icons, like bunches of defunct keys,
candle-stumps, and empty snuff-tins. The clay of the trench wall
was malleable as Plasticine, and from it we'd make brick cities —
Lilliputs of Belfast — on the plain above, and bombard them with
marbles or pebbles, for a condition of the city was its eventual
destruction. Then men came with cross-staves and theodolites,

and paced the landscape; shortly after, a giant yellow earth-moving machine moved in and tore a swathe across the war theatre; and our blitzed stage properties vanished forever under the chevroned caterpillar-tracks of Brobdingnag. The houses started to go up, attaining hitherto unknown levels. I used to watch the bricklayers ply their trade, as they deployed masonic tools of plumb-line, try-square and spirit-level, setting up taut parallels of pegs and string, before throwing down neatly gauged dollops of mortar, laying bricks in practised, quick monotony, chinking each into its matrix with skilled dints of the trowel. Had their basic modules been alphabet bricks, I could have seen them building lapidary sentences and paragraphs, as the storeyed houses became emboldened by their hyphenated, skyward narrative, and entered the ongoing, fractious epic that is Belfast.

THE ULSTER
CINEMATOGRAPH THEATRES

I have a tangled recurrent dream of the dense urban space of Arthur Square and its confluence of five streets – Corn Market, Ann Street, Castle Lane, William Street South and Arthur Street, each with its tributaries of arcades, alleyways and entries. It is a precinct crammed with shops, stores, offices, public houses, cafés, cinemas: here are Joseph Braddell & Son, Gunmakers, Fishing Rod and Tackle Manufacturers; Guest, Keen & Nettlefolds, Ltd., Iron & Steel, Bolt, Nut & Screw Manufacturers; Wm. Rodman & Co., Heraldic and General Stationers, Fancy Goods Warehouse, Print Sellers, Gilders, Picture Frame Makers, Photographic and Artists' Materials Depot; M'Gee and Co. Ltd., Military, Naval and Ladies' Tailors, Inventors of the Ulster Coat and Slieve Donard Coat; the X.L. Café and Restaurant; Gillis & M'Farlane, Mayfair School of Dancing; W.J. Kidd & Sons, Boot Upper Manufacturers and

Leather Merchants; and The Ulster Cinematograph Theatres, Ltd., (Imperial Picture House & Café), where I saw my first film, Disney's version of the Jules Verne classic, *20,000 Leagues under the Sea*, issued in 1954, and starring James Mason as the enigmatic Captain Nemo. The film diverges from the book in several instances, most notably at the end, where the *Nautilus* and Nemo's island hideaway are blown up by an atomic bomb; in the book, Nemo drives his vessel into the maelstrom, where 'at the tide, the pent-up waters between the islands of Ferroe and Loffenden rush with irresistible violence, forming a whirlpool from which no vessel ever escapes', recalling Edgar Allan Poe's story, 'A Descent into the Maelstrom', passages of which put me in mind of the tornado in *The Wizard of Oz*, which was, I think, the second film I ever saw:

> Looking about me upon the wide waste of liquid ebony on which we were thus borne, I perceived that our boat was not the only object in the embrace of the whirl. Both above and below us were visible fragments of vessels, large masses of building-timber and trunks of trees, with many smaller articles, such as pieces of house furniture, broken boxes, barrels and staves . . .

And the schoolhouse in Poe's story 'William Wilson' (surely a precursor of Wilde's *The Picture of Dorian Gray*), in its inscrutable internal dimensions, resembles my dreams of Belfast:

> But the house! – how quaint an old building was this! – to me how veritably a palace of enchantment! There was really no end to its windings – to its incomprehensible subdivisions. It was difficult,

at any given time, to say with certainty upon which of its two stories one happened to be. From each room to every other were sure to be found three or four steps in ascent or descent. Then the lateral branches were innumerable — inconceivable — and so returning in on themselves, that our most exact ideas in regard to the whole mansion were not very far different from those with which we pondered on infinity.

Pleasurably lost, I wander through the palpable dream, touching its surfaces of brick and granite, sniffing the soot-flecked air; usually, it is night-time, but the shops are all lit up and open, forming bright inviting porticos. Sometimes, with a *doppelgänger* jolt, I recognize this is the real world, only slightly altered from when last I visited, or was invited, and I acknowledge my shadow. Finding myself in the sleep department of a vast emporium — I have just climbed its marble Versailles staircase — I resist the urge to bury myself in a double bed, since this is a lucid device for escaping the dream, should one wish to; instructed by an exit sign, I am led down some steps, and emerge in the upper lounge of the Morning Star in Pottinger's Entry, inhaling its immediate smoky beery aura. The barman is none other than William Hartnell, who played the head barman in Carol Reed's 1947 film, *Odd Man Out*, which starred James Mason as a fugitive revolutionary, Johnny McQueen, and I am reminded again of the similar roles of Nemo and McQueen, both highly dedicated criminal idealists. One attempts to rob the wages office of a linen mill to finance his operations; the other loots sunken galleons. Both are haunted by their past; both conspire against the Empire.

The basic plot of *Odd Man Out* (taken from F.L. Green's novel of the same name; Green collaborated on the screenplay) is simple: the robbery of the mill is botched, and McQueen,* although we have been given to understand he abhors violence, accidentally shoots dead a wages clerk and wounds himself. The get-away driver panics, and McQueen is left to wander the city, pursued by the authorities and by his own men, who have arranged for him to escape by boat; *en route*, he encounters a number of characters who have various motives for helping him, or selling him. The weather gets progressively worse, as the almost-incessant rain turns to snow; at the end, McQueen and his girl partner are cornered at the harbour gates. She takes a gun and fires at the approaching officers; they return fire; she and McQueen are both shot dead.

The city in which the film is set is not named, but is immediately identifiable from the opening aerial shot, which pans in

---

*Reed is generally faithful to Green's text; but in the book, 'the Chief of the militant Revolutionary Organisation . . . was Aloysius John Murtah . . . known throughout the land as Johnny.' I had thought that McQueen might be a version of Quinn, from the Irish Ó Coinn, a descendant of Conn; appropriately, the ancient Irish hero Conn bears the epithet 'of a hundred battles'. However, according to my quizmaster and singer friend, Brian Mullen, McQueen is generally recognized to be from Mac Shuibhne, son of Sweeney, also anglicized as Mawhinnney and McWeeney: and the mythical Sweeney is a King of Ulster who, driven mad by the events of the battle of Moira, imagines himself to be a bird pursued, flitting eternally through the trees, an outcast from society. Sweeney is one of the main protagonists of Flann O'Brien's novel, *At Swim Two Birds*, which Reed might have read. One might also ponder the homosexual, or royal, implications of 'McQueen'; and James Mason's notoriously unstable 'Oirish' accent offers a further ambiguity, that of the nationalist leader who comes from elsewhere, like Hitler, Napoleon, or Seán Mac Stiofáin (John Stephenson), a commander of the IRA in the 1960s who disguised his English birth by adopting in a weird accent possibly influenced by Mason.

from over Belfast Lough – literally, 'across the water' – showing us docks, factories, church spires, before focusing on the Albert Clock, which will become a repetitive icon in the unfolding drama, as we read its four faces from various narrative angles, and the toll of its bell reminds the participants and us of the passing of inexorable time. The city is a Daedalian construct, a precursor of Reed's Vienna of *The Third Man*, in which even the street scenes, with their strong Caravaggio chiaroscuros, look like interiors, their darkness sporadically relieved by lighted pubs and corner shops; hearse-like cars glide through the gloom, or are parked resignedly at kerbs. As McQueen begins to suffer from bouts of delirium, his cul-de-sac series of places of refuge – an air-raid shelter, a derelict brick-kiln, a bath-tub in a junkyard, the baroque delapidation of an artist's studio – come to resemblethe cells and chambers of the prison he has escaped from. Belfast is a prison; McQueen is an internal exile.

One such famous scene takes place in a bar called the Four Winds, a meticulous reconstruction of the Crown Bar – reconstructed, I imagine, because the film technology of the time could not be accommodated within the actual space of the bar, particularly given Reed's deployment of skewed *Doctor Caligari* camera angles. The Crown, like many old Belfast pubs, has a row of compartments – booths, or 'boxes', as they are known here, though Green calls them cribs – which can be snibbed from inside, thus ensuring privacy for whatever transactions occur within; there is a bell system for summoning a waiter: internal space within internal space. In one of these boxes within a box, McQueen, reluctantly abetted by William Hartnell, finds temporary respite from his pursuers. Many years later, Hartnell was to put his dapper authority to good use when he played the first Doctor Who, the pseudonymous protagonist of the eponymous BBC TV science fiction serial. The Doctor is a Prospero or Nemo, a Time Lord exiled from his peers, flitting through the universe in his dimension-bending vehicle, the 'Tardis'. The outward aspect of the 'Tardis' is that of a British police telephone box, but its inner surface area is many times greater, forming an intestine maze of chambers, ante-rooms and corridors. One of the serial gags of the plot is the Doctor's hit-and-miss relationship with his craft (and surely the name is a joke, from the Latin *tardus*, slow); manipulating the sixties futuristic control-panel, checking all the calibrations, pulling out the Nemo organ stops, he plots a course to an intended destination; almost invariably, he weighs in at the wrong place and the wrong time, in the middle of a local revolution, or an alien invasion.

The Crown Bar Box is a kind of time-machine, whose interior can accommodate the conversational buzz of about a dozen characters, each with tall anecdotes to tell, whose different times and places interpenetrate the fabric, making a noise like the atmospheric crackle of several short-wave radios yakking simultaneously, hardly interrupted by the giving of a complicated order to the bemused waiter. In these circumstances, time goes by with great rapidity, until 'time' is called, and grave white-aproned barmen move among the throng, clinking empty tumblers, glasses, bottles. Then you find yourself pitched out into the starry breeze of a night beyond the open door, already eager for the sobering vinegar tang of fish and chips.

Meanwhile, back in the *Odd Man Out* set, Mason is entering a jail delirium again, freaked out by the thrum and buzz of social blather from the world beyond the crib; and we are reminded again of Reed's elegant deployment of sound to hint at other, parallel dimensions. The sound-track pulses with the noise of the city, which is punctuated, at important desultory intervals, by the bass saxophone fog-note of the escape-vessel, and the afore-mentioned boom of the Albert Clock. Reed's ear has picked up a cue from this passage in Green's novel, and has amplified it, so that it becomes an aural map:

The others were silent. They were listening to the passage of police cars in the neighbouring streets. The sounds were lifted by the rising wind and carried over the whole district. Occasionally a shriek ascended like the thin tip of a flame twisting and detach-ing itself to float away and expire or become obliterated by the noisy passing of a private car or lorry on the main road. From somewhere far distant, the sound of a tramcar speeding along a straight road was audible like the noise of life itself in all its indif-ference to the personal tragedy. A train's whistle blew for several seconds, and this was followed by the clang of shunting-wagons in a marshalling-yard. And from the docks came the slow-majes-tic note of a ship's siren. The three men standing irresolutely in the windswept, empty street heard it. Momentarily, it lifted their sordid lives to the contemplation of life beyond the streets which their own bitter purpose had made deadly. It proclaimed the ocean and wide lands, and rendered small and trivial by compar-ison the meagre territory and the unrelenting civil strife that were all that these three outlaws had known from earliest infancy.

And last night, as I slept, my dreams were infiltrated by the atmospheric throb of a surveillant helicopter, vacillating high above the roof of the house like a rogue star; I heard the *doppel-gänger*-doppler noise of ambulance and fire-appliance; I heard dogs howl disconsolately, as someone, not too far away, tinkered with the same wrong note of a blue, piano-keyed accordion. Just after dawn, I was wakened by the clinking of a milkman's electric float, and remembered empty bottles being used for petrol bombs, fusillading against the incongruous drab-and-olive camouflage of armoured cars, as the riot-torn dark street flickered like an annex of an iron-foundry or inferno.

The dream shifts again, and I am trapped in a grey force-field between the Shankill and the Falls. A magnetic storm has skewed the normal compass of the district, and the poles are all the wrong way round, repelling when they should attract. Directions are revised, as previously communicating streets are misaligned. The powerful anti-gravitational friction has caused tectonic faults to open up, from which emerge, like flotillas salvaged from the bottom of the North Atlantic, the regurgitated superstructures of defunct, Titanic industries: tilted, blackened spinning-mills; the loading-docks of great bakeries at dawn, illuminated by the smell of electricity and yeast; waterworks in convoluted ravines – dams, races, bridges, locks, conduits, sinks, culverts, sluices, ponds, and acqueducts; tentacles and cables of Leviathan, swarming to the surface from a buried ropewalk; catacomb-like brick-kilns.

Some of these apparitions are more palpable than others, and may be walked around or in, and explored, once one has worked out how to reach them, for the streets turn into stairs or wynds when least expected. Some have a wobbly mirage tinge about their edges, their reality already decomposing on exposure to the semi-lucid air; when you brush against them, they collapse, and vanish with a sound like falling soot. Sometimes, their demise results in a new regime, and I find myself in a neat terraced street of two-up-one-down houses, their façades painted in blue and red hues, white half-moons scrubbed before the doors, and identical vases arranged with sweet william in all the windows.

Children are playing. One has attached a rope to the neck of a lamp-post, and spins round it in a dwindle swing. One trundles the hoop of a bicycle-wheel rim with a bit of bent wire. Another bounces a ball between her legs against a wall. Two are burling a skipping-rope, as an endless loop of five trips in and out in syncopated time. Three hop on squares scotched on the granite pavement. Four are taking giant steps and baby steps in staggered sequences. Seven are playing hide-and-seek, but only one is visible. Six in a game of ground-tig have found four window-sill asylums. A minor troop of leather-belted boy scouts drills up and down the cobbled middle of the street, blowing a Lillibulero tune on tin kazoos. Unconsciously, I fall into step, until I suspect a trap. Only then do I remember the two chunks of dynamo-magnet in my pocket. I take them out, and push their North poles together, feeling them vibrate and hum. They touch; the street-scene shimmers briefly, and I step through its fog into home territory, rubbing my eyes, like an escapee from a film matinée, stumbling into daylight.

I am standing before the door of my grandmother's house at 3 O'Neill Street.

O'NEILL STREET

I see a lit coronet of gas hissing under a blue kettle, as it begins to
whistle up a head of steam on the top of the 'stove', as we called
this domestic appliance, whose overhead rack was habitually
draped with drying socks and drawers; an almost-cool oven contained recently washed empty jars of various sizes for jam-making
time, when a purple vat would simmer for hours, and blackberry aromas lingered around the kitchen in their aftermath. I
loved the warmed, clean, glass jars, the long-handled aluminium
ladle filling them with glop; the sacramental discs of waxed paper
tamped on to the jam-skim; then a larger circumference of
crimped-edged lid would be applied, and bound by a rubber
band. I would be allowed to stick on the dated labels.

I recognize I have just indulged in some kind of Transferred
Memory Syndrome, whereby my mother's kitchen in 3 Mooreland Drive gets blurred and shadowed, combining with the

scullery of 3 O'Neill Street in the foxed mercury of a deteriorating mirror. I feel myself to be of baby-length, crawling between my granny's slippers, sniffing their woolly bobbles and the dust-balls trembling on the cool linoleum. This had a trellis pattern, and my fingers could explore its avenues, alleyways and arbours for a small eternity of time. An enormous fractal space could be discerned within the microcosmic confines of O'Neill Street. Its ostensible plan – a 'kitchen' room and a meagre scullery down-stairs, two box-bedrooms up – once examined, led to nook-and-cranny narrative regimes, whose focus was the hearth and its Dickensian component parts: the black, hob-accompanied cast-iron grate; the conjugated poker, tongs, brush and shovel; the dented brass fender, and its hinterland of tiles; fresh coals on the fire, beginning to pout and bubble and spit; the tiles flickering with the same effect; the miniature Grecian urns embroidered on the two plinths which support the mantelpiece; the mantelpiece agog with ornaments, of which two, at least, have survived the demolition of O'Neill Street some twenty years ago.

The first is a thimble-holder, carved from one bit of wood in the shape of a thumb-sized owl perched on a hollow tree-stump; it is nicotined with age, but where it has been scuffed by acciden-tal history, there are traces of a blond wood that might be ash. I have it before me now, trying to return its quizzical gaze, for its eye-beads of black resin have been slightly misaligned. Its ears have long since been knocked off, the scars worn smooth by gen-erations of caressing thumbs and fingers. This owl was and is a small, powerful icon. Looking into the ink-well abyss of its thim-ble-receptacle, I re-imagine fairy-tales in which such black holes are adits to an underworld, patrolled by speaking dogs, I remember, in the Falls Park, the scoop in the bole of a tree, which had acquired a mossy basin sometimes filled with rainwater, where I would conceal coins and come back to retrieve them weeks later; I knew, then, that no one else had stumbled on this portal to the universe, and only I had access to it. Then, the gravel walks on which I ran back to my family assumed a grave significance of dance-step patterns, which I tried to follow with my Plimsoll footprints; I'd run faster, faster, till I took off like an owl, and, gliding low, I could intercept my shadow, and tell it to slow down.

The owl reminds me of its kinship to the bat, both night foragers, denizens of barns, attics, belfries and hollow trees; of hieroglyphic deities; of how the apparition of the Great White Barn-owl can be attributed to the banshee, how owls are general harbingers of doom; of harvest-mice, scurrying amid their cereal arcades, transfixed by a pair of searchlight eyes; of the time-bending, oracular call of the owl.

The second ornament is a milkmaid figurine of Dresden mode. So, I remember Dresden, which I visited briefly some years ago, not long after the fall of the Berlin Wall. They were in the initial stages of rebuilding the Frauenkirche, a Baroque mass of rubble tumbled between the remnants of a tower and the apse, and had begun to sort out its chaos; neatly numbered stones lay arranged on steel racks. I was aware of such jigsaw techniques from the Ulster Folk Museum, which relocated old buildings to its domain at Cultra; but there, the curators were merely taking apart and putting together again a 1:1 scale model; here, the whole enormous lapidary havoc was beyond me, a Humpty-Dumpty task as impossible as piecing together O'Neill Street from its dislocated, scattered fragments. Yet, reconstruction of the Frauenkirche proceeds apace, and they reckon to have the edifice finished by the year 2006.

Walking into a kitchen house in 'Rowland Terrace' in the Ulster Folk and Transport Museum, to give it its full title, I am returned to 3 O'Neill Street, even though the Rowland home has, since its relocation, lost its patina of being lived in, and buzz of conversations past. And, though Rowland Street came from off Sandy Row, on the opposite side of Belfast's sectarian divide, I recognize its furniture and ornaments: the mantel-clock; the dresser backed against the staircase; the Singer treadle sewing-machine, which in O'Neill Street occupied a niche opposite the foot of the stairs, between the chimney-breast and the yard window. The Singer looked like a prototype time-machine in its shellac-black, gold-scrolled body-armour and fitments of chromed-steel chattering parts; for one pedal movement of the treadle, the seamstress got about sixty split-seconds of stitches, as she distributed the fabric of needle-punctured time away from her in piecework fashion.

When not in use, the Singer was hidden from sight beneath its curved wooden cover, that looked like a small catafalque or tabernacle on an altar; yet one could still sense, within that dark interior, a darker, magnet-heavy, die-cast presence brooding in a must of gramophone machine-oil. De luxe models folded surreptitiously, on greased hinges, into a matrix of the table, and when the operator concealed the prostrate machine with a fitted panel, the whole console was transformed into a piece of furniture – a davenport, perhaps, or an occasional table with its case of dried flowers placed on a frilly doily. This is an engaging management of space, where the Singer is horizontally entombed between the table's laminates like an Egyptian fossil. There is a hide-and-seek philosophy about it, reminding me that when I looked up 'davenport' (I wanted another word for 'writing-desk') in *Chambers 20th Century Dictionary*,* I chanced on 'davenport-trick', 'an artifice by which a man can free himself from ropes wound round him and tied. [From two imposters who practised it (fl. 1845-65).]' The next four entries read:

> **Davis apparatus**, a device making possible escape from a crippled submarine [From the inventor].
> **davit**, one of a pair of erections on a ship for lowering or hoisting a boat. [App. from the name *David*].
> **Davy, Davy-lamp**, the safety-lamp used in coalmines invented by Sir Humphrey *Davy* (1778–1829).
> **Davy Jones**, a sailor's familiar name for the (malignant) spirit of the sea, the devil.- *Davy Jones's locker*, the sea, as the grave of men drowned at sea. [Origin unknown].

An inspired alphabetical sequence, which gives the bones of an elaborate narrative, a Captain Nemo–Houdini routine, where we visualize a globe-helmeted, leaden-booted figure in slow motion on the snowy TV-screen ocean floor, bearing a flambeau: upwardly streaming, empty word-bubbles.

---

*What an appropriate name for a dictionary, with its implications of legal wranglings in book-lined inner sanctums, of precedents and antecedents, of rooms within rooms.

So I would sit in the submarine control-space of the Singer, guiding it through cloudy grottoes; sometimes, as my attention wandered, I would find myself gazing upwards into the steep crook of the stairs instead, thinking of the coal-hole underneath them and how it was reached by way of the scullery, where I hear the boom of the stove being lit with one of those will-o-the-wisp sparking devices.

The coalman appears like Lucifer in a flash of clapped-out light, smelling of squibs, the whites of his eyes glaring from beneath his Pharaonic headgear. There are white dots on his knuckles as he clutches the twisted ears of the black dead weight on his back. Reaching the scullery, he stoops into the portal of the coal sack galaxy, undoes the ears, and jettisons a tumbling load of fractured lumps. The slack, exhausted bag is taken back to the lorry, flopped down, and another, packed with knobbles, is taken in for deposition. Long after he had disappeared, the coalman's cloak of coal-dust aura lingered in the silty air.

The coalman and the sweep were kinsmen, alter egos allied in a carbon-burning life, whose aeons' residue was furred impalpably within the chimney. Yet both were independent agents, and the sweep was a solitary genius, teetering on his slow high bicycle down foggy gas-lit side-streets, balancing the *fasces* of his trade on his right shoulder. Arriving at the venue, he would unroll his equipment, and drape the fireplace with a pall; operating in behind it like a blind man, he socketed a length of cane into the brush-head, then another, feeling his way in integers of telescopic stalk. Arriving at the end of it, he'd ask us children to go out responsibly on to the street to check the apparition of the black chrysanthemum: up periscope!

Now it is time for the lamplighter to make his rounds in the dusk. I used to see him from my bedroom window, propping his short ladder against the cold, cast-iron pole, opening the Aladdin glass door, applying his taper. The gaslamp popped and flared, then steadied to a bright oasis. Across the city, lights came on in ones and ones, linked by subterranean realms of gas.

I am not quite asleep yet. My father sits on the bed. I feel his comfortable, draped weight on me. He coughs, as if it were a prelude to a great orchestral concert, or a Midnight Mass – a fusillade before the quiet of the Introit – then stubs out his cigarette, and begins to tell a story:

WHITE STAR STREET

Will Gallagher was a blacksmith; he maintained a smithy on the main road out of Carrick. Here he would spend days and parts of most nights working hard at shoeing horses. He'd work Sundays and Holy Days, for he had little fear of God; and in those bygone days, when train and motor-car remained to be invented, a smith had bags of work, since horses were a most important mode of transport.

Every night, his day's work done, Will would drop into the Wishing Well, and drink till well past closing time. One night, in a drunken knot of conversation, he began to give off about this and that, about the hard life of the smith, and the sweat of his brow, et cetera.

— It must be, says he to one companion, there must be an easier way to earn your bread, than to be humped over an eternal furnace, working from dark to dark, and my back near broken.

— There is, indeed, his drinking partner says, have you ever
hear tell of the Black Art?

— I have, says Will, you mean to sell your soul to the Devil?
And he started to think about it. He spoke no more that night.
After a while, he went home, still pondering the implications of
the Black Art.

He'd heard somewhere that the way to contact the Devil was
to recite the Pater Noster backwards. So he shut his eyes, and for
the first time in many's a long year, knelt down by his bedside,
and began to say the Lord's Prayer the wrong way round. No
sooner had the last word passed his lips — or should I say, the
first — than His Satanic Majesty appears in a zap of black lightning.

— I am Lucifer, he says, why do you summon me from the
Nether Regions?

— I'd like, says Will, to sell my soul to you, for I reckon I'm
going to hell in any case.

— OK, says Satan, what would you like in exchange for your
soul?

— Well, says Will, I'd like one of them inexhaustible purses,
whereby no matter how much I withdraw from my account, I
will always be in the black. And I'd like, of course, the standard
three wishes: the first wish, should anybody sit in that chair in the
corner, that he cannot be released from it except at my behest;
the second — should a body lift the broom in the corner, he'll
stick fast to it, till I tell him to let go; and the third — should anybody lay his hand on the appletree in the back yard, he'll be
magnetized to it, until I give the word.

— It's a deal, says Mephistopheles, and he throws a bag of gold
at him.

There was another bolt of lightning, and the Cloven Hoofed
One vanished.

Will peeped into the money bag: it was filled to the brim. He spilled some bits of gold across the table; the bag stayed full. He began to dance a jig and a reel.

— I am rich, immeasurably rich! Free forever from the forge!

From then on, he spent his days and his nights in the pub, running the gamut of wine, women and song, till, one day, the seven years were up, and Your Man appears once more in a fart of brimstone.

— Willie Gallagher, says he, your number's up; the seven years are spent; and now I've come to take you to the Lake of Fire.

— Fair enough, says Will, let you sit down in that chair and take your ease, for your feet must be killing you. The Lord of Flies sat down. When Will came back, wearing his hat, Satan tried to extricate himself, but could not. His nether region was stuck to the seat.

— Let me out of here, he says to Will.

By God, says Will, I will not — well, maybe I will, if you give me another seven years.

— Oh, all right, then, says Old Nick, and he was gone again in the blink of an eye.

Relieved of the presence of the Black Prince, Will went on the tear again; and seven years went by like seven weeks. One night, he was wakened by a thunderbolt: there was Old Scratch at the foot of the bed.

— Come with me, O Billy Gallagher, says he, and you will come, for I'll not sit down in your damned chair.

— Fair enough, says Liam, I know when I'm beat, but would you mind giving the floor a bit of a sweep while I go and get my hat, for you're a tidy man, and I know you'd like the house to look good for whoever might come after me.

The Devil lifted a broom from the corner and began to sweep

the floor. But he found that the broom had taken on a life of its own; nor would it let him go.

– Get this brush off me! shouts Lucifer.

– By God, says Will, I will not – well, maybe I will, if you go back to the Flags of Hell and leave me alone for another seven years.

Mephistopheles had no option; he vanished in a cloud of smoke.

The seven years went by, as had the other fourteen. One night, Willie was about to go out to cure his hangover. An almighty clap of thunder hit the house, and there stood His Black Nibs at the door. He gripped our hero by the shoulder, and said: – I have you now, Bill Gallagher, and I'll never let you go, until I see you in the darkest pit of Hell.

– Well, says Liam, I guess the game is up, and if a man has to go, he has to go, but tell me this, Satan, do you ever get thirsty?

– Thirsty? says the Devil, do you not know anything about my habitat? The brimstone lakes? My minions turning boys like you on spits? You'll know all about thirst when I've got you there.

– Well, says William, there's a fine crop of Cox's Orange Pippins on that tree in the back-yard. Away out and pick yourself a couple for the journey, while I lace up these boots.

Your Man goes out to the back-yard. No sooner had he laid his hand on an apple, but he found it stuck fast; and turn and twist as he might, he could not get free.

– Release me from this tree!

– Indeed I will not, says Billy: you can stay there till the Crack of Doom, and after it, as far as I'm concerned.

– I'll give you another seven years!

– You will not, says Liam, for I'll not free you from the tree till you swear blind to me that you'll go back to Hell and leave me alone for the rest of time.

The devil had no option; he vanished in a shower of sparks.

Now Will was on the pig's back. No more Devil to annoy him, and years of raking to look forward to; but that night, Will Gallagher died in his sleep. He found himself at the Pearly Gates. St Peter looks out, and says:

— Is it you, Willie Gallagher? The boy that sold his soul to the Devil? Get out to Hell from here, and don't come back! And he slammed the gate in his face.

Down goes Billy to the Gates of Hell. The Devil looks out, and says:

— Get out of here, you twister. There's no room for you here, with your chair, your broom and your Cox's Pippins.

— Well, where am I to go then? says Willie. Peter won't let me in to Heaven, and you won't let me in to Hell.

— Hold on one sec, says Satan, and he came back with a rush-light in his hand. Here you are, says he, away off and make your own hell!

So, from that day to this, Liam Ó Gallchóir wanders the bogs of Ireland. And should you be travelling the moors some night, you'll see a wandering star, and if you try and track it down, it will recede from you forever; for it's will-o'-the-wisp, carrying his private Hell.

My father calls this story, which I have translated from his Irish, *Liam na Sopóige*, from *sopóg*, according to Dinneen, a wisp, a handful of straw, or a torch 'of bog-deal splinters, or of straw, mounted on a pole for night-fishing' (here Dinneen, in his customary fashion, presents us with a dramatic little genre vignette, and we imagine these fishermen, in catchless lulls, passing the time in telling serials of the ones that got away). L. Mc Cionnaith's* *English–Irish Dictionary* (2nd edition, 1943) provides some interesting variations: *lochrann soluis na sídhe* (fairy guiding-light), *sop reatha*, (wandering wisp), *solus sídhe na bportaigh* (fairy light of the bogs), *teine sídhe* (fairy fire), and *teine shionnaigh* (fox-fire, which the *OED* defines as 'the phosphorescent light emitted by decayed timber').

I carry these little wisps of language about me in my free hand as I consult *Brewer's Dictionary of Phrase and Fable* (new edition, no date, but the flyleaf is dedicated, in a careful italic hand, '*To S.W.V. Sutton, Christmas 1929, with his father's love*', which seems an oddly formal address, and a suspicion arises that maybe S.W.V. wrote it himself, as the repressed father could not allow himself such written vows of affection).

Brewer's† great ramble of a book refers me, under Will-o'-the-wisp, to these entries:

Friar's Lanthorn. One of the many names given to Will-o'-the-wisp, confused by Scott with Friar Rush (q.v.), whom Sir Walter seems to have considered as 'Friar with the Rush(light)'–

> *Better we had through mile and bush*
> *Been lanthorn-led by Friar Rush.*
>
> Marmion

---

* Both Dinneen and Mc Cionnaith were Jesuit priests, and their training in dialectical oratory and moral taxonomy must have stood them in good stead in the field of lexicography.
† Another clergyman, the Rev. Cobham Brewer, Ll. D., though of what denomination I do not know, but from a reading of other entries, notably that for 'Catholic Church', I would strongly suspect him to be High Church of England.

Ignis Fatuus. The 'Will-o'-the-wisp' or 'Friar's Lanthorn' (q.v.), a flame-like phosphorescence flitting over marshy ground (due to the spontaneous combustion of gases from decaying vegetable matter), and deluding people who attempt to follow it: hence, any delusive aim or object, or some Utopian scheme that is utterly impracticable. The name means 'a foolish fire' it is also called 'Jack o' Lantern', 'Spunkie', 'Walking Fire', and 'Fair Maid of Ireland'.

> *When thou rannest up Gadshill in the night to catch my horse, if I did not think thou hadst been an* ignis fatuus *or a ball of wild-fire, there's no purchase in money.*
>
> Shakespeare, 1 Henry IV, iii, 3.

According to a Russian superstition, these wandering fires are the spirits of still-born children which flit between heaven and the inferno.

We are now wandering well off the beaten track as, following Brewer's suggestion to look up Friar Rush, we find that 'in printer's slang a friar is a part of the sheet which has failed to receive the ink properly, and is therefore paler than the rest. As Caxton set up his press in Westminster Abbey, it is but natural that monks and friars should give foundation to some of the printer's slang.' Here, at least two interpretations are possible, and I can see a good case being made for sudden apparitions of white-habited monks, ghosting the ink away from the sheet by their presence; or maybe we can attribute the term to the perceived untrustworthiness of these ecclesiastic fellows, whose literate closed orders were viewed with some suspicion by the lay population. Indeed, the five Friars cited by Brewer – Bungay, Gerund, John, Rush, and Tuck – all partake of some degree of subterfuge or rascality; they are Odd Men Out. Rush himself is 'a legendary house-spirit who originated as a kind of ultra-mischievous and evil-dispositioned Robin Goodfellow in medieval German folk-tales (*Bruder Rausch*, i.e., intoxication, which shows us at once that Friar Rush was the spirit of inebriety)', and I see a cartoon picture of a flushed drunk monk with a wench on his knee, hawking occasional gobs on to the rush-strewn tavern floor, pounding with his other fist the thick oak refectory table to emphasize the climaxes of his rambling, still-Jesuitical rhetoric of *laissez-faire* morality, since 'his particular duty was to lead monks and friars into wickedness and keep them in it'.

Bungay, 'a famous necromancer of the 15th century, whose story is much overlaid with legend', had the ability to raise mists and vapours on the occasions of important battles to confuse the enemy, and was known to have gained extensive work experience under the Franciscan monk, scientist and scholar Roger Bacon (?1214–92), who was first in devising lenses to correct vision, according to *Collins English Dictionary*. Gerund is the eponymous anti-hero of a satirical romance by Jose Isla (1703–81), 'ridiculing the contemporary pulpit oratory of Spain; it is full of quips and cranks, tricks, and startling monstrosities'. John, a prominent Rabeliasian character, was able to gabble his matins and vigils faster than any of his fraternity, and often 'swore lustily'. Which brings us to Tuck, 'pudgy, paunchy, humorous, self-indulgent, and combative clerical Falstaff', surely a prototype of Billy Bunter in Frank Richards' *Greyfriars School*, where Harry

Wharton is Robin Hood, and Bob Cherry Little John. These
schoolboys maintain a decent English code of honour throughout
their japes and escapades, resembling the jolly-well-met-fellows
of the labyrinthine Forest, whose mazy paths and shades and dappled glades were re-imagined by us children in Belfast in the
1950s in the willowy scrub-land which we called The Jungle,
adjoining a bank of the Owenvarragh river a long few hundred
yards or so south of our new, small, speculatively built suburb of
semi-detached houses made of 'rustic brick', a concept I confused then with 'rusty', since its building-blocks seemed to have
been corroded and pitted by coarse ochre-orange and deep red
iron oxides, interspersed with grits of black and purple.

Now I can smell the newly plastered walls of the pristine
house in Mooreland Drive our family moved into from the
Lower Falls, our new-found voices echoing within its empty
rooms, floating up its wooden staircase acoustic, as our footsteps
rang on the bare pine boards of the floor, sounding out its underlying hollow of dimension, where an IRA man could be
concealed when on the run, reclining like a temporary mummy
in his ideal otherworld of imminent republic. We thought it possible, then, that we might discover trapdoors leading to the
narrative ballad of Sherwood, where the Merry Band had dug
camouflaged pit-falls into which the Sheriff's samurai, encumbered by their beetle-case elaborate armour, were encouraged to
stumble, never to get out except when given a sporting hand by
Robin of Lockesley and his band of key cronies – Little John,
Friar Tuck, Will Scarlet, Allen-a-Dale, George-a-Greene, and
Maid Marian – whereupon the agents of the Empire would

immediately throw in their gauntleted hands with the rebels of Sylvania, convinced, by these hoods' demeanour, of the justness of their cause. So the English language was born of this unauthorized liaison, as Anglo-Saxon cohabitated with Norman French.

I see them as double agents lying parallel under the floorboards, or hidden in an attic, fugitive idealists like Johnny McQueen of Carol Reed's film *Odd Man Out*, who are lost in its Belfast Caravaggio interiors of *noir*. The axis of the name 'Belfast', in all its ambiguity, occupies a momentary rushlight clarity.

THE CHURCH OF THE HOLY
REDEEMER

If *Odd Man Out* suggests that Belfast is a universal city, I cannot help but see bits of Belfast everywhere. Berlin, Warsaw, Tallinn, New York, to name some, have Belfast aspects; and recently, in Paris for the first time, I picked up this book of photographs that I want to explore, since its various *grisailles* remind me of the light of Belfast, or rather, a remembered light, since the bulk of the images date from the period 1947–51.

The photographs, by Willy Ronis, are of the Belleville-Ménilmontant district. Beautifully composed and contemplated, they simultaneously reveal and withhold. No. 41, *Devant l'église Notre-Dame-de-la-Croix, place de Ménilmontant*, for example, is a baroque conundrum, signalled initially by that preposition 'devant' (in front of). *Devant*: yet more than half of the picture is taken up by what looks like a side-chapel of the main church, whose tower and the first stage of its spire make up the background; either that, or two churches coexist in an unlikely contiguity. I look at it again; perhaps there *are* two different establishments. The texture of the light suggests an intervening space, as it parallels the buttresses and window-columns, fading in defined verticals back from the viewer or the lens, till the dimmed tower and spire seem to hover in another recessed realm.

Below this architectural enigma is a horizontal frieze formed by the back-yard wall of a shop or dwelling whose gable end is the left-hand frame; poised against the wall, in various conversational clichés, a minor Bayeux of characters; the rest of the foreground is occupied by a big black motor-vehicle resembling a limousine or bus, or hearse. Its roof is covered in flowers: the scene, it would appear, is of a wedding and a funeral, the wedding confirmed by the sunlit presence of a woman wearing brilliant white among the small throng of guests. She has a white jacket on, chaplet, veil, just-below-the-knee-length skirt, white, sling-backed, wedge-heeled shoes. She cradles a bouquet of white flowers in her left arm.

Although I must have stared into this photograph for some hours, off and on, it is only now that I've been able to resolve the problematic Rorschach blot draped against the flowers on the roof of the vehicle. One could interpret it as a black flag, or shroud; but it is, in fact, a man, his rump strained towards us and his head invisible, as he stoops to attend to the wreaths. Momentarily confused by this Charon phenomenon, I started, paradoxically, to doubt the hearse; perhaps it was, all the time, a wedding limousine, and the wreaths were bouquets; but no –

through a side window of the car, now, I can detect the barely shimmering fringes of a pall. Squinting at it, I am led to see another detail not glimpsed before, where, at the bottom right edge of the frame, a trouser-leg and shoe have just entered the ambiguous moment.

Ronis finds such happy accidents in other locations: in *Rue de Belleville/Rue de Rampal*, for instance, the crush of shoppers milling at this corner of junk shops is elaborated by the strident blur of a woman who has just entered from stage right. His *Rue de Solitaires* shows a distressed milliner's, the hats displayed on stands or faceless dummies' heads; the shop is nameless, yet the street has two signs, the same name repeated in different typography below a skewed ornamental bracket which throws a gnomon shadow across an iron window-grille. This is a temporal pointer which resembles its other, the perfect isosceles triangle which has crept in on the lower left-hand foreground, a shadow thrown by an invisible presence, indicating the precision of the time-frame, and guiding us beyond it.

The enigmatic *Passage Plat* takes this technique to a beautiful extreme. Here, everything is guideline, poised against a huge misty canvas sky of photograph. On the left, a soaring elongated tree is bursting into sparse leaf. The focal point is a man with his back turned towards us. He seems to contemplate the distance, having climbed the last five steps of a supposed long stairway and arrived at an eminence or plateau. The blurred nave of a church lies just below him, and its Gothic spire balances the tree.

The same church is seen from different angles in some six or seven other photographs; as I compare them, I realize it is no

other than Notre-Dame-de-la-Croix, and that the photograph I
first described is, most likely, of one church. In *Rue des
Couronnes/rue Henri-Chevreau*, it is viewed from the interior of a
café framed in a window of its ornamental doors; another
window shows two figures – a woman holding the hand of a little
girl, both wearing transparent, fold-up plastic mackintoshes,
gone all crinkly with the drizzle that they hurry into, towards the
blurred church of the imminent horizon. You can almost hear
them trot across the shiny, scallop-patterned pavé.

In *Cour rue de Retrait*, the print is nearly all pavé, those versions
of the granite setts of Belfast, mostly now all torn up. It is full of
different weights and textures of bumpy oblong embedded light.
Off to one side, a child is about to run away from us into a
garden.

Returning to *Devant l'église Notre-Dame-de-la-Croix*, I remind
myself of why it first attracted me, the accident that its rose
window resembles that of the Church of the Holy Redeemer,
more commonly known as Clonard, from the district it inhabits.
Clonard is from the Irish *cluain ard*, high water-meadow, and is
bounded on the north by the Farset River, from whence it
declines towards the Clowney Water (*cluaineach*, water-mead-
owy) in the west. I went back to Clonard yesterday. As I opened
one of its heavy, brass-lined vestibule doors, a near-audible pneumatic rush of church aroma crossed the threshold: wax, terrazzo
flooring, incense, polished oak, ghosts of sodden coats, and altar-
flowers, the black serge smell of confessionals. A beeswax odour
lingers, despite the fact that the votive candles have gone electric,
and are operated by a bank of individual switches, so that lighting

the candle of your choice among the near-gross on display requires some minor computational skill; but electricity has rendered defunct the traditional aesthetics of candle placement. Wax is a consumptive, dying medium; electricity, in its incandescence, never wanes, but must be switched off. It is odourless. Drip-free. Guaranteed not to gutter. Here, the definition offered by the *Catholic Encyclopaedic Dictionary* is relevant:

> CANDLES, VOTIVE are lighted by the Faithful and set up to burn before the Blessed Sacrament, relics, shrines or images. The origin of the custom is obscure, but from the earliest times a symbolism attached to use of candles – notably in the case of the paschal candle. As the incense which sent up its cloud of fragrance was a symbol of prayer, so the candle consuming itself was a type of sacrifice. In the Middle Ages it was common for grateful clients to 'measure themselves' to a particular saint; *i.e.*, a candle was set up of the same height or weight of the person who had received or desired some favour.

This self-immolation by proxy, it seems to me, is procedurally difficult when given electricity. Wax is a process; electricity, in its on-or-offness, is digital. One cannot know how many prayers are terminated by a power-cut. And the electric candle goes against the rubric grain of prayer-time, which, though formulaic, is flexible. I know of no research conducted in this region, but it is imagineable that no two wax candles, lit simultaneously, will expire precisely at the same moment; each has its own specific gravity, and will bear the fingerprints and DNA of individuals. Yet it is also part of a wider community: lighting a candle in a votive shrine, one applies its virgin wick to that of an already-burning other, in an efflorescent act which owes its being to someone else's prayer, and we enter a realm where all the lights of the shrine could trace their geneaology to one primordial flame; one's candle, placed within that constellation of prayer, takes on a serially compounded significance, another asterisk within the cataracted narrative. Marathons of Olympian time are implicated.

Pondering these issues, I wandered off the nave into a transept. It was getting dusk. A verger or a sacristan appeared. I watched him pace slowly up to the shrine, and switch the candles off in sequence, leaving one still lit at the apex of a triangle, like a Christmas star.

ELECTRIC STREET

Every night, on retiring, I would tent the bedclothes over my head to make an underwater grotto, whose interior of furls and crumples was thrown into chiaroscuro by the beam of the annual torch I got in my Christmas stocking. I was practically unaware of my body, since it formed part of the structure – supporting columns of the knees, flying buttresses of elbows – and my breathing was a rhythm of the coral tide. In this context, the torch was a one-man submarine, in which the bulb behind the window-lens was me.

Then I would return it to its primary function, relishing the snick of its off-on switch, the clunky weight of batteries slotted end to end within its grooved tin tube. Cocooned in its light, I'd open a book I'd dog-eared the night before. Black clichés hummed and buzzed on the yellowed pages, dissolving them in an expanding *O* of flame, charred edges eating the words from inside out, revealing the eye of the story, in which I became its simultaneous hero and observer.

I am a British agent parachuted into enemy Bohemia, my

mission to spring the German anti-Nazi physicist, whose calculations, scrawled in chalky symbols on a blackboard, and then wiped clean, resided only in the convolutions of his brain. The Schloss in which he is imprisoned is an Elsinore of winding clockwise stairs, lancet turret windows overlooking crenellated parapets, and passageways within walls, complicated as the ventilation system of an ocean liner. Crawling through it like a travelling rat, I find a monocular eyelet in an arras high above the banqueting hall, and spy the SS in their perfect, tight-fit, silver-braided, black uniforms, as they communicate impeccably in Nazi English. They quaff fine wines poured from cobwebbed bottles into cut-glass goblets, and I am tempted to shoot the ash from the end of their leader's Havana corona.

Then I remember with the tip of my tongue the tiny suicidal pebble of cyanide embedded in a molar, and imagine its purported scent of bitter almonds, cyanide from Greek for blue, from the blued lips of the victim, I would like to think, but possibly it is integrally blue – who knows, since we only glean these things from books, words of vitriol and strychnine, ratsbane, arsenic, Agent Orange, datura, hemlock, Paraquat, nicotine and acrimony: an aura of country houses, the weekend permeated by the waft of blue cigar-smoke and red herrings, a seething plethora of motives. It's time, I think, to get Poirot on the job, or Holmes, whose London reminds me of Belfast in its teeming narrative dimensions and its atmospheric genre fogs:

> Back in the fifties, I'd look forward to October or November, when, every other day, smog would permeate and cloak the still-dark morning streets with various murks of yellow: Outspan

orange, saffron, Coleman's mustard, burnt Sienna, honey, jaundice, lentil, nicotine. Snug in the lull between waking and getting up, I'd massage the cold tip of my nose, thinking of it being pressed against the opaque window-pane. Outside, the habitual metronome of the blind man's cane was dulled and thickened by the intervening blanket as he made his way to work in the Basket Factory. His ticks were tocks. Zigs became confused with zags, and I would savour, with a slow advance deliberation, the prospect of my being lost on the way to school.

After breakfast, muffled in my overcoat and balaclava, I would step into the incandescent wall of coalsmoke smog. I'd inhale its acrid aura through my woollen mouthpiece. Launching tentatively into it, I'd feel my way with fingertips: doors and hyphenated window-sills; verticals and horizontals; the untouchable gloom at the end of a gable wall. From here I'd take a right up Milton Street and reach the blurred oasis of a still-lit gaslamp. The thoroughfare ahead was heralded by muted parps of car-horns, as if a traffic-light had stuck at amber.

As I come on to the Falls Road, I try to visualize its shop-front sequence: Angelone's Ice Saloon; Muldoon's the Barbers; McPeake's 'Wallpaper, Radio and Drugs'; Kavanagh's the Butcher's; O'Kane's Funeral Parlour; Smyth's the Tobacconist's; the haberdashery whose name I can't remember. I can't find it in the Street Directory for 1948 I've just perused, with its advertisements for defunct traders: John S. Brown, 'Manufacturers of the celebrated "Shamrock" Linens and Hand Painted "Raytone" Double Damask Table Cloths and Napkins'; Wilson, McBrinn and Co., 'Wholesale Manufacturer of Men's, Youths' and Boys' Garments, Sole Manufacturers of the famous "Sunshine" Flannels; also the "Captain", "Middy" and "Sailor" Serges in all garments'; and A.W. Hamilton, 'Ship Repairers, Boiler Makers,

Sole Ulster Representative of the Schori Metallising Process, Manufacturers of Gates and Railings, Milk Bottle Crates, etc.'

It reminds me of those freezing February days when, perversely, the marble season would begin and your knuckles are skinned and raw, chapped blue and purple from squinting and shooting 'marlies' in their complicated planetary rituals and ricocheting paths. Or two of us are sent out into an opalescent fog to skid and skate across the black bottle-glass rink of the granite yard. We are the milk-collectors. The galvanized iron crate burns frostily into our palms and fingers. It clinks and tingles as we teeter back, the pair of us like out-of-synch zinc buckets on a milkmaid's swaying yoke.

I step into the sudden fug of the classroom radiator-warmth. When we take the bottles out they're frozen solid half-way down their half-pint length. We rack and clunk them up like snowman soldiers on the regimental cast-iron pipes. Gradually, a sour-sweet thaw will blend its milk-aroma with the other fug ingredients: chalk-dust, pencil-shavings, Plasticine, sweaty socks, damp raincoats, schoolbag leather, ink, lino, blotting paper, oak and varnish, the interiors of pencil-boxes, the exhalation of our breath against the De la Salle Brother's blackboard-black soutane. Snow, too, is in the air; it will soon snow down like algebra. We will watch it crowd the window, then settle down to write in red and blue lined exercise books.

We dip our steel-nibbed pens repeatedly into the speckly delph wells, until our fingers become cramped and inked with blue. We copy out the alphabet, following the Brother's chalky copperplate. Years later, we would graduate to fountain pens: Parker, Conway Stewart, Waterman. They had gold nibs and thick Bakelite casings of Fabergé-like mock tortoiseshell and pearloid themed in various mosaics of blue or green or red: ruby, garnet, ochre, carmine, solferino; olive, loden, beryl, avocado,

Paris green; sapphire, cobalt, peacock, hyacinthine, Oxford blue. Meanwhile, all the motor cars were black. The last trams on the Shankill Road were blue as the Gallaher's Blues cigarette packet, and their trolleys emitted ink-blot stars in the grey December afternoons. Buses were fire-engine, *doppelgänger* red.

The conductor punches out the pink tuppenny ticket of Belfast Corporation Transport. Usually, I'd climb into the smoke-fogged Upper Saloon and occupy its front seat and pretend to drive, revolving my imaginary wheel and gazing down into the stream of Fords and Humbers, bikes, milk-carts, brewers' drays, linen emporia vans and mineral water lorries. The desultory red of an Inglis' bread-van, the yellow of a Hughes', illuminated the occasion. I'd float proud and high above it all, looking space-man-like at these familiar Dinky aliens.

Or sometimes, going on down-town expeditions with my mother, we would take the lower Saloon, her faint rouge mingling with the red upholstered leather aroma. She would lean into me as the bus curved down the road, past Lemon Street and Peel Street, past Alma, Omar, Balaclava Street, until we disembarked at Castle Junction. Coming up to Christmas, four o'clock was nearly dark, and Royal Avenue was lit by tall, spaced light-poles bearing glassy orchids of electric sapphire blue. The massive clock above the Bank Buildings shone like a Roman-numeralled moon. Snow and tinsel glittered in the shop windows. Salt crystals crackled under our feet.

I was most impressed by Robinson and Cleaver's window display, where an impossibly talented Meccano boffin had constructed a Platonic model of a working windmill the height of a nine-year-old boy. I would pause with my nose pressed against the cool glass and admire this complicated paradigm of engineering with its berry-red and holly-green components: girders, flanged plates, trunnions, flat plates; double brackets, channel bearings, obtuse angle brackets; pawls and ratchets, sprockets, bush wheels, crank shafts; nuts, bolts, washers, spring clips, threaded couplings. The intricacies of its construction were too much to grasp, like the dimensions of the Titanic or the dense, cross-hatched melée of shipyard cranes, scaffolding and gantries that towered above the east bank of the Lagan.

Four or five Meccano revolutions of the windmill sails went by before my mother gently dragged me off. Robinson and Cleaver's big, revolving, brass-lined doors engaged us with a faint pneumatic hush as we were swept into the foyer. Neon-lit cosmetic names – Coty, Yardley, Givenchy – surrounded us in mirrors. Lipsticks and eye-shadows. Cold creams. Compacts. Colour charts. We glided on the deep blue carpet and took the Versailles marble staircase to the first floor Ladies' Garments Department. Here, taut corsets were displayed on headless torsos. In the corner of my eye I registered the flesh and blush tones of diaphonous 'Spirella' bras. I would be relieved to escape to the sober warmth of the Men's and Boys' Outfitters, with its dark serges and muted Thornproof, Donegal and Harris tweeds. As we passed through the store, we'd sometimes pause before a tall first-floor window to gaze down momentarily at the bobbling stream of shawls, hats and flat caps, or upwards to the luminous green cupola of the City Hall, the almost blue green, starry Christmas Tree emblazoned on the dusk.

Such occasions would necessitate a hair-cut. After pondering the revolving mystery of the barber's pole – where did the candy stripes come from, where did they go? – I would go in and sit on the bench to wait my turn, reading the cardboard advertisements for Brylcreem, Styptic Pencils and 7 O'Clock razor blades, and wondering what they did with the hair shearings at the end of the day. I'd imagine franchises with Wig and Mattress Manufacturers. Or not. Mattresses were horsehair. It reminded me that when you rounded the corner from Muldoon's and walked up Durham Street, across the Boyne Bridge into Sandy Row, you'd see red-coated King Billy on his white horse prancing in the Boyne of a gable wall. I'd wonder if his long, scrolled, auburn locks were wig or hair.

Now I am staring at my head without a torso, my hands invisible and paralysed beneath the barber's nylon shroud. I try not to wince as the cold die-cast metal clippers snip and snag my ears and raw neck. He asks me my name and where I go to school, as if he were a mirrored Grand Inquisitor, compiling the denominations of the Parish. I am about to answer when he throws a jolt of freezing oil into the top of my skull. Then he violently kneads my head before he calms and draws a plumb-line parting on my cranium with a sharp steel comb. Afterwards, I walk and blink into the brisk cold air of Hallowe'en as if emerging from a picture-house.

Early showers of rockets whooped and burst their yellow stars against the deepening blue. Shawled, lip-sticked boys clattered by on high heels in the orange-and-russet-scented dusk. The smell, too, of pineapples and gunpowder and greengrocers' barrels ammunition-loaded with brazil and monkey nuts. Outbreaks of squib fusillades put me in mind of the First World War, and I'd see the cracks between the paving stones as a complex of trenches, me as Baron von Richthofen in his red Fokker tri-plane which I'd previously constructed from Airfix. Arms outstretched in aerial manoeuvres, I purled and pirouetted my way home to crash-land in the hallway.

On days like this, my father would have worked the early shift and would be dozing on the sofa in his navy-blue postman's uniform, his eyes and nose invisible beneath the authoritatively drooped black peak of his cap. His bag hung on a nail behind the hall door, and I'd explore its tan canvas interior for lengths of coarse twine or missives from the far-flung corners of the British Empire, written-on with 'Unknown at This Address; Return to Sender'. When he'd wake he might tell me a story like 'The Bottle Imp' or 'The Talking Horse'. By now, the room was nearly dark and he'd illustrate the narrative with deft time-lapse squiggles of his glowing cigarette-end.

That night in bed, rehearsing the momentous events of the day, I'd visualize these neon joined-up writings on the inside of my eyelids. Now I saw the oak names carved into the school desks, one on top of another till they're indecipherable, the obliterated dates. Now I saw the lapidary names of streets in Roman capitals. I took up calligraphy again as I admired the blue-boiler-suited craftsmen inscribing signs of shops with careful brush and oils. I imagined writing on a slate, then wiping it all clean and writing it again. I saw black graffiti on white-washed gable walls: *Remember 1690, Remember 1916*. I saw the Battle of the Somme in newsreel black and white, the throng of shipyard workers pouring out from under the *Titanic*.

Come Spring, I knew my father and I would climb Black Mountain, panting up the broken limestone, cold-stream-pouring pathway from the Whiterock Road, up into the air-mail tissue-paper sky of Easter, far above the city. When we'd attained the celestial summit we'd sit down on the undulating heather, and he'd light up a Park Drive cigarette and point it towards the various details of the urban map spread out below: the biggest shipyard in the world; the biggest ropeworks; the green cupola of the City Hall; the biggest linen mill; Clonard Monastery; Gallaher's tobacco factory; my school; the GPO; and in between, the internecine, regimental terraces of houses and the sprawled, city-wide Armada of tall mill funnels writing diagonals of smoke across the telescopic clarity of our vision. I could see the colour-coded kerbs of Union Jack and Tricolour. I saw my tiny self appearing at the front door of 100 Raglan Street, staring up through the absolutely smogless air, into all the ambiguities of blue: Virgin Mary, Denim, Boiler-suited, Prussian, Rangers, Oceanic, Irish Sea, Atlantic, Gallaher's and Esso. I saw the petrol rainbow of an April shower and vanished into it, contemplating how I would get lost *en route* to school.

These memories were initially set down as a preface to a book of images, *Belfast Frescoes*, by the Belfast artist John Kindness. His work is described by Julian Watson, its publisher, as follows:

> With the surprise of an old but still magic comic, or the marginalia in an ancient manuscript, here is a memoir of a childhood in 1950s Belfast, told in pictures and short sentences. Here also, through the remembered vision of childhood and in what is left suggested rather than spoken, is a description of present times.
>
> It is odd that such an idiosyncratic and personal creation had a seemingly bureaucratic beginning. In the summer of 1993 John Kindness was approached by the Public Art Development Trust to submit a proposal for an artwork for the Belfast lounge at Heathrow Airport. The idea came to him that there would be a long gash in the impersonal international airport formica-clad walls. Revealed behind – as if by some peculiar alternative technology – would be remains and traces of something altogether more personal and specific, rather as ancient frescoes are found beneath crumbling plaster in long-neglected buildings.
>
> As it turned out, the Airport did not proceed with any commissions. Archaeology there might have to wait for a few centuries, but the idea took a more immediate hold on John and

with a depth he may not at first have anticipated, as all manner of remembered detail returned to his mind.

Even though there were no longer any walls for his frescos to be concealed in, he started work on the series in early 1994. Each of the resulting twenty panels is made in lime fresco on pieces of slate measuring 12 × 24 inches . . . This little book is designed by the artist. We wished to reproduce all the frescos in their original sequence with simplicity and directness.

Ostensibly simple these images might be, but their design is complex. My original brief was not to write about them, but to respond to them from my own angle; fittingly, John is a Protestant and I am a Catholic, but our Belfasts correspond, and we used to have great crack together in Belfast folk clubs in the late sixties. Each panel is underwritten by a brief commentary in careful schoolboy calligraphic roundhand, like the one I used for writing-up my stamp collection; and each panel has a frieze; both adumbrate the main subject in a playful and ironic commentary. For example:

Early in the morning in our house there was a cigarette that moved around in the dark, it was my father getting ready to go to work.

A lit cigarette has floated out from an opened flat pack of Gallaher's Blues, a macho untipped cigarette once popular with the better-paid class of working Belfast men. The packet is a beautiful archaic defunct dark blue. Below it, a teapot and a teacup; both contain, or bear on their surfaces, images of a blue *Titanic* (its funnels like four lit cigarettes) about to hit the iceberg. To the right, a boy in blue striped pyjamas is getting up from his tousled yellow-eiderdowned, iron-framed bed, reaching like a swimmer or a sleepwalker for the handle of the nearby door, which is shown in cross-section, in its various grains and joints.

Frieze: In the bottom left-hand corner a vertical lit cigarette sends out a long plume or sentenced message of smoke, curling up to the top edge to become clouds and billows, in which suns, moons and stars, stylized like those on an astrolabe or old-fashioned clock dial, appear and disappear, and Leviathans and packet-steamers ride out a storm.

Or

If you draw on a page with lemon juice or milk, it is invisible until you hold it in front of the electric fire and it goes brown.

The boy artist Kindness is wearing a grey shirt, maroon and grey striped tie, rust-coloured Fair Isle sleeveless sweater, grey knee socks with maroon and green knee-bands; he is seated on a too-low stool at a knee-height desk, pen poised above a blank page resting on its surface, which also bears a lemon and a small glass tumbler. Reading from left to right, are the following: a page torn from a spiral-bound jotter on which we can make out these words, written in sepia longhand, 'Robin Hood shot a nude riding through the glen He told Friar Tuck to run like . . .'*; two

---

*My memory of this children's risqué ditty is somewhat different. The verse I know, a parody of the theme song of the TV Robin Hood serial of that time, goes, 'Robin Hood saw a nude riding through the glen/Friar Tuck ran like fuck to warn the Merry Men/When they got there, Maid Marion was bare/And Robin Hood, Robin Hood, was in the nude.'

halves of a cut lemon; an italic-nibbed stationer's pen with moiré blue handle; a scrap of paper on which is sketched a childish, embrowned female nude; another tumbler of water; a metal foil Co-op milk-bottle cap; and a one-bar red electric fire with a blue fabric-covered flex snaking up to terminate in a brown Bakelite plug and wall-socket.

Frieze: A nib in the bottom left corner leaks an upward plume of blue ink or smoke, whose spirals, as they reach the upper edge and run along it, become lemons suggestive of breasts; they are punctuated by nibs whose waisted pattern degenerates into female torso curves.

It is appropriate that Kindness, in these works, has taken slate as his ground material: not only slate, but actual roofing slates (you can see the nail-holes in the corners) since Belfast was as comprehensively roofed with that material as it was built of brick. On stormy days slates would fly from the roofs; if we had to venture outside, we were warned to stay well in to the walls lest we be decapitated; and broken slates had several uses – they could be written on and with, and short lengths could be fashioned into castanets, or stone-age knives and scrapers. It was good to be inside on such nights, as the whirlwind fife-and-drum ensemble of the storm crepitated overhead, and you thought of the stars being driven out of their courses. Wind whistled down the chimney, disturbing the glowing coals, making them flare and pop, echoing the atmospheric wheeps and sigmas of the Clydesdale wireless as we tried to tune into The Weather.

THE CLYDESDALE SUPPLY
COMPANY

In the 1948 Directory, Royal Avenue is crammed with offices and businesses and retail outlets. Many important bodies are ensconced here: the Ulster Tourist Development Association, the Central Catholic Club, Pathe Pictures Ltd., the Belfast District Ancient Order of Foresters, the Blind Welfare Association, the N.I. Road Transport Board Head Office, and the Star Coal Company. Here, too, are costumiers, gunmakers, grain stores, dance studios, and insurance brokers.

As dusk begins to take the form of soot-fleck starling-flocks, it settles on the cornices and sills and architraves of Royal Avenue; filaments of neon blue tremble in their glassy hemispheres as the new electric street-lamps are switched on; lights come on in ones in small office windows, silhouetting the occasional audio-typist or silently dictating businessman.

These office warrens teem with many interim interiors of agents, auditors and caretakers: No. 10, for instance, is adumbrated by no fewer than thirty-nine premises within its five tall storeys. Imagining myself climbing the long stairwell to the Clydesdale Supply Co., radio dealers, I am put in mind of the ponderous drum-major tasselled hooves of a Clydesdale horse as it drags a load of bagged coal past 3 O'Neill Street, where I am listed towards my granny's Clydesdale wireless, left ear pressed to its grille as I spin its needle-sentinel through the glowing blips of Athlone, Hilversum, Leipzig and Marseilles, hearing the solid thrum of its speakers beneath the dotty Morse and atmospheric static.

In the small hours, at the height of the Troubles, when incidents of arson or assassination occurred routinely, I used to listen to the short-wave police radio, from which I learned the alphabet of *Alpha, Bravo, Charlie, Delta* . . . So convincing was the aural landscape, that I sometimes believed the police could overhear me, or at least know that I was listening to their stillicides of window-wiper swash, as they crawled through West Belfast in unmarked cars. Such paranoia was common then, and perhaps necessary, given the proliferation of bugs and other, increasingly sophisticated surveillance devices (one of which can pick up the vibrations of a window-pane at some incredible distance, and translate their shivers into conversation, the glass acting as a tympanum).

At this point, the efficacy, or otherwise, of children's tin-can two-way radios occurs to me, their empty Ovaltine receivers connected by a cricket-pitch length of postman's string. Although your correspondent was within normal earshot, you suspended this belief for the buzz of imaginary distance: your nearby accomplice would suddenly dwindle off into a little-known adjunct of the Empire – Sarawak, or Borneo, perhaps – and reproduce its sound-effects of squawking birds and monkeys whooping through the trees, as he dispatched an urgent order for machetes. I'd immediately requisition an aircraft, and take off in it. In less time than it takes to tell, I'd find myself in the eye of a tropical storm, the needle on the petrol-gauge shivering at zero . . . and then:

For perhaps another two minutes the engine maintained its customary note. Then it spluttered. It cut out, came on for another few seconds, spluttered again, and then cut, as Ginger knew, for the last time. The airscrew came to rest. He held straight on, which was all he could do, in an uncanny silence, broken only by the boom of distant thunder. For what seemed an eternity of time he stared down into the opaque bowl below him, waiting for the end.

It came slowly. The mist seemed to harden. It became deeper, more solid, in colour. Then, through it, appeared a phantom world of uneven ground from which sprang stunted, misshapen trees and giant weeds. Easing the control column back as near as he dared to stalling point he floated down into them. At the last instant he flicked off the ignition and flattened out for a pancake landing. As the aircraft began to sink bodily he lifted his knees to his chin to prevent his legs from being trapped, covered his face with his arms, and waited for the inevitable crash. The machine checked, shuddering, as the undercarriage was wiped off. The safety-belt tightened on his stomach like an iron band. Then, with a splintering of wood and rending of fabric the Auster bored into some bushes, flinging him against the instrument panel. It tilted on its nose, and then, quite slowly, sank back. Silence fell.

Then it was time to wind up the episodic tin-can radio, and go indoors to snuggle by the fire and dip again into more of *Biggles and the Black Raider*, 'Another adventure of Air-Detective Bigglesworth and his Air Police', by Capt. W.E. Johns, first printed in 1953 by Hodder & Stoughton. I bought this book in Harry Hall's second-hand bookshop in Smithfield, in what year I cannot tell; but I do remember glimpsing its cerise spine and sans-serif title on an almost-unreachable shelf in a cold, damp, booklined alcove. Palpable fog had crept in the massive gate, whose archway bore a keystone lion's head with open, lapidary jaws. The monumental piers resembled those of factories or prisons or entrances to the underworld.

Opening a second-hand book, breathing visibly over its pages, I think of all the hands it's passed through, of their fingerprints, and careful signatures on flyleaves; I think of personalized *ex libris* plates; of invented coats-of-arms; of books being tokens of a Sunday School, distributing awards for 'Regularity, Diligence and Good Conduct'; of dates and dedications; of those readers, to whom it was a present, and who didn't read it; of all the dead who read it; of old tobacco-dust, embedded between pages; of creaking bindings, and of hinged, tissue-papered illustrations; of the *X* in Xmas . . .

Breaking free from this mnemonic chain, I find I've wandered into nearby Gresham Street, where, in 1948, the main articles for sale were books, bicycles and radios, recurring like salient motifs in a post-war spy thriller, evoking book-codes, valves and dynamos. The proximity of the General Post Office suggests mercurial telegram boys on red push-bikes. The two bird-fanciers, Montgomery at 7–9, and Creighton at 11, handlers of winged messengers and stoolie-pigeons, must be implicated too.

These latter outlets were the precursors of a pet-shop empire that, in the 1960s, occupied a good third of Gresham Street, their windows packed with rickety cages twitching with mice, gerbils, budgies, rats and goldfish: it was an almost-visible olfactory zone of animal-feed and cat-litter mingled with the horse's droppings that were current on the street at that time. And I can see a ponderous Clydesdale take a blinkered right turn down Upper North Street into Royal Avenue, taking us almost back to where this chapter started. Not quite: alighting from the back of its cart, where I've just hitched a lift, I take a left, and reach the Belfast Central Library.

LIBRARY STREET

I am dreaming below the dome of the Belfast Central Library, imagining its radii of knowledge streaming out to the smaller branch libraries – Falls, Ormeau, Shankill, Donegall Road, Tullycarnet – the dome like the focus of a pulsar, or a flying saucer, emitting radio-beacon light-rays. I feel the whole thing ready to tremble, lift, and slip off into outer space to wander in dark forever through the incandescent galaxies.

I wake to the drowsed aroma of a wino sitting next to me, his nose slumped in a volume of *Encyclopaedia Brittanica*. Libraries attract crazies and eccentrics, who wander the circle of the reading-desks, coughing chronically, twitching with staccato tics. I recognize one by his Elastoplast-patched left lens: I used to see him often, in the neighbourhood of Botany, moving rapidly through the crowded alleyways, writing agitatedly in a black flip-back notebook. I have never caught his one good eye; but once, glancing sidelong as I tried to hurry past him, I got a brief glimpse of his open page, crabbed with uninterpretable symbols. Yet another has his left sleeve pinned in a habitual Napoleon pose, his right hand poised for an imaginary sword. Or, at the request desk, I often bump into the bespectacled youth who has placed an order for *Mein Kampf*. The hiccup man is not far behind.

In the library, nobody is what they seem. Ostensible normals will try to slip you a tract printed in a typeface full of question-marks and bullet-points. I have before me a particularly interesting example of the genre, proclaiming The Church of Retrospective Predestination: 'HAVE YOU BEEN BORN YET?' its headline reads. The text is backed up by several authoritative quotes, such as, 'And the rest of the acts of Hezekiah, and all his might, and how he made a pool, and a conduit, and brought water unto the city, *are* they not written in the book of the chronicles of the Kings of Judah?' (II Kings, 20: 21), or 'Thine eyes did see my substance, yet being imperfect; and in the book all *my members* were written, *which* in my continuance were fashioned, when *as yet there was* none of them.' (Psalms, 139: 16). The basic tenet of this sect is that only by looking back at our lives can we make sense of them, as we chart their many *déjà vus* and unexpected nexuses; and sometimes, I find myself on the verge of subscribing to it, especially in the course of writing this book which I cannot read until I've written it. In this context, I recall an entry in Samuel Taylor Coleridge's *Notebooks*, where, high on laudanum, he is writing by candlelight and is convinced that the words appear on the page by their own volition; all his quill does is follow them. I remember writing the quote on the blank side of a blue, Belfast Central Library requisition slip, but I cannot put my hand on it now. How many episodes have thus slipped into the province of the unwritten shadow to this one?

Notes on beer-mats, Rizla paper packets, sales slips, envelopes and bookies' dockets; quotes on Post-its, tax bills, tracts, receipts, and bus tickets; memoranda Biroed on the back of my hand; addenda scrawled on shopping lists and business cards, and books of matches: directions for a future not yet written, and which might never be. And yet, these lost incunabula must still have a function, an intimate, hand-to-brain, recording-loop connection, similar to the automatic-pilot digits of musicians, which remember patterns inaccessible to normal thought. I often get up from bed in the early hours and go downstairs to the kitchen to scribble down some insomniac inspiration for this book, and vividly remember it in the morning, just because I'd written it; I've no need to go back to the actual chronicle. Why, you might ask, don't I have a notebook by my bed, like a dream-diary? It seems to me the journey downstairs is a necessary one: it is a process of refinement, palpable on the soles of my bare feet as they experience the various textural *frissons* on the way – the coarse-weave bedside dhurrie, the cool black-painted floorboards, then the prickly hessian landing-and-stair carpet, consequently the *faux* marble dining-room lino, and finally the freezing kitchen tiles. Phrases can be shaped by that declension, and my chronic inability to find my slippers, lost as they are in the dark, dust-balled purgatory under the bed, their gasping mouths bereft of feet.

Trying to think of all the shoes I've ever worn, I feel an

instep-ache of memory, stepping into my father's huge, impassive brogues and their cold, puckered insole ridges, running my fingers over their Braille wing-tip upper punctuations. From time to time it would occur to me that the shoes could be submarines, inching in tandem pedal-movement over the convoluted sea-bed of the Persian hearth-rug. I would man them with injection-moulded toy soldiers (sailors, unaccountably, being unobtainable), and depth-charge them, from my Gulliver perspective, with empty cotton reels. This latter item made a useful tank when you tractor-notched its twin rims with a pen-knife, and constructed a driving-mechanism from a thick elastic band drawn through its core and attached to a pencil-stub. You wound it up like clockwork, and watched it crawl across the casualties you'd strewn on the Persian battlefield, some taken out of action by the die-cast, spring-loaded metal cannon and its matchstick ammunition. Yet the lethal matchstick was also a perfect first aid splint for a veteran decapitated lead soldier, as you inserted it into his neck-cavity, and impaled the disembodied head on the match-head, thus recalling eighteenth-century executions.

These were the then-ubiquitous 'Swift' matches, produced by Maguire & Paterson at their impressive, block-long Ulster Match Works on the Donegall Road, some four or five hundred yards up from the Star Factory. I still think of the powerful, cross-town, North-West axis formed by the Match Works and Gallaher's Tobacco, Cigarette and Snuff Manufacturers at 134–148 York Street, which were, according to my father, the most extensive premises of their kind in the world. Belfast was also reputed to be the home of the biggest linen-spinning mill, the biggest shipyard, and the longest ropewalk, all of which superlatives were depicted on the Swift box, printed in an indigo or denim blue, its eponymous bird like a willow-pattern hieroglyph arrested in the eastern sky. It was, of course, a bird's-eye view.

There is something intoxicating or mesmeric about a matchbox, as you shake it to hear its maraca complement of fifty, which, when you slide open its drawer, appears like a phalanx of stilled sentinels. Amateur craftsmen used to assemble complicated cabinets or sewing-repertoires from empty match-boxes. Magic tricks were performed with them. Slotted one into another, they became a goods train, involved in some important skirmish.

Children were notorious for detaching the sandpaper striking-strip and pleasurably sucking it for its spunky* gluey crunch;

---

*Chambers' entry for **spunk** is worth quoting in full: *n.* a spark (*dial.* esp. *Scot.*): a spirited, usu. small or weak, person (*dial.*): spirit, mettle, courage: touchwood, tinder (*obs.*): a match (*dial.*): semen (*vulg.*). – *v.i.* to take fire, flame up (*arch.*): to fire up, to show spirit (*U.S.*): to come to light (*Scot.*, with *out*). – *n.* **spunkie** (Scot.) a will-o'-the-wisp: a fiery or mettlesome person: whisky (*Burns*). – *adj.* **spunky** spirited: fiery-tempered [Cf. Irish *sponc*, tinder, sponge – L. *spongia*, a sponge – Gr. *spongia*].

The Revd Dinneen (*An Irish–English Dictionary*) does indeed give **sponnc** as 'sponge, tinder', but not 'a match', which is what my Ulster Irish understands by it, and I learned not to use this word when asking Connemara men for a light, since they interpreted my request as 'Have you got any semen?' Their word for match was *match*. Typically, though, Dinneen comes up with some other angles: 'the spark of life', which I take to be a Jesuitical euphemism for semen, and 'the herb coltsfoot (used as tinder, *al.* as tobacco and as a specific)', which brings to mind an elaborate rural idyll of spunky little men in worn serge suits hand-rolling coltsfoot cigarettes, or tamping the dried herb into clay pipes, reminding us of the Irish wake tradition of circulating pipes of hemp about the company, and you wonder what sort of high they got from this frisky coltsfoot stuff, as they ignited it with flint and steel and tinder produced from flat tin tinder-boxes which, I imagine, never having seen one, to be like they used to lick the bulbous red heads too, deliberately mistaking them for 'cherry lips', a small, loose, wine-gum type of sweet once very popular. These were dispensed from open trays and scooped into serrated-edged, hand-sized paper bags, wherein they used to stick promiscuously together, and you'd enjoy dislodging them, introducing them in ones into your mouth, and kissing them until they melted. The bigger, boiled sweets — brandy balls and butter balls, clove rock and cough-rock — came in screw-topped ecclesiastical jars that you'd love to get your arm stuck into, to be sleeved by glass. I used to think of such jars as reliquaries, wherein the limbs of saints might be displayed, and the faithful were healed by merely gazing at them, such was the force-field of their mutual attraction.

Scented with vanilla and tobacco, the interiors of corner shops had a chapel-vestibule gloom, in which brass weights clinked religiously on scales, and a nicotine light exuded from the dark wood panelling. Russell's, on the corner of Odessa Street and Sevastopol, was one such venue, where my granny would send me for a ha'porth of snuff — chunk-chink of the manual typewriter cash-register — which came in a paper twist, while broken candy came in pokes. My father sometimes manufactured candy in domestic portions, boiling up Demerara sugar and butter in a

---

bicycle-repair-kit receptacles, or glasses cases. The magical giant dogs of Hans Christian Andersen's 'The Tinder-Box' then spring to mind, with their eyes the size of bicycle wheels, or windmill sails, or the screw of the *Titanic*, and I see the eyes of the coltsfoot smokers begin to spin and boggle in their sockets, as they inhale themselves into another dimension, and go walkabout in the underworld, carrying their little wisps of rushlight.

saucepan, letting it seethe and reduce before glopping it on to a flat greased tray, all the while singing, *sotto voce*, 'This old man he had a horse-elum, had a horse-elum, had a horse-elum; this old man he had a horse-elum, down in Demerara . . .' Sometimes he'd butter his palms and wind the still-warm malleable candy into a rope, which he'd snip with my mother's dressmaker's scissors into humbugs. These made a passable imitation of Callard & Bowser's Rum & Butter Toffees, to which I was addicted for their initially indomitable rock-hardness, impossible to chew as vulcanite, until you rolled one in your oral cavity for hours, feeling its clunk against your teeth and gums; at last, able to masticate it, you could clamp it in a dental matrix, thereby making conversation useless. Major fillings were lost this way; now, their silvery amalgam puts me in mind of mercury, or of soldered electrical components, or the miniature radios which spies were reputed to have built into a hollow tooth, together with a bullet-point of cyanide, which was bitten into when the game was up.

My first extraction was by gas, at the Tooth Clinic in Academy Street. The apprentice dentist inserted a rubber bit between my teeth and put a black protuberance over my nose; years later in the Ulster Folk and Transport Museum, I would re-encounter this disguise in the shape of an antique airman's oxygen-mask, as I took it from the dummy's face and breathed into it: that tang of fear, the sudden slope away from things, the smell of a pilot-light as the air goes gas-flame Bunsen-burner blue – like the onset of a migraine, as you fall or fly into the deep – and the dentist's chair has become an ejector-seat, in which its decrepit khaki occupant reclines like Tutankhamun.

Under the influence of gas, I flew to Ancient Egypt. There, I met similar Daedaluses, and masters of a Zodiac cryptology, whose complex pyramid and pylon architecture was a wonder of the world, especially when spied on from a flying boat, and one perceived its wiring-diagrams of constellations, or the lights of vast Los Angeles, firefly millions of amoeba blips in contraflows on freeways. I get that same buzz driving home from Aldergrove Airport, as I, descending from the Antrim plateau, take the high curve of the Horsehoe Bend, and look out from the corner of my right eye into the panorama of illuminated Belfast, my metropolis.

THE PANORAMIC
PHOTOGRAPH COMPANY

High Street, looking east, 1786

Since the modern camera did not exist, this is a photograph of an engraving. The main feature is the Market House, with its curious diamond-shaped clock hung on a gibbet-like support; here, in 1798, Henry Joy McCracken would be hanged. Five inn signs depend from similar devices. One is illegible; the others display a Phoenix, a Maltese Cross, a Harp, and a Crown.

In the foreground, two dogs are chasing each other, while a third looks on. A tricorn-hatted gentleman is chatting up two ladies, one of whom is looking over her shoulder, possibly at the shawled woman carrying a baby. Two cloaked figures conduct some business, and there are other knots of twos and threes in the background. In the far distance, a gang of men or sailors converge on the tangle of masts, spars and shrouds, where the Farset debouches into the Lagan.

The engraver's master-stroke is his depiction of a horseman about to disappear into the archway of the Donegall Arms Hotel. In this split second, only the rear legs of the engorged horse are visible. It is nineteen minutes to three o'clock.

High Street, looking east, 1851

This, too, is an engraving, although the first photograph had been taken in 1826 by Joseph Nicéphore Niépce, using the action of light on asphalt solution; but it looks more like a photograph than its predecessor.

Some good arrested-action detail here, too: the stage-coach poised in front of the Donegall Arms Hotel; an accompanying clutch of bystanders or prospective travellers; a small child tugging at its mother's skirts, as she is engaged by an Abe Lincoln lookalike, in stove-pipe hat; and, in the near-immediate foreground, a peg-legged man carries a placard on his back. I can't make out the words. The time on the public clock is illegible.

Castle Place and High Street, looking east, early 1880s

The picture was taken around noon on a summer's day: you can tell by the drawn awnings and the shadows, so brief as to seem concealed beneath the full skirts of perambulating women. Being a photograph, its narrative intent is both accident and design; yet, you try to read the poised hither and thither of the citizens, arbitrated in magnetic angles to each other.

Some customers are about to board an open-roofed

horse-tram, overseen by an erect policeman. His stance is nearly mirrored by a small newsboy carrying a stack of newspapers too big for him; this would be the early edition of the *Belfast Telegraph*, and I can almost hear his traditional call of 'Err-lai: Tall-ai! — where the colon is a glottal stop.

A horse and cart are parked opposite Robb's Department Store, part of which incorporates the façade of the old Donegall Arms Hotel.

I admire the ornamental standard gas-lamps. On the evening of 30 August 1823, according to the correspondent of the *Belfast Newsletter*,* immense multitudes of people gathered in the High Street 'to witness the lighting of our streets with gas'. The principal light, powered by twelve bat-wing burners, was so bright 'that a letter was read by it near the quay, 60 yards distant from the pillar'. He continued:

> The light now used is of the purest kind, shedding on the streets a brilliant lustre — pleasing but not dazzling — and more resembling the clear effulgence of a cloudless atmosphere illumined by the moon, than any artificial beams heretofore produced by the imitative power of man.
>
> Living objects in our streets thus illuminated were distinctly seen, even at remote distances — and did not as formerly resemble shapeless masses, now moving in obscurity, and now tinged, in part, with a doubtful gleam of light twinkling on them from dull or expiring lamps . . .

---

*See Jonathan Bardon, *Belfast: An Illustrated History*, Blackstaff Press, 1996.

In the High Street, in September 1816, the last public hanging in Belfast, of two weavers who set fire to a cotton manufacturer's house in Peter's Hill, took place.

Castle Place and High Street, looking east, 1968

It must be a wet Sunday afternoon. Castle Place is deserted, and the only signs of animation are the dummies in Robb's shop windows, where a solitary red double-decker diesel bus is parked. I see it as red, even though the photograph is monotone, just as I know it is bound for the Antrim Road, since I used to court a girl resident there about that time. I might have boarded this very bus and sat in its upper deck, dragging at a cigarette, impatient for the cool rainy avenues of Cliftonville and Brookvale; and, to pass the time, I would remember the driver winding the movie-camera handle of the closed, interminable loops of routes and termini, peering through his periscope, sometimes backtracking, anticlockwise, when he found he'd skipped his scheduled destination.

Before the buses were the trams, and Castle Place was known as Castle Junction; here, the radial routes of Belfast conspired to form an asterisk.

Demolition of Hercules Place, looking north, 1879

The view is from Castle Junction. Outside the Provincial Bank, an awry throng of gawping spectators; beyond them, a blur and haze of demolition, the skyline gapped. In the right foreground, someone has been double-exposed as two overlapping ghosts.

Marcus Patton reports that 'in 1804, the Sovereign of the town ordered butchers to sell meat only in Hercules Lane and Arthur Street, and by the middle of the 19c Hercules Street was populated almost exclusively by butchers . . . and as they frequently killed animals on the premises it was a most unhealthy and unsavoury area.'

O'Byrne* paints a different picture:

On a Saturday night in Hercules Street the place seemed filled with life and light. Above the heads of the thronging people the flaring gas jets at the end of their long brass brackets made bright as day the crowded thoroughfare.

With its rows and rows of butchers' shops – there were forty-seven in all – it was a quaint, odd, many-coloured picturesque street, surrounded by a maze of twisting lanes and alleys and byways, in which a stranger might go astray, only to be rescued and set right again by the Bellman, to the amusement of the dwellers therein . . .

Under the old, sagging houses, the pavement was encumbered with pedlars' stalls and barrows, with all kinds of trade going on in the open air. Water-carriers and hawkers, farmers and fishfolk, merchants, pedlars and huxters, egg-wives and waggoners, all seemed to find their way to Hercules Street . . .

A peep into an old book containing a list of the inhabitants of Hercules Street, and fancy brought us back to where its people sat beside their supper fires a hundred years ago.

And one picture does for all.

A wide kitchen, ruddily bright from the big fire that burns

---

*Cathal O'Byrne, *As I Roved Out*.

cheerily on the old-fashioned hearth, a red-tiled floor, with wain-scotted walls and a ceiling of old oaken timbers; a wooden settle on which its owners' fathers and mothers sat before them, some dusky old chests and presses in which are stored away for safe keeping the precious and costly robes and gowns, the women's Sunday finery, with heads of lavender and sprigs of rosemary to keep away the moths. And inside the same old presses are stores of household linen, hand-woven, the glory and pride of its fortunate possessors, and the sprigged and embroidered white linen petticoats, so stiffly starched – to be fashionable – that they could stand alone.

A great dresser, covered with blue and white crockery-ware and copper pans, shining brass kettles, great half-brown crocks, wooden basin and gleaming glass, the latter made in Ballymacarrett, where the queer, beehive-shaped chimneys of John Kane's glass works can be seen across the river to the left of the Long Bridge.

At the back of the houses the old, vast cowsheds and stables are sweet with the smell of cattle and dried meadow-grasses, where great high-piled loads of hay seem forever to be arriving, bringing with them into the narrow, dusty way, the scent of moist fields and reaped grasses and the perfume of honeysuckle hedges. All through the summer days great sheep dogs lie asleep on almost every doorstep, and old, wise-looking, bearded goats wander about at will.

I have quoted Cathal O'Byrne extensively because I love this ramble of fantasy, with its brilliantly realized details: he makes you see the ghostly floating petticoat without a corset or a torso, the vitreous-glazed dark brown outside of the crocks, and their speckled white interior bowls, reminding me of Gerard Manley Hopkins's 'fresh-firecoal chestnut-falls'. You can easily visualize O'Byrne's unhyphenated sheep dogs, snoozing in rows as far as the eye can see, and trying to count them makes you feel dozy yourself. Thankfully, they tend to wake up on occasions, whereupon they emit an alternate *woof* or *baa* to jolt you from this reverie; or you might be surprised by the sudden absence of one on the half-moon scrubbed before a doorstep, and you ring its owner's bell to enquire why his woolly sentinel is not on duty; it transpires that the sheep-dog is sick and is ensconced in a bed in the return room, with its hooves or paws up in the air, undergoing one of the periodic bouts of identity crisis endemic to this breed. Meanwhile, a wandering goat has eaten your shoes which you left at the threshold, in the Chinese-temple fashion of those days, where everyone enjoyed the feel of their woollen sock-soles skating heel-for-toe across the black oak floorboards, polishing them with palimpsests of social discourse, in the balletic, pointed gestures of a Scottish so-called dance.

Then there is O'Byrne's great subjunctive floating past tense, neither perfect nor pluperfect: 'a wooden settle on which its owners' fathers and mothers sat before them': we see their ghostly presences take on lineaments of flesh and blood, instantly acquiring tricorned hats, coiffed hair, dainty Regency high heels, frock-coats, oriental waistcoats, milkmaids' puffed-sleeved blouses, many-petticoated high-waisted frocks, and other various embroideries of *broderie anglaise* and cuffs shot with Carrickmacross lace. Their grown children, with children of their own rolling around under their feet like lambs or pups or kids, do not seem to mind the droning pieties their parents speak from beyond their shared grave, for, although one does not have to heed ghosts, one should treat them with reverence, and appreciate their aromatic presences of blue lavender and spiky rosemary.

I have been dipping into *As I Roved Out* for nearly forty years, off and on; and sometimes, in the course of writing this book, I acknowledge O'Byrne's ghostly presence at my shoulder. The edition I first knew was the abbreviated one of 1957, and I can see its pale green spine in my father's book-case in the 'parlour', alongside the darker, gold-blocked green of the Reverend Patrick S. Dinneen's *Irish–English Dictionary*; and I feel there is a great complicity between the fantasist and the lexicographer, as exemplified by the Reverend's definition of *bearradóir*: 'a cow that eats the hair of her tail or of other cows' tails.' And in Dinneen I detect a shade of that other compromised Jesuit, Gerard Manley Hopkins:

> In coming together to honour the memory of Fr. Dinneen,* I am inclined not to any mood of sadness but rather to follow the line advocated by G.B. Shaw on the death of another famous Irishman when he advised to 'put out your brightest colours . . . His memory is still green in his native parish, where he is recalled simply as 'The Dictionary Man' . . . As the century closed, Fr.

---

*Fr. Dinneen – His Dictionary and the Gaelic Revival, lecture by Noel O'Connell, Honorary Secretary of the Irish Texts Society; given in the Irish Club, London, on 29 September 1984 in the presence of H.E. The Irish Ambassador Mr Noel Dorr to mark the 50th Anniversary of the death of Fr. Dinneen on 29 September 1934.

Dinneen was in a ferment of zeal and activity for the Irish language to the point that he made a traumatic and dramatic decision. He resigned from the Jesuit Order in 1900. Much speculation has occurred about such an unusual event but I feel happy to accept the tradition in his family that he simply wished to devote himself full-time to the Irish language but his superiors would not permit it.

As Noel O'Connell points out, 'his Dictionary is not merely a compendium of words and their meanings. He gives examples of usage and idiom that have seduced the reader over the years into many fascinating byways.' I have often opened Dinneen in a *sortes Virgilianae*, like now, at p. 959, where my thumb is resting in the margin at this word, *scartha*, which basically means 'separated', or 'apart', but Dinneen's examples are, as always, fascinating:

> *táim scartha le céird*, I have given up my trade; *chomh scartha leis is tá an adharc leis an muic*, as devoid of it as the pig of horns (saying); *a n-earball scartha amach ó fhuaimeint tighe*, the last of them driven from the shelter of their homes; *ní scartha duit le caidreamh na saoithe sean*, you must not give up the society of those learned in antiquities; *táim crom scartha ar an saoghal*, life weighs me down.

Here we detect a Jesuitical, biographical ghost behind the lexicographer priest, as he justifies his grappling with the language, in and out of the language. I am especially drawn to his 'the last of them driven from the shelter of their homes', whose Irish makes an interesting etymological tangle. Here, the word for 'the last of them' is *earball*, 'a tail; a remnant; the end'. In Ulster Irish, this word is pronounced *ruball*, which makes me think of English *rubble*, and terraces of devastated Belfast brick houses fled by their inhabitants; at the same time, *ruball* suggests the curlicued tail of a pig, which I see snoozing on a kitchen floor. Then there is his 'shelter', *fuaimeint*, a word I never knew until now,* which he defines on p. 492 as 'vigour, force, effectiveness; sense; foundation', and I wonder what it might have to do with *fuaim*, 'sound, noise, clamour, report, echo', as I get the thrum of a solid bass note below the floorboards which give me shelter, and the music of the phrase, which I say to myself now, *a n-earball scartha amach ó fhuaimeint tighe*, has the ring of an imperial or civil war, as the foundations of the state are turned upside-down.

Then I replace Dinneen on his shelf beside O'Byrne in my father's book-case which, when I opened its leaded glazed doors with its permanently in-situ key, exuded a sudden ink-horn smell of books and wood, wood which is *adhmad*, as in *adhmad urláir*, 'the floor or bottom timbers of a boat; a poem', and I enter yet another dimension.

---

*though it must derive from *L. fundamentum*.

ST PETER'S PRO-CATHEDRAL

Some time in the sixties, my mother decided to convert the loft, a broad, triangular-prism volume of dark beneath the roof. An odd-job man wired it, and he devised a cunning, steep, right-angle staircase up into it, and he laid a floor on the joists. He put a window in the gable. He put up batten-and-plywood dado-height walls to make a nave of the space, with two enclosed, prismed aisles on either side, above the eaves; and he put in sliding doors through which you hunkered to gain access to its lumber-gloom. Inside, in a game of hide-and-seek, you experienced a tea-chest musk. The dulled Platonic outlines of cardboard boxes came to hand; rummaging the interior of one, you'd rediscover the shape of a shoe among the bric-à-brac of elephant book-ends, wicker-handled tea-trays and discarded lamp-shades. Then, when your eyes became accustomed to the light, you found there were broken chinks of light at the edge of the eaves, and the dotted rivets of the water-tank were buttons of light.

The converted loft was my bedroom for several years. Relatively heavy objects, defying normal gravity, were wont to float up into it, even the family book-cabinet, which lodged itself against the party gable wall like a high altar under a triangular ceiling-canopy. The cabinet comprised a book-case screwed into the top of a writing-bureau. The bookcase had three shelves and two leaded glass doors. The bureau had three drawers beneath a 45° angled flap; when you opened it, two synchronized, green baize-covered armatures slid out from concealed sockets, to support the flap, whose obverse was the ink-stained leather-covered surface of a writing-desk. Consequently, pigeonholes and smaller drawers were revealed within, crammed with fraying correspondences and dog-eared family snaps: arcades in a Lilliputian Byzantium, smelling of faded ink and the gum of postage stamps.

I open the flap again in my mind, and compose myself like an express postal-worker on an antiquated night mail-train, assigning letters to their destinations like an automatic pilot, swaying with practised ease against the lurch of the carriage, as a long white rope of smoke unfurls from the snort of the locomotive chattering through the dark, past sleeping villages and back-yard pigeon-lofts in conurbations, under aqueducts and viaducts and into tunnels.

Alternatively, the cabinet could be an organ console; but mostly it behaved as a writing-desk, and it was here that I first began to write, in the late sixties and early seventies. I kept a kind of journal then, in a 13″ × 8″ unruled notebook with marbled endpapers that I got from a friend's father who worked in Her Majesty's Stationery Office. I haven't thought about it for years, but now that I've remembered it's stored in a drawer of the desk I'm writing at, I bring it out and flick through it, experiencing again the embarrassment I felt when last I looked at it. But one of the less embarrassing entries seems germane to this present sequence of explorations:

5th June, 1970: . . . such strange dreams I had last night. My sleep seemed an unbroken story in dream, a strange story unfolding in the night. Linked by images of death & injury. At one stage I knew I was dead, I was a skeleton wrapped in a black rustling shroud. My friends walked with me & knew I was dead. I came back to life. Somehow my skeleton disappeared, absorbed into flesh again, scarred flesh. My legs were broken & stitched together. My left knee was a mass of cracks and hardened blood.

I wish I could remember it all clearly – there was some coherent pattern to the train of events.

One thing I do remember now – a tram which led you back into the past. It was a sort of excursion. You paid a few shillings & the tram moved off, supported apparently by thin air. As it moved, the scene around slowly shifted & altered through past time. There were only three passengers – myself & 2 girls, I can't remember who they were, I knew them slightly. Much of this scene took place around Milltown, I think.

I think this was inspired by a notice for City Bus Tours I read yesterday – or perhaps it was today. A lot of today's events link with last night's dream in an odd metaphysical way – death, injury, the tram journeying to the past – past & future inextricably mixed.

The tram is also an extension of the recurrent dream I have had since a child – it always differs a good deal, but the basic elements remain the same – the red bus I can never catch. I stand at the stop, hold out my hand. The bus slows down, then suddenly revs up and moves off. It happens over and over again. Frustration? I don't know. Now that I think of it, this dream was also there last night.

The dream of the bus is always connected with the past – not my past, but a past I have no personal knowledge of – about 1930 (when there were no buses.) But I know too that this is the past of my childhood, even though it is before my time. It usually takes place at the Dunville Park stop or at the Grosvenor Rd. lights, or sometimes somewhere around Ballysillan. (Why there I cannot imagine – this area of town occurs quite frequently in my dreams, though I don't know it very well – that and the Ardoyne area. It is all quite transmuted, of course – I invent streets & roads which don't exist. Round York Street & Dock St. I have invented many streets which don't exist – strange diagonal side streets full of derelict buildings, crumbled Victorian pubs, leading to York St.)

Oh, and Smithfield, of course – this occurs quite frequently, I invent vast secret halls approached by winding staircases, full of motheaten leatherbound books. Always a curious air of decadence, of crumbling, almost a physical decay like crumbling flesh. The halls of books are tended by old women with parchment skins & stale perfume, slightly sinister . . .

And today, before it occurred to me that I might quote my self of twenty-seven years ago, I happened to be in Smithfield – not the Smithfield of the latter dream, which was destroyed by firebombs on 6 May 1974, but the 'sadly pale replacement for the much-loved Victorian covered market' (Patton) built in 1986–7. There, in a second-hand bookshop, I bought the little pamphlet I have before me, No. 67 in Benn's Sixpenny Library series (I paid a pound for it), *Architecture*, by the nicely named Christian Barman. I had opened it at this passage, which links urban space and dreams:

> Long before the bankers of Lombard Street were the bankers of Lombardy, from whom that street takes its name. And there was also, in Northern Italy, that other street, the great Street in general, of whose existence the people, as they wandered round the outside of their churches, were gradually becoming aware. This discovery of the street was the first step in the progress of the new architecture to which the name of Renaissance has been given; and it is in Italy that it was first made.
>
> The truth is that during the preceding centuries the street had been so far overlooked that it could hardly be said to exist at all. It was just a hole in the town. Like the hole in the hub of a wheel extolled by the Chinese philosopher, it was a very important hole. Yet no one ever troubled to look at it. The churches and surrounding houses were observed, and between them there was just space, straight or crooked inlets from that greater Space that lapped the sun and stars. In architecture the movement known as the Renaissance is principally the discovery of the walls of these inlets. In its way it was at least as great a discovery in architecture as the discovery of the unconscious mind in modern psychology.

And, appropriately, one of my current recurrent dreams of Belfast focuses on streets dominated by a church, St Peter's Pro-Cathedral in the Lower Falls. Looking at it on the Ordnance

Survey plan of 1931 (a modern map would not show the demolished streets, or versions of them, in which the dream takes
place), I note how the church is like the hub of a crooked wheel,
with streets bounding it and radiating from it: Alexander, Derby,
Milford, Ardmoulin, Irwin, Baker, Massarene, Scotch, Bow,
English, Cinnamond. Completed in the neo-Gothic style in 1866,
the church occupies what looks like medieval space, although
the streets do not exist by virtue of its presence, as they would
have done in medieval times; their *raison d'être* is to house the
workers in the spinning mills and foundries that made Belfast a
once-great city. In my dream, St Peter's has acquired a piazza,
sometimes wet and empty save for a scattering of cobblestone-
grey strutting pigeons, sometimes packed with the stalls, booths
and awnings of an open-air market, where the conflicting litanies
of dealers' cries are rained on by the mewing of the seagulls
wheeling overhead, and the air is laden with the scent of oranges
and herrings. The buildings fronting on to this confabulation are
eclectic: Chelsea town house, Glasgow tenement, Venetian
palazzo, Oxford bookseller's with compass windows, Amsterdam
tall house overlooking its reflection in the water, Belfast grocer's
corner shop, Parisian boutique, New York diner, Dublin pub,
New York deli, Warsaw synagogue, Berlin brothel, Bolognese
haberdasher's in an arcade, Delhi shirt-shop, Beijing tea-
emporium, Havana humidor, Vienna café, San Francisco oyster
bar, Copenhagen doll's house outlet, Chicago kosher butcher's,
Dieppe wine-merchant's, Los Angeles thirties automobile show-
room, Carson City drive-in movie theatre, Constantinople kiosk,
Byzantine bazaar-booth, Buenos Aires private library, the

Workshop for the Blind on the Shankill Road, the Alexandria Memory Institute, Santiago copper-shop, lonely gasoline pump of Intercourse, North Carolina, Vladivostock ice-store, Tokyo shoe-shop, Kyoto temple, Laredo saloon, Kufra Oasis drinking-fountain, Mumbles ice-cream parlour, Roundstone cartographer's, Newmarket bookmaker's, the Boston Aquarium, Cork picture-framer's, and ubiquitous McDonald's.

Of course, not all of the buildings on this menu appear simultaneously in any one version of the dream; but the space they occupy accommodates more than would appear feasible, and they are liable to mutate as the dream progresses, depending on what route you take through it; and the façades of the grand piazza will be different every time you enter it.

The weather, too, can be very changeable, shifting from blustery showers to sunny calms in minutes, and rainbows occur frequently, reminding me of the interior of St Peter's, where stained-glass shadows tremble on the marble embrasures of windows. I often enter the church for shelter, usually arriving in the middle of an elaborate ceremony whose function I only dimly know; but this does not entirely matter, since the participants, moving in a cloud of ritual and incense, are oblivious to the other goings-on which take place in the lobby area immediately between the porch and nave. Here are whispering dealers in holy pictures and indulgences, little men in long black crombie overcoats, some displaying their wares on cinema ice-cream-girl trays, others with interior pockets sheaved with luridly printed tracts. Here you can purchase little brass glass-faced reliquaries that look like toy compasses, about the diameter of an old florin, with a florid acanthus-leaf circumference; they contain a splinter of the True Cross, or a smidgin of linen snipped from the shroud of a saint, and feel surprisingly heavy for all their small size in your hand. The more authentic of them cost about ten florins. Meanwhile, sextets of shawled women walk in rounds, intoning interweaving rosaries, and a bawling baby is being baptized at the nearby font. Four men are playing cards in the shadow of a confessional. Fourteen genuflectors follow the Stations of the Cross. Individuals are lighting candles at the many side-shrines, their faces momentarily illuminated by them. Others, entering this immanence, dip their finger-tips into the necessary stoups of holy water, feeling its cold kiss on their foreheads as they bless themselves. An unseen organist manipulates his stops of *voix celeste* and *vox humana* in a reverie of practice, climbing and descending scales of meditation, moving from funereal to hymenal mode in the space of a bar, allowing himself almost-deliberate mistakes so as not to make them again on the important occasions in his diary of engagements.

Leaving the church, I walk down Milford Street, take a right at Macmillan's Place, again a right at Durham Street, to find myself in Barrack Street looking at my Alma Mater, St Mary's Christian Brothers Grammar School. It is some time in the sixties.

BARRACK STREET I

I remember the second-term light that fell through the high sash windows of the fourth form in St Mary's, and the chalky dust-motes sifting downwards through it, as the Mathematics master scribbled formulaic elaborations on the blackboard; he doubled as a Latin teacher, since both subjects were logically complicit in their aim of inculcating order into adolescent minds. Mr X had a pen-chant for entwining his wrists in the looped cord which operated the pawl-and-ratchet mechanism that cranked open the top light of the window, as he dangled his weight at an angle to the perpendic-ular, contemplating an aspect of non-Euclidean geometry, while he conjugated a Subjunctive Mood. Were this a story I am telling you, some prankster would have abraded the cord with a schoolboy's blunt pen-knife; as it was, we feared X's eccentricity too much to tamper with the course of nature, and his falling flat on his face one day was due to inertia and the relative load-bearing properties of braided materials. It is to his credit that he rose from prone with some aplomb, like an Olympic gymnast springing to a crucifix, end-of-routine stance from a jack-knife somersault – as if the accident had been premeditated, and formed an important flourish in his curriculum vitae. Later, he would use the memory of this routine as a retrospective device to illustrate the Ablative, 'which expressed *direction from*, or *time when*, but was later extended to other functions'.

Another of the tall windows formed a second-storey portal for the Invisible Boy. This entertainment consisted of a simple but mysterious manoeuvre, whereby one boy in the class was delegated, or persuaded, to climb through the opened window; then, finding his feet on the boot-wide cornice that ran below the sills, he would inch his way along like a reluctant suicide, till, fingers of one hand gripping the edge of the brick embrasure, he would disappear from internal view. Understandably, the Invisible Boy was only promoted during periods of rookie teachers, or those about to be retired; trying to remember the exact point of this operation, while recognizing its clandestine thrill, I think it had something to do with knowledge being power, that we were privy to a thing our master did not know, that the class complement was minus one; also, elements of ritual sacrifice were there, since the Boy was an elected scapegoat, or a proxy, for his classmates, and his apparent freedom was an obverse prison. Nevertheless, each boy knew him as an *alter ego*, and through the Boy each boy could experience bi-location.

Spreadeagled, frozen for forty minutes on the second storey, I was once a Boy myself. Of necessity – it was otherwise impossible to balance – I faced the wall; yet it seemed I had eyes in the back of my head as I recalled the dizzy sudden view I got as I first gazed through the open window, till, half-way through my sentence, I fell into a reverie of West Belfast: there had been a recent shower of hail, and roofs and tops of backyard walls were frosted with it; mill chimneys, neo-Gothic spires, were silhouetted against a yellowish-blue sky; and, far-off, up on Black Mountain, a sudden ray of sunlight glanced across the whitewashed farmhouse at the corner of the Hatchet Field. I felt the verges of a flying dream.

In these lulls or slips of time, high above the muted afternoon of non-school business – the subdued clanking of a tram, the thrum of a linen mill, the distant cries of infants playing – one could see how time could be manipulated by one's place in it.

Being sent out during class-time on an errand (or message, as we called it), the open street is wider and more empty than it had been. Recently fallen rain chuckles along the gutter in a minor Styx, before falling into the cast-iron deep of a storm-grating. The granite setts of the street are all wet sunshiny bumps and glittering mica specks; the pavement is an ongoing oblong universe of parallels, faults, joins, cracks and adjuncts, where, between the slate-blue flags, intervening avenues of moss bear microscopic flowers. Scooping a green strip of it out from its habitat with a hooked index, I realize, now, that its stripped underlay of soil must be a residue of soot, dog and horse shit, dirt, tobacco-dust and flax-dust, whereby the waste products of the city are recycled into every crevice, into bronchial passages and alleyways, and violets bloom among the tumbled ruins of abandoned brickfields.

It would take me a geological age, or no apparent time at all, to reach Greenan's shop on the corner of Waterville Street and Clonard Gardens, where, when you plunked your thumb on the worn brass thumb-scoop of the latch, an interior bell dangled and tinkled on its connective string. You walked into the empty space, feeling invisible, hovering on one side of the high wooden counter, till Mrs Greenan, in her dressing-gown, materialized among the aromatic fugue of soap, sweets, cheese and cigarettes, and reminded you of your routine order. I used to believe that my father's rhyme appertained to this establishment:

> Oul' Granny Grey, she kep' a wee shap
> Jist a cupla dures from ar scule
> An' the shap wiz a kitchen windy
> An' the counter jist a wee stule . . .

and so on for a few more verses of nostalgia, till Granny Grey ends up keeping her wee shop in Heaven, or *Havin*, as the Belfast accent has it.*

Doubling back to school from Granny Greenan's, I began to appreciate the urgency of my mission, as I clutched the oblong tin of Erinmore tobacco in one hand, small change in the other; already, I could see the master enjoyably prising open its vacuum-sealed lid with a special device on his smoker's pen-knife, as the

---

*I note here the inadequacy of orthography, which cannot represent the cadences of actual speech; and there is no one Belfast accent, but, as in any city, many. My own granny's accent is no longer heard; it died with her generation; but accents evolve and change, and *her* granny's accent would probably sound foreign to our ears.

premonition of tobacco hit his nostrils; and he would allow us to doodle, or do nothing, while he extracted a cartouche of its moist plug and cut it into bits on his left palm with a blunt blade of the knife, before rubbing it into crumbs and thumbing it into his briar bowl, whereupon he lit it with a Bo-Peep safety-match, which burned down to a spidery, expired stalk before the tobacco ignited properly. Then his tamping implement would be deployed, a second match applied, till the whole pipe began to glow and gurgle, emitting vowels of contented smoke.

Responding to this coded message from the future, I would zig-zag like a secret agent, Early Christian Boy assigned to smuggle the Communion Host through Roman lines to a sacrament-deprived catacomb, because I knew the subterranean routes of storm-drains, sewers, and culverts. Yet, the militia also were alert to their existence, and patrolled the manholes vigor-ously; decades of torch-bearers and their leashed cohorts of bloodhounds wandered sluggishly among the shadowy arcades and tunnels, ankle-deep in water. Standing upright in a dark niche, immobile as a holy statue, I trembled on the verge of mar-tyrdom; the police, eventually, would stumble on me, and interrogate my whereabouts; and I would die, rather than sin.

During these imagined epics, the ornaments and flowers in empty parlour windows were arranged like icons in a running sub-text, and the lions' heads on doors grinned silently, as they held the bits between their teeth. By now the street was a time-bound amphitheatre, with Clonard Monastery as one ruined wall of a Colosseum, which cast its ancient gnomon shadow on the whole proceedings. Whole empires crumbled, as the moss between the flagstones seethed with microscopic life. The sky was blitzed by photographically developed clouds, blown in a hurricane into the present from its own inexorable detritus, as time collapsed about it, and only the eye of the storm could determine what would be; afterwards, the survivors in potato cellars would emerge to rub their eyes and poke about the abandoned bits and pieces of their sky-borne farms. Somewhere up there, a whole house still sailed in the vortex, all its crockery and Tilley lamps intact, pictures and mirrors tilting gently from the perpendicular. I am reminded of the elaborate traveller's-tale bungalow, eaten inside-out by a termite army, who digest its every wooden item, but leave behind a shell of what had been, until the unsuspecting aftercomer touches it, and the simulacrum crumbles into dust.*

For all these reveries, I was not unpunctual in my return. The time I've taken to describe these mental byways is much longer than their actual span, for each can be perceived holistically, in kaleidoscopic, frozen moments; and time is telescoped within them. Think of those minutely detailed, mundane dreams in which you wake, rise, brush your teeth, put on your clothes, etcetera, and go to school or work, enjoying all the routine

---

*Sometimes the termites 'will do things so fantastic that they might almost be practical jokes. Forbes, an English traveller, relates in his *Oriental Memoirs* that, returning home after spending a few days with a friend, he found every engraving that hung in his rooms completely eaten away, frames and all, not a vestige remaining; but the glass that covered them had been left in its place, and carefully cemented to the wall, so that there should be no fear of its dropping and perhaps making too much noise.'

Maurice Maeterlinck, *The Life of the White Ant*

panacea of a day, etcetera, until you wake again, perhaps for real, and must endure the process once again: these dreams only occupy some fleeting moments, according to some observers; but they seem a form of *déjà vu*, or a basis for prognostication. An ornithologist informs me that starlings flock at dusk in standard, routine patterns, so that each day is the same to them; and what we see as wheeling, baroque outbursts occupy a predetermined flight-path; the birds are both conductor and the score, their movements only deviated by the ambient humidity or temperature. As we discussed this phenomenon – birds chattering, dotted and quavered on telegraph lines – another amateur suggested the analogy of a fireworks display, whose nebulae exploding in the night above you have been engineered to manage such effects, yet each is slightly different in its calculated spontaneity.

Over and over, though we flit incessantly into the moment, our pasts catch up with us, and apprehend us at the endless intersections, where fingerposts are unreliable, and mileages are tilted. I realize, now, that I've travelled back from secondary to primary school by the arbitrary short-cut of a synapse, down one worm-hole of the riddled memory, which stores everything we've ever known, and more, if we could only find the portals to its vast, inconsequential realms, where the laws of time and space work in reverse. In this non-Euclidean geometry, the interior of a surface is infinitely greater than its exterior. There are boxes within boxes, elaborately carved versions of each other: not copies, since one chromosomal detail, according to current evolutionary theory, must differ slightly from its predecessor, till, by a Chinese-whisper process, the microscopic generations appear garbled to their ancestors; we are assuming, here, that they evolve from the outside in, whereas the converse is just as likely to be true, since space is a function of time, and vice versa.

Time spent inside is not equal to that spent outside. The mouthful of 'St Mary's Christian Brothers' Grammar School' was reduced to 'Barrack Street' in common parlance, a nomenclature which corresponded both to space and history. There was speculation that the ghosts of sentrymen or screws patrolled the doors of classrooms, and this vision of a prison was encouraged by the military carriage of the black-robed, black-buttoned, black-booted Christian Brothers. Sometimes, the routine periods of time would be disrupted by sporadic bursts of poltergeist activity emanating in the chemistry laboratory. Will-o'-the-wisps had discovered its whiff of phosphorus and Bunsen-burner gas to be conducive to their being; occasionally, pipettes and retorts exploded mysteriously over the benches etched with names and acid. Dissident, spilled globules of mercury rolled and hissed on the floor; the shelves trembled with powerful chemical substances, as if an underground train of association ran below the whole establishment, shaking its foundations.

Inserting myself into the remembered cell of a classroom, I realize again that the Invisible Boy was a kind of paradox or oxymoron, simultaneously free and unfree, there and not there; his reality depended on the observer. Now I recall that in another ground-floor room, a deviant of the Boy was perpetrated. Here, a wainscot-high row of coat-hooks ran along one side of the room; in winter, they were festooned with damp, visually impenetrable gaberdines, behind which the newly incumbent Boy would be required to hunker uncomfortably. A particular kink of this version was the elevation of its scapegoat aspect to a point of sadism. Curled foetally, the Boy, as present absentee, would be cajoled by furtive kicks and fisticuffs to give himself away; yet this stratagem was liable to backfire, since, were the Boy's cover blown, the whole class would be implicated. On one occasion, someone stuck a compass-point into Him, whereupon the Boy's responding utterance was muffled by a collective outbreak of whooping-cough; it was agreed, thereafter, that such weapons should be decommissioned. Complicit in invisibility, we suffered Mafia or IRA extremes of honour, for our Catholic education had imbued us with the desirability of martyrdom: perfect train-ing for a man on the run, who, if arrested, would die rather than inform or sin; and I have dreams of being such a figure to this day, finding myself apparently trapped in a cul-de-sac between the Falls and Shankill Roads, desperately searching for a manhole.

Given our underground status, we constantly employed our-selves in hide-and-seek techniques, rehearsing the dimensions of concealed space. We knew the cramped, gas-tainted meter cup-boards under stairs, larders stifled in potato-earth and spice aromas, and the camphor alcoves between chinking gowns in wardrobes. Incessantly, we scanned the urban plan for short-cuts, entries, deviations from the known routes; we monitored the traffic-flow and, hopping on to the backs of flatbed lorries, practised being desperadoes on a train. We preferred the roles of Indians to those of Cowboys. We would keep our eyes peeled, and our ears to the ground, absorbing the moves of far-off regi-ments. We uttered gargled locomotive noises, and the telegraph wires trembled and buzzed with advance information; long before the dots and dashes were decoded at the next Morse halt, our *alter-ego* outlaws would have tumbled out of the box-car, down a steep embankment, thus allowing stuntmen to display their body-double skills. We could accurately gauge the chronology and provenance of horse-shit, as we crumbled it and sifted it between our thumbs and fingers. Thinking of uniformed riders, we were put in mind of the Royal Ulster Constabulary, who perambulated the environment on high, bottle-green bicycles, operating their swaying dynamos and thumb-switch Sturmey-Archer gears, as they ticked like fat bombs along urban byways, apprehending miching youngsters in their out-of-school routines. Then they would conjure a pencil-stub from a special pocket and lick the graphite apex before inscribing the *nom de plume* of the truant in a black, flipped-open notebook. It suddenly shut with a snap of garter elastic, as the false name and address were registered.

Thus another chapter was closed.

BARRACK STREET II

We were constantly interrogated, since much of our routine learning was by rote. Rote did not end with primary school alphabets and tables, for it entered into full plethora mode in grammar school. We learned lists of Latin, French and Irish words, together with their proper conjugations and declensions, their voices, tenses and moods; we sang names, dates, places, populations; we got poems, songs and recitations off by heart. We were expected to enumerate and name the angels' hierarchies, and know the function of the sacred vessels and accessories:

> For the celebration of Holy Mass the priest needs two Sacred vessels – the *Paten* and the *Chalice*. The Paten is a small plate of gold or gilded silver, on which is placed the *Host*. The Chalice, also made of precious metal, contains the *Wine*. The Host is made of pure wheat flour and is baked between two irons. The Wine is unadulterated juice of the grape naturally fermented.

In preparation for Mass the priest places on the cup of the Chalice a small Linen Cloth. It is used to wipe the Chalice before the Wine is put into it, and to wipe it again after Communion. This cloth is called the *Purificator*.

Over the Purificator the priest places the Paten, on the top of which he puts the *Pall* – a small square of stiff linen which prevents dust or other impurities from falling into the Chalice during Mass.

Completely covering the Chalice is the *Chalice Veil*. It is a square of silk, fashioned of the same material and having the same colour as the vestments the priest wears.

On the Veil is placed the *Burse* in which is carried the *Corporal*. The Corporal is a linen cloth, approximately a foot square, that serves as a small tablecloth on which the Sacred Vessels rest during Mass.

The *Ciborium* is a vessel made of precious metal. It is usually larger than the Chalice and is covered with a lid. In it are kept the Sacred hosts reserved for Communion.

For exposition of the Blessed Sacrament the *Monstrance* is used. It is made of precious metal and is designed to hold the Blessed Sacrament in public view for the adoration and to be raised in blessing the Faithful. It contains the *Lunette*, a crescent-shaped device of gold or silver used for holding the Host in an upright position.*

All subjects had a greater or lesser degree of this liturgical exactitude. There were correct answers to everything, and they were inculcated by the universal administration of pain. Some

---

The Sunday Missal for All Sundays and the Principal Feasts of the Year.

eccentrics wielded canes and yardsticks as their ruler of choice; most preferred straps, which were custom-built to each master's specifications. Some liked a broad, flat implement, more full of sound than fury; veterans of a meaner temperament deployed thin, whippy, licorice-black sticks of leather, which left a scarlet weal on your palm or the veins of your wrist. Sometimes these expertly- stitched weapons contained a line of brass thrupenny bits – about three or four shillings' worth, depending on length – to give them *gravitas* and sting. They made a sound like *stet*. The paradoxical Mr X maintained a fine strap of Wildean green, which came into play only when sarcasm had failed, and then but languidly. Brother Y rubbed dubbin into his to preserve its whiplash flexibility; Z treated his with Vaseline.

Different techniques and subtle disciplines were brought to bear on us, from the erratic, head-high flail of the novice, to the short instructive snap of the wrist-expert. The dapper little Mr M was one of the latter, who had honed his skills to exquisite degrees by the exercise of golf and callisthenics. As a History teacher, whose lessons consisted mainly of questions, Mr M's paradigm of education was a popular games show of the time, *Double Your Money*. Here, the contestants were required to answer initially simple questions: after getting the first right, they won, say, £5; if they got the second, £10, and so on, in a double-or-quits routine; as the questions got progressively more difficult, the contestant would hover between greed and prudence, egged both ways by a vociferous audience, as he provided them with vicarious thrills. Small fortunes were won and lost. Mr M fancied himself as an impresario of quiz, and his version of the show, *Double Your Slaps*, put a new twist on the concept of reward. In this rubric of negative morality, a wrong answer elicited a stroke of the black strap. The boy under the spotlight could then opt to take his leather *frisson* there and then – *stet* – or defer it, and go on to 'double his slaps', in the hope that, by correctly answering just one question, his accumulated debt (or earnings) would be absolved.

A simple mathematical calculation shows that after seven consecutive wrongs, or failures to respond, a boy would be entitled to sixty-four slaps, which number reminds us of the parable of the chessboard, whereby the brilliant sculptor, or architect, is asked to name his fee, and specifies one grain of rice to be placed on one square, two on the second, four on the third, and so on, and the Emperor looks at him as if he wasn't all there and says, are you sure, but the builder says, go on, I'll be content with that; and by the time the whole board is covered, the bits of multiplied rice exceed the number of atoms in the known universe. And some contestants did rack up some astronomically impressive numbers; here, a catch occurred, for the time that M might spend in dealing out this vast sentence had to be reduced, pragmatically; otherwise, there would be no time for the show, and nothing would get taught. M's solution to the problem had a simple, sporting beauty, in which his rules of barter operated to make a golf ball worth six slaps, or a generous dozen, when he was in good form; and he would knock a few digits off the sum of punishment to bring it down to a reasonable number of balls a boy could afford to buy. In a theatrical aside, he would suggest that

Smithfield Market was an ideal venue for such purchases, where a clutch of second-hand balls could be had for a few pennies.

A neutral observer might admire M's method, encompassing, as it did, a wealth of disciplines: Behavioural Science, Law, Civics, Algebra, Black Market Economics, Physical Education, and Ostensible History; Reeling and Writhing might also be included in this Wonderland, or was it Through the Looking Glass? Perhaps it is not surprising that this holistic philosophy should extend beyond the confines of the classroom; but in retrospect, the manner of its proclamation seems distinctly odd.

At 68 Divis Street – I have just confirmed it in the 1948 Directory – was Gribbin, Jas., Bootmaker, who maintained a sideline as Manufacturer of Straps for the Discerning Educator. Here, not being able to afford the elaborately stitched, custom-built items, we would purchase lengths of half-inch-thick bootsole leather, and fashion our own instruments of punishment, and consent to beat each other, in a mirror image of our betters. It was a version of conkers, in which the strap was one conker, and your opponent's hand the other –

Iddy iddy onker
My first conker
Iddy iddy ack
My first smack

– and the winner was the one who could take the most smacks. I have buried this experience so far in the back of my mind that I used to attribute it to false memory syndrome; but I have met other victims of that era, and they confirm it. Sometimes I get a glimpse of a freezing yard – the concrete arena like a bottle – crammed with boys slipping, falling over one another – or hunkered at a game of marbles – leap-frogging – chained to one another – then unravelling in knots along magnetic force-fields – playing hand-ball at gable walls – falling off low walls – the odd boy or two draped over iron railings, morosely sucking their spikes – then isolated pairs of strap-holders, pursuing their grave rituals of domination – the sound of one hand clapping in the throng.

Meanwhile, boys bursting with testosterone lounged in the cramped open-air urinals, squeezing their pimples, puffing and inhaling furtive cigarette smoke, in a bonding mechanism generally ignored by the authorities. A peer, lately returned from France, would produce a blue talismanic pack of Gitanes; one was passed around like a drug, and we would gasp at its authoritative strength, as if choked in smog, or the musk of scented French girls. Then some son of a publican or bookmaker, exerting his high status, would up the ante with a beautiful hinged box of Rameses II, distributed by Stephano Bros., Philadelphia PA., 'manufactured from the mildest superfine quality selected YENIDGE TURKISH TOBACCO, and from the best rice paper; made in proper Egyptian style – EGYPTIAN CIGARETTES, TURKISH TOBACCO.' I am smoking one right now, by way of an experiment in time, as it scorches my tongue and wafts its sudden fug of burning socks and horse-dung into the kitchen where I write. Now I've just stubbed it out – it's still smouldering – I remember something that I haven't thought about or visualized for years, my father's Vatican souvenir glass ashtray, which was a miniature of the great piazza of St Peter's and its huge basilica:

VATICAN, The. The official residence of the pope at Rome, so named from being built on the lower slope of the Vatican Hill; figuratively, the name is used to signify the papal power and influence and, by extension, the whole Church. In addition to the papal apartments, those of the palatine prelates, officials, and staff, the apartments of state and the chapels (the Sistine, Pauline, papal private, of the Swiss Guards, etc.), the palace itself includes the chief library of the world, the archives of the Roman Church, five museums of antiquities, two picture-galleries, and a polyglot printing-press; an astronomical observatory is attached. The apartments of state, etc., have been described as the most stately and least luxurious of any mansion of the world; the rest of the palace is one vast workshop. Since 1929 the palace with its gardens and other immediate surroundings has been recognized as a sovereign state.*

Vatican, surely, must have something to do with *vates*, as defined by the *OED*: '1. A poet or bard, esp. one who is divinely inspired; a prophet. 2. One of the classes of the old Gaulish druids. Hence *Vatic*, *ical*, adjs. of, pertaining to, or characteristic of a prophet or seer; prophetic, inspired.' Naturally that *seer* reminds us of the Holy See, which, though it derives from *sedes*, a seat, suggests a holy alliance of vision and authority; the Jesuits,

---

*The Catholic Encyclopaedic Dictionary.

I understand, still maintain a state-of-the-art or art-of-the-state observatory on the Vatican Hill, whereby they reconcile the sidereal universe, post-Galileo, to the *primum mobile* of divine intention. So the Vatican is a kind of Star Factory, whose telescope picks up the music of the spheres, broadcasting it *urbi et orbi*, with all its polyglotal organ stops pulled out.

At this point in time, it seems to me that flicking ash on to the glass piazza, or grinding cigarette-butts into it, would reek of sacrilege; I see the confraternities and consororities of pilgrims crushed into it from all the diocesan angles of the globe, babbling panic-stricken in their multitude of tongues, as the glowing red giant nose of the UFO descends on them like a precursor of Apocalypse. Yet, it could be argued that the Vatican *cendrier* had a sacramental function, as ash reminds us of our own mortality, and Wednesdays of incense: it was a small, heavy, pocket icon, a *memento mori*. Smudged and spotted, it resembled X-ray images of cancered, nicotined lungs, or classroom posters of the soul, dotted with mortal-black and ash-grey-venial stubs of sin.

I roll up and light an Old Holborn cigarette to bring me back to school in Barrack Street:

> *A dillar, a dollar*
> *A ten o'clock scholar*
> *What makes you come so soon*
> *You used to come at ten o'clock*
> *And now you come at noon*

– and indeed, there is something paradoxical about school

time and its division into periods of forty minutes, reminding us of the Forty Days of Lent; of the number of days of the Flood; of years of the Israelites' wandering; of the days of the fast of Elias; of Moses on Sinai and of Our Lord in the desert; of Quadragesima; of quarantine; of the Forty Hours' Prayer, 'the solemn exposition of the Blessed Sacrament for the space of forty hours, more or less, being the time our Lord lay in the tomb, continuous adoration being maintained by relays of watchers'. It is no wonder that school periods sometimes took an age, or that, cancelling our presences within it, we would absent ourselves from the system. Playing truant, we went on the beak or the hike or the bunk; we miched, or mitched; we bobbed and fagged off; jigged and jouked; played the nick and the kipp and the lag; we went wagging it; we went plunking, skiving, sagging, ticking, twagging school; we skipped and hopped and dodged and scarpered, as we took French leave and exited into the city, to explore its yawning avenues and dark arcades.

SMITHFIELD

It was great to get lost in Smithfield.

No inhabitant of Belfast needs any description of the general
aspect of Smithfield. It seems a storehouse, or rather salehouse,
for all the nondescript wares which can be collected from whatever quarter. How such heterogeneous articles contrived to
come together in one and the same place, and set themselves
down there, side by side, in truce and amity, is a problem which
it perplexes the mind to solve. One would think of the 'rudis
indigestaque moles', but that, after all, it is not quite a chaos of
formless things – only a glorious disorder of things of some shape
and name, but such as no one, perhaps, ever saw before, or ever
will except in Smithfield, brought together within so limited a
compass. It might seem as if there had been a design to surprise
the passer-by, by the strangeness of the contrasts and combina-
tions, such as we might see in a huge kaleidoscope – only
substituting ugliness for beauty; or, as if all the warehouses and

shops in the town had poured out all their refuse contents into this one common repository and receptacle. It is easy, however, to see that a singular social medley must be found collected and associated within the precincts of Smithfield. Honest industry, on whatever scale it is pursued, is worthy of all honour; and the merchandise of this place is not without its advantages to a numerous class, both of traders and purchasers. It is reported very currently, however, that many goods find their way into this mart by other than the established means of honourable traffic; and I have known some friends who have had the pleasure of finding there, and buying back, their property, after it had unaccountably disappeared from their houses or their tables.

Revd W. M. O'Hanlon, *Walks among the Poor of Belfast*, 1853

That Smithfield, and the Smithfield of my memory, are no more.

Now mostly absorbed in the Castlecourt complex, this was a rectangular square between Castle Lane, Millfield, North Street and Royal Avenue. It was laid out in July 1788 in an area at the end of Berry Street known as 'The Rails', to replace the markets held till then in the High Street. It may have been named after the London meat market, but there is a record of John Gregg leasing 'grazing for two cows' at 'Smith's Field' in the early 18c. The Smithfield of popular memory was a quadrangle of small shops containing three covered arcades of junk stalls, mostly built in 1848, but the central area was built up and roofed over by the Borough Surveyor in 1884. This treasure trove of old books, old pictures, old radio components, mostly elderly dealers, and customers of all ages and classes, was destroyed by fire-bombs on 6 May 1974. Despite the prompt provision of portakabins to bring the traders back, Smithfield had lost its stock as well as its atmosphere, and it never recovered . . . Four workers burnt to death in a fire at the Lucifer Match Factory here in 1882.

Marcus Patton, *Central Belfast: An Historical Gazeteer*, 1993

I visited Smithfield the morning after the 1974 blaze. It looked like a minor Dresden, with only the stone piers of its gates still standing; yet I was reminded of how difficult it is to burn books, for reams of them survived among the smouldering ruins, their margins charred, but the dense compact volumes of their interiors still intact. As children, we used to observe the same post-bonfire phenomenon, when all that remained of sofas were their cobra springs, and even books that had been wholly burned retained, like carbon-paper flimsies, their pages of ash, until someone poked them with a stick and a wind blew them away in whispered nothings; I still wonder how the book-burning emperors maintained their censor illusions, when relics, shards and signatures of books must have been retrieved from the pyres by lovers and disciples, who, in the aftermath, would slip them to each other in the undergrounds of samizdat, and memorize their bits of text; and, where two or three of them were gathered in an upstairs room, or in the gloom of a catacomb, they would stitch their remembered episodes together, pretending to make a quilt for a wedding or a funeral; and the temporal authorities could not suppress the stories of this collective phoenix.

Concurrently to writing this, I had been reading Alberto Manguel's *A History of Reading*, and at this moment, 7.15 p.m. on 8 April 1997, about thirty minutes have passed since I opened his book at page 304 and was smitten by a pleasant shock of *déjà vu*: here is reproduced a favourite photograph of mine, which I first saw when it (or, to be precise, the left-hand half of it) appeared on the front cover of the *London Review of Books*.(I can't, here and now, give you the issue, since it's pinned to the display-board in my office, in Stranmillis Road; I see it in my mind's eye, as I write, and feel curiously bilocated). The image, to me, is emblematic of Smithfield. Manguel writes:

> And sometimes, when the stars are kind, we read with an intake of breath, with a shudder, as if someone or something had 'walked over our grave', as if a memory had suddenly been rescued from a place deep within us – the recognition of something we never knew was there, or of something we vaguely felt as a flicker or a shadow, whose ghostly form rises and passes back into us before we can see what it is, leaving us older and wiser.
>
> This reading has an image. A photograph taken in 1940, during the bombing of London in the Second World War, shows the remains of a caved-in library. Through the torn roof can be seen ghostly buildings outside, and in the centre of the store is a heap of beams and crippled furniture. But the shelves on the walls have held fast, and the books lined up along them seem unharmed. Three men are standing amidst the rubble: one, as if hesitant about which book to choose, is apparently reading the titles on the spines; another, wearing glasses, is reaching for a volume; the third is reading, holding an open book in his hands.

It is, indeed, a beautiful image, and there is something hieratic and priest-like about this trinity of readers – one, indeed, seems to be wearing a dog-collar – each involved in his private realm of contemplation, as if interceding with another universe, their backs turned to the ladders in the ruins. Reading their different postures, we are reminded of ourselves: that backwards craning of the neck to scan the spines of an upper shelf; that exploratory stoop, the index finger hooked into the headband; that poised, absent-minded stance, where the reader's eyes are absorbed in the light which falls on an open page.

I see myself maintaining these postures in Smithfield, reaching up on tip-toes, for example, for this calf-bound book I next take up, Vol. VI of *The Works of Henry Fielding*, comprising *Joseph Andrews*, 'The Preface to David Simple', and 'The Preface to the Familiar Letters between the Principal Characters in David Simple, and some others', these latter pieces taking up only thirteen pages. As I weigh it in my hand, it has the feel of a pocket icon, and I appreciate again its rock-solid binding, the five thistle motifs gold-blocked between the raised bands of its spine (it was printed in Edinburgh 'by and for Martin & Wotherspoon' in MDCCLXX); opening it, I see again the Phoenix colophon of Hon. John Browne, Newport, hand-stamped in embrowned ink on the frescoesque, damp-stained, foxed inside front cover, and the scrawled, still-black signature of Wm. Gibbon, something illegible, 1872. Skimming the book, letting the leaves flick by my left thumb in a rewind animation sequence, I remember how movies or films used to be known as 'flicks'; as I arrest it at two open pages, my eye is carried to the bottom of a page, where I notice that the first word of the next page is reproduced, or anticipated, indented in the right-hand margin. I like this 1771 device, which simultaneously stops you and carries you forward, in a knit-purl fashion, and you could make a mini-narrative or arbitrary précis of the matter by conjugating these dropped stitches, a yarn made all the more mysterious because it contains hyphenated bits, broken by whatever way the typesetter thought fit to justify them, for example, 'pray, deed, they, too, upon, martyr, -sently, -ship, O love, -gar, -ness, more, your, passion, returned, but, fellows, you, Mr, that, was, they, -tainty, or, all, unless, mistake, time, -wouse, Joseph, poor, The, thief, CHAP.', which gives a tolerably fair, if etiolated, encryption of Chapters V–XIII.

It strikes me that this hook-and-eye principle is applicable to my own method of writing, where I have to make a link or bridge from the end of a chapter to the head, or body, of the next, sometimes in quite an arbitrary fashion; it is also part of the ever-recurring problem of getting sentences to follow each other, like a troupe of circus elephants, trunks hooked into tails, or the tall-tale filing system cited by Manguel, where, 'in the tenth century . . . the Grand Vizier of Persia, Abdul Kassem Ismael, in order not to part with his collection of 117,000 books when travelling, had them carried by a caravan of four hundred camels trained to walk in alphabetical order.'

Taking the last words on the pages of a random chapter of this book, 'From Abbey Road to Zetland Street', as printed out in my fair copy, I get the following: 'have, old, top, it, makes, reflec-tion, numbers, thimbles, directory, aeroplanes', which is a pretty good mnemonic; but of course a quite different, and much shorter, series will appear on the finally published pages of this book, this caravanserai. The pattern will be different, but

226

nonetheless as valid. Pattern, the second word of that last sentence, recalls knitting, and my niece Róisín's saying, in response to some idle remark about pine-needles fallen on the road, 'Are those the needles that you woolly with?' She was about five at the time, I think; not that I heard her speak it, but it was one of those implanted-memory syndromes of family folklore, which are so strong that they can cross branches of a family tree, and I can visualize an absent Róisín sitting beside me in my sister Caitlín's car, as we drove along a shiny black tar road strewn with pine-needles, and the circumstances nudged her memory of Róisín's *bon mot*. My sister, indeed, has a great memory, and remembers me doing things I cannot recall; but I can observe myself doing them through her comedy of words. She also has a great mind for the words of songs,* and must have a couple of

*Caitlin is also moderately ambidextrous and, in the manner of Leonardo, used to practise mirror-writing. When she was a young girl she used to make up mini-sagas about Princess Nosrac Niltiac and her brother, Prince Nosrac Naraic, our reversed *alter egos*. The Nosracs inhabited a Through-the-Looking-Glass realm not unlike Hollywood Transylvania, and were famous for travelling the country in disguise, performing various feats of charity and advocacy for the peasantry, who were oppressed by absentee or anti-Royal overlords. A secret passage led from a palace attic down through a zig-zag stair within the cavity wall to a larder in the cellar, from whence it took you under the moat, and you emerged from a far-off wishing-well into an April-dappled glade. There was, indeed, a serial princess of this ilk who featured in a weekly girls' comic of the fifties and sixties, *School Friend* (not *Schoolfriend*, which has entirely different connotations). I've just asked my wife Deirdre if she remembers it, and *en route* she tells me a possibly apocryphal story of how the present Queen of England, Elizabeth, when a princess, used to go on disguised walkabouts with her younger sister Margaret, the one who smokes and drinks. As it happens, I have a copy of the 1956 *School Friend* annual before me, having dragged it out from under a pile of books in the back room in the course of writing this footnote, and I am most disappointed to find that the said princess does not feature here, though there is a jolly good illustrated yarn about The hundred off by heart: I sometimes think of her brain as a knitting-machine, as she word-processes the pattern of the songs into wearable garments, and racks them up in camphor-scented wardrobes for future retrieval; naturally some, in difficult-to-get-at recesses, get forgotten about, but not lost, and sometimes make themselves available for selection when she's looking for another item; here, maybe, we're talking fifties juke-boxes, which, like typewriters, have their knitting-machine aspects, not to speak of dishwashers, and there is something humanoid about the armature which flips over the black disc in the manner of a blackjack dealer. Also, juke-boxes look like the bonnets of American cars with their sunburst chromium grins and curved windshields; I'm trying to remember if they sported anything like tail-fins, which would have made them look like science-fiction rockets, whereupon the windshield would become the transparent visor of a Dan Dare space-helmet. Coincidentally, 'juke' if spelled 'jook' is what I used to believe was Ulster dialect for 'look'; but one rhyming-slang etymology traces it to the fifties motor-bike rider Geoff Duke, whom you only got to see when he

---

Silent Three, who have a habit of donning monks' cowled robes and black eye-masks in order to advance the plot ('. . . at school, the three chums formed a secret society known as The Silent Three. While out for a stroll on the cliffs, Betty had wandered ahead of her chums. And suddenly . . .). Other stories include 'It All Began with a Carnival Costume', 'Dilly's Dizziest Day-dream', 'Solak – a Dog Under Suspicion', 'The Disguise which Bluffed the Boys', and 'Trix's Amazing First Flight'. But no Transylvania, which might have belonged to another similar comic (do I vaguely recall School Chum?). All the same, I can picture its mad King Ludwig of Bavaria Eurodisney castle, and the pretty princess with her hair done up in plaits, flitting about her business in a milk-maid's yoked tight-bodiced dirndl dress over a drawstring-necked blouse with elbow-length puffed sleeves.

took off his helmet; *Chambers* gives 'jook' as Scots 'to duck, to dodge', which is possibly a related issue, as I never fail to see a sly boy jooking round a corner when I hear this word.

At any rate, my mother was a great woollier, and I used to be baffled by the practised ease with which she translated a pattern from its multiplicity of tightly printed symbols into a visibly expanding, multicoloured Fair Isle cardigan – which strikes me as being a bit of an oxymoron, given that Cardigan is in Wales, though the garment is named after Lord Cardigan, who probably rarely set foot there. For a moment I indulge a fantasy of the Shetlands (official name until 1974, Zetland), where Fair Isle is situated, as a Welsh-speaking archipelagic colony, and envisage the great Shetland-pony-wool-spinning, wind-powered factories, the extensive, unwalled orchards of windmills perched on the sides of mountains; or perhaps the people speak a Celtic–Norse–Scots–English creole which is an important field of study for Swiss linguists, who arrive in flocks in the summer like migratory birds, and rarely winter there, so that many of the multiple choice words for fog and sleet are not found in their thesauruses. In the winter the folk pass the long Northern nights about the fire in composing a saga about the Swiss, who have been coming to Zetland for generations, and whose cast-off watches and obsolete tape-recording machines have become objects of devotion. Then the Swiss return in summer to record the next cycle, thus ensuring that it will not be lost to future generations; mostly, the saga deals with the unrequited episodic love of foreigners.

Of course, if one follows the grammatical logic of the construction 'Fair Isle cardigan', the shoe would be on the other foot, and the Zetlanders would have invaded Wales, whereupon a cinematic image of a fleet of dragon-boats skims across the inward eye like a squadron of swans, evoking the Early Irish monkish marginal quatrain:

> Bitter the wind tonight,
> combing the sea's hair white:
> from the North, no need to fear
> the proud sea-coursing warrior.

I like this version by John Montague for its nice internal assonantal rhymes based around the *ee* of the sea sound, its enjambement of *fear*, giving it all a shivery impression; and I think the phrase 'negative capability' could be bandied about here, since we can see these Vikings even though they don't exist for now, just as the invisible traveller in the Basho haiku walks unbidden into our brain, as Harold G. Henderson's literal translation* has it: *This/road/:/going-person/be-none/(with)/autumn-nightfall.* We imagine him carrying a staff or a sickle, flitting in and out of digital being. Returning to the Norsemen, you can see the target-practice shields slung from the gunwales like the roundels on the wings of Second World War Royal Air Force fighter-planes, and the guy standing at the front, or is it the back, with his long hair flying round him from under his earphones-horned helmet, pointing his sword in the general direction of Ireland,

---

*In his *An Introduction to Haiku*.

encouraged by the general spy knowledge that the round towers laboriously constructed by the Irish are strategically silly, given that all you have to do is light a fire around the structure once the monks, withdrawing their ladders, have climbed into its top storey.

Checking my old *Brewer's Dictionary of Phrase and Fable* for a possible entry for round towers, I can only come up with *Roué* and *Rouen*, both of which deserve to be quoted in full:

Roué. The profligate Duke of Orleans, Regent of France, first used this word in its modern sense (about 1720). It was his ambition to collect round him companions as worthless as himself, and he used facetiously to boast that there was not one of them that did not deserve to be broken on the wheel – that being the most ordinary punishment for malefactors at the time; hence these profligates went by the name of Orleans' roués or wheels. The most notorious roués were the Dukes of Richelieu, Broglie, Biron, and Brancase, together with Canillac and Nocé; in England, the Dukes of Rochester and Buckingham.

Rouen. *Aller à Rouen*. To go to ruin. The French are full of these puns, and our merry forefathers indulged in them also, as, 'You are on the highway to Needham' (a market town in Suffolk), i.e. your courses will lead you to poverty.

The Bloody Feast of Rouen (1356). Charles the Dauphin gave a banquet to his private friends at Rouen, to which his brother-in-law Charles the Bad was invited. While the guests were at table King Jean entered the room with a numerous escort, exclaiming, 'Traitor, thou art not worthy to sit at table with my son!' Then, turning to his guards he added, 'Take him thence! By holy Paul, I will neither eat nor drink till his head be brought me!' Then, seizing an iron mace from one of the men at arms, he struck another of the guests between the shoulders, exclaiming, 'Out, proud traitor! by the soul of my father, thou shalt not live!' Four of the guests were beheaded on the spot.

However, 'tower' yields an interesting concept: 'Towers of Silence. See SILENCE.' Under *Silence*, 'the Towers of Silence. The small towers on which the Parsees and Zoroastrians place their dead to be consumed by birds of prey. The bones are picked clean in the course of a day, and are then thrown into a receptacle and covered with charcoal.'

Before reading this definition, I had reckoned that the Towers of Silence might appertain to the Stylites, or Pillar Saints, described thus by Brewer's:

> A class of early and mediaeval ascetics, chiefly of Syria, who took up their abode on top of a pillar, from which they never descended. The most celebrated are Simeon Stylites of Syria, and Daniel the Stylite of Constantinople. Simeon (d. 596) spent sixty-eight years on different pillars, each loftier and narrower than the preceding, the 1st being 66 feet high. Daniel (d. 494) lived thirty-three years on a pillar, and was not infrequently blown from it by the storms from Thrace.

One cannot help but wonder about the logistics of such operations, as we imagine baskets of food or faeces being raised or lowered on ropes by a supporting cast of aficionados, and the buzz of having such a drop-out character to provide for and look up to must have been immense, if we are to believe the

Revd John-Bernard Dalgairns, whose treatise, *The Holy Communion*, deals with such issues in passing:

> With this tendency to error in the race from which he sprung, one would have expected to find marks of fanaticism about St. Simeon Stylites. Yet no one has less about him of the arrogance or obstinacy of delusion. He comes down from his pillar at a word of advice from the neighbouring monks. He casts away the chain that bound him at the suggestion of a visitor. Above all, the good which he effected marks him out as an apostle. There is something wonderful in the apparition of this man, with beautiful face and bright hair, raised up on high, night and day, adoring God. He stands in the same relation to the saints of the solitary desert, that the Dominicans do to the cloistered Benedictines or Camaldolese. Not in the desert, but in the vicinity of vast wicked Antioch,* he stands on his pillar and he preaches. Once he grew weary of the streams of people who were continually flocking from all parts of the world, even from distant Britain, to hear him; he bade the monks shut up the enclosure round his column, because he wished to be alone with God. At night a troop of angels came and threatened him for quitting the post assigned to him by God. He began again at once his weary work. For thirty-seven years his sleepless eyes looked down with pity and compassion on the crowds who came to consult him. Cheerfully, and with temper unruffled by the burning heat, or the pitiless pelting of the mountain storms, he listened to all and consoled them. From three o'clock in the afternoon till set of sun he preached from that strange pulpit to the most motley

---

*His mountain was forty-five miles from Antioch, but easily accessible.

congregation ever assembled to hear the Word of God. Wild
Bedouin Arabs, mountaineers from the highlands of Armenia,
and from the cedars of Lebanon, banditti from the Isaurian hills,
blacks from Ethiopia, were mingled there with perfumed counts
of the East, and prefects of Antioch with Romanised Gauls and
Spaniards. The Emperor Marcian was once among his audience.
Even the objects of St. Chrysostom's indignant eloquence, the
ladies of Antioch, who never deigned to set their embroidered
slippers on the pavement of the city, quitted the bazaar and their
gilded palanquins to toil up the mountains, to catch a glimpse of
the saint outside the enclosure, within which no woman
entered. Wicked women looked from a distance on that strange
figure, high in air, with hands lifted up to heaven and body
bowing down with fear of God; and they burst into an agony of
tears, and then and there renounced their sins for ever.

Imagining the multilingual babble of these congregations, I think
of how my sister's children were reared bilingually, in Irish and
English, as my siblings and I were. I used to lull myself to sleep
with language, mentally repeating, for example, the word *capall*,
the Irish for horse, which seemed to be more onomatopoeically
equine than its English counterpart; gradually, its trochaic foot
would summon up a ghostly echo of 'cobble', till, wavering
between languages, I would allow my disembodied self to drift
out the window and glide through the silent dark gas-lit streets
above the mussel-coloured cobblestones. I was bound for the
Star Factory, where words were melted down and like tallow
cast into new moulds.

Thinking about pre-language, I come up with the earliest
dream I remember, where I am adrift in a universe devoid of

words; here, 'cloud' and 'star' are meaningless vocables; but I am sitting on what resembles a cloud, and the uncountable stars blaze all around me. This does not seem an entirely unusual position to be in, although the cloud has a curious non-terrestial texture, feeling both hard and soft at the same time; and I am ensconced in aeons, minutes, seconds, centuries of time, huge other clouds of it slowly toppling and thrashing like waterspouts collapsing themselves in the distant regions of the future, occluding whole galaxies; sometimes, they bump into one another, and flicker and boom with rapid desultory sultry lightning. Whatever I am, I sit on my private cloud for a small eternity, before a bolt zaps me across the universe with immeasurable angelic force, to land me on another identical cloud; and the sequence repeats itself again and again, till it seems it must go on forever.

Luckily, there is an out. When I realize the recurrent nature of this dream, I can harness a cloud to take me to the moon, from whence I can take the moonbeam causeway back to earth, gliding in through the window-pane into my bed, where I snuggle within my skin and close my eyelids, hoping to dream of a bridge to the next chapter.

BRICKLE BRIDGE

Compare the bridges of the city to bar magnets: the traffic acts like iron filings drawn into force-fields; and often the bridges are jam-packed with metal vehicles throbbing motionlessly, polarized above a river or a mesh of train tracks.

At dusk, a parallel phenomenon can be observed, as clouds of starlings congregate and billow over and above the bridges. A pedestrian, leaning over a parapet, might gaze into the black magnetic Lagan, and see parabolic swarms of mini-millibirds whirl among the cloudy shoals beyond the rows of just-lit street-lamps. When he looks up, they swoop and tower above him, forming dense and complex auguries, wheeling unpredictably into the future which, in retrospect, becomes inevitable, as their twists turn faster than the split blips of an atomic clock; and before you know it, they have got to where they will be.

Co-ordinated, countless sentences of starlings flit and sway in baroque paragraphs across the darkening sky, as they compose exploded founts of type. It is coming up to the time of the year when the clocks go back. An Autumn chill is in the air, and shadows lengthen in the inky Lagan. The multitudes come home to roost in serried nooks and crannies, under eaves, on pediments and capitals, stilled and castellated on the tops of ornamental porticos, on balconies, cornices and window-sills, in sooty alcoves and gazebo turrets, lining the balustraded parapets, perched on the spokes of cartwheel windows and weighing down the hands of the Albert Memorial Clock.

The same Royal lends his name to the Albert Bridge, downstream from the Queen's Bridge. In the 1960s, traffic congestion on the latter necessitated the construction of the Queen Elizabeth Bridge; recently, this kowtow nomenclature was abandoned when the imaginatively named Lagan Bridge afforded further relief to the palpitating arterial roads. I have to admit I love this bridge: driving on its flyover, admiring the stylized white lines printed on the clean black tarmac, I feel I am taking off from an aircraft carrier — I think of HMS *Formidable*, for instance, launched by Harland and Wolff in 1939 from East Belfast, where I am coming from in 1996. I soar on a gradual aerial curve above the harbour and the docks, seeing them in new, sunlit perspectives, like Wordsworth on Westminster Bridge:

> *Earth has not anything to show more fair —*
> *Dull would he be of soul who could pass by*
> *A sight so touching in its majesty:*

This City now doth, like a garment, wear
The beauty of the morning; silent, bare,
Ships, towers, domes, theatres and temples lie
Open unto the fields, and to the sky;
All bright and glittering in the smokeless air . . .

This brings to mind its opposite, the Belfast of 1947, envisioned in the opening shot of Carol Reed's *Odd Man Out*, as the aerial camera pans down into a mass of chimneys and mill-stacks churning out ocean-liner cigarette-smoke over spires and cupolas. Momentarily, I have a *déjà-vu* of the tobacco-scented plush interior of a post-war cinema with its dim oyster-shell wall-lights, the screen flickering with the silver exhalations of a thousand smoking couples; and the votive glow of the EXIT sign brings me back to the red blip of my father's cigarette-end scribbling phrases on the dark, as he relates the story of a film. I remembered *A Night to Remember*, for example, long before I saw it, for my father had told its story, the sinking of the *Titanic*, many times, and the actual film, when I first saw it in the Broadway cinema in the fifties, only served to corroborate his descriptions of the implacable properties of icebergs and supposedly watertight bulkheads, and the temerity of building Babel boats. I felt the chill of his Atlantic language.

Titanic Memorial: 1920, by Sir T. Brock of London: Flowing marble statue of a sombre female figure of Fame looking down on two sea-nymphs holding a drowned man, on a grey granite base with basins at front and back. Gold-leafed inscription recording the names of those gallant Belfast men . . . who lost their lives on

the 15th of April 1912 by the foundering of the Belfast-built
RMS *Titanic* through collision with an iceberg, on her maiden
voyage from Southampton to New York. These included the
ship's designer, Thomas Andrews, and her doctor, John Simpson.
The memorial was initially erected in Donegall Square North, in
front of Robinson & Cleaver's.*

In fact, the memorial was removed (to the grounds of the City
Hall) because it was thought to represent a traffic hazard; but the
subterranean public toilets, which occupy an otherwise unneces-
sary island directly in line with the memorial's previous location,
still remain, though recently closed. Here, cramped in a dank
stall, one could think oneself to be in the bowels of a U-boat; the
plumbing hissed and whispered as if under marine pressure, for a
depth-charge had gone off nearby, an illusion perfectly maintained by the IRA bombing campaign of the 1970s (it is gratifying
to note that the toilets' glass brick roof, or pavement, has survived unscathed).

Also in the grounds of the City Hall, by the same sculptor, is
Queen Victoria, victim of a fictional bomb:

> Centrally placed in the front lawn . . . is the marble statue of a
> dumpy Queen Victoria standing holding an orb that has been
> truncated through time or vandalism into a small begging bowl.
> The statue base carries bronze figures linked by heavy swathes,
> of a mob-capped girl holding a spindle, a boy reading a scroll,
> and a shipwright in apron and hobnail boots clutching a model
> steamship. At the climax of George Birmingham's novel *The Red*

---

*Marcus Patton, *Central Belfast: a Historical Gazetteer.*

Hand of Ulster, a shell fired from Belfast Lough by an English battleship 'made flitters of the statue of the old Queen that was sitting fornint the City Hall', greatly to the annoyance of the loyal people of the city.*

Strangely, the IRA never saw fit to bomb the same statue, though it did others, notably that of the Revd 'Roaring' Hugh Hanna in Carlisle Circus; just a matter of yards away, the equestrian statue of King Billy which surmounts the Clifton Street Orange Hall had his sword blown from his hand; 'it has now been replaced, but not quite at the right angle'.†

Nor, so far as I know, did the IRA ever attempt to bomb any of the bridges of Belfast; perhaps East Belfast, on the other side, lay out of sight and out of mind, as it did to me for much of my life.

Queen's Bridge: Bridge of Newry granite across the Lagan at the end of Ann Street, built to the designs of Sir Charles Lanyon and John Frazer at a cost of £27,000. It was opened in 1844, and widened (by cantilevering out) by J.C. Bretland in 1885, when the ornamental lamp-posts from the Glasgow Sun Foundry were added to the parapets. This replaced the old Long Bridge that had been erected in the 1680s. It had been narrow, little over twenty feet wide, but spanned 840 feet and was twenty-one arches long, seven of which collapsed when rammed by a ship in 1692 (after

---

*Marcus Patton, *Central Belfast: A Historical Gazetteer*.
†C.E.B. Brett, *Buildings of Belfast* (revised edition, 1985). The statue is of bronze, ten feet high, weighs thirty-seven hundredweights, and the stirrups, saddlecloth and pistol-holster were cast from the originals in the possession of the Baroness von Steiglitz.

being weakened, it was said, by the crossing of the Duke of Schomberg's heavy cannon in 1689).*

Boyne Bridge: 1936: Steeply humped concrete-walled bridge replacing the Saltwater Bridge shown on 1791 map, so called because it marked the tidal limit up the Blackstaff River. The old bridge, two arches of which are said to be encased in the present structure, was built by Edward Viscount Chichester in 1642, and its three arches were known as *The Great Bridge of Belfast* until the Long Bridge was built. It was also known as *Brick-kiln Bridge* or *Brickle Bridge* from the vicinity of brick-kilns that had been used to build the Castle and many 18c buildings.†

Most of Belfast is built of brick. Brick is riot-friendly, especially when broken into halves, more easily to fit the hand. It then became a *hicker*, in Belfast dialect, a thing to be *chucked*, or thrown: these words might be related, since Chambers cites one usage of *chuck* as 'a small pebble or stone'; *hicker* might derive from *hack*, 'a bank for drying bricks'. The hicker is one ingredient of the ammunition *Belfast confetti*, which originally referred to a not-so-welcome shower of shipyard-workers' bolts and rivets, and later, by extension, to any *ad hoc* compendium of hand-launched missiles, which might include slates, buckets, iron railings, jam-jars, ball-bearings, and coal, as well as the usual assortment of small bombs contained by coffee-jars or milk-bottles; once I saw formes and clichés of type, looted from Ticard's

---

*Marcus Patton, *Central Belfat: A Historical Gazetteer*.
†Ibid.

the printer's in Durham Street, being fired at the army. Another great element was the *kidney-paver*, a small human-organ-shaped cobblestone which fitted to the hand as if preordained by geological authority. Kidney-pavers are now completely extinct, since the civic authority which put them there in the first place tore them up one by one from their matrices, and replaced their habitat with concrete. Then the street would be occupied with military-mortar cement-mixers and a team of sappers in mismatching uniforms of greasy serge suits, a pair of whom would tamp parallels along the wet concrete street with a plank set on edge, two sets of rocking-horse handles attached to its ends. For a day and a night, or more, the street would be a no-go zone, demarcated by the serial monocular glow of red bull's-eye oil-lamps hooked onto wooden rails between saw-horses, as the aromatic burning oil you sniffed was cut by acrid coke-smoke from the watchman's brazier that had red holes punched in it. Nevertheless, some boys would not be deterred by this prospect, and would dare each other to leave their matrix footprints in the Hollywood Boulevard wet concrete.

Ticard's the printer's lay near the Protestant vs. Catholic fault line of the aforementioned Boyne or Brickle Bridge, and here the 'Battle of the Brickfields' would be regularly re-enacted. On both sides of this divide, its denizens were known to have knocked down the back-yard walls of their own dwellings in order to provide themselves with cross-community ammunition.

Herein lie some interesting etymological meanders: according to Dinneen, the Irish for 'The Battle of the Boyne' is *Briseadh na Bóinne*, i.e., the breaking of the Boyne; and brick has its root in *break*, allied to the flaw in Irish linen known as a *brack*. Chambers' *brickle*, 'apt to break, troublesome', is appropriate in the context, and *brock*, whether it refers to food-scraps, broken down stuff, or to the animal, is also relevant; and the badger is a *brockit* beast, as he lends his distinctive fur coat to the concept of variegation, especially in black and white. To me, all these bricky words sound like Irish *breac*, speckled, which extends to mean, in the verb *breacaim*, 'to cover a paper with writing'. Cuneiform-covered clay tablets of Babylon occur to me, as I inscribe these words in a Challenge A4 feint-ruled notebook with a red-inked Japanese Zebra 'Zeb-rolle' 0.5 pen that bleeds through a little to the other side of the page, giving it a speckly effect. This is not a serious problem, since I write the main text on the recto, using the preceding verso as a scribble pad for notions I might use in the future, or for possible revisions: for instance, I've just scrawled *Lilliput Laundry*, possibly to remind myself of its bizarre Ulster-pawky-humorous nomenclature, or of the classic SF film *The Incredible Shrinking Man*, or primarily, perhaps, of those indelible pencils used to label laundry and school-uniform name-tags. You sucked the point of the pencil to make it work, empurpling your tongue with gentian violet, and the DNA of your spit was engraved in the letters of your name, and it was possible that future scientists might make an identifiable schoolboy clone of you.

Sometimes, though, in the spirit of experiment, I would write an occasional main page text on the verso of the previous, whose faint mirror image could be seen as a prelude to be improvised on, making me think of scientists atomizing carbon particles onto a blank page in order to make visible the missing contemporaneous notes, using, like clown policemen, those devices with squeezable rubber bulbs. I think a larger, mechanically powered version would have proved useful to the pursuers of the Invisible Man, and I seem to remember the Man had problems with smog, when he became a Jekyll-and-Hyde wraith; or with falling snow, when he looked like a wounded terrorist angel lost in the dark city, his slow footsteps blurring rapidly behind him in the blizzard, and the dominant sound-track is the tolling of the Albert Clock, permeated, sometimes, by the dissonant bass fog-horn of the complicit vessel that must leave at midnight, and you know the whole thing is bound to end in tragedy, as the Man becomes Nemo.

But, rewinding to the holographologists, I see them in their white coats, brown shoes, and clingfilm-gloved hands, peering through Holmesian magnifying-glasses that have vanity-mirror ivory handles, deciphering the verso ghost-writing of my drafts, whose rectos I can barely read myself, sometimes, as they often resemble a barbed-wire hedge of emendations, carets, stets, arrows, underlinings, question-marks, and cancellations.

Then I have to go and tidy the whole thing up, as I'm doing now, running my fingers over the keyboard of the 'personal word processor' acknowledged early on in this book, which only recently replaced the portable electric Corona typewriter I used for most of the fair copy; and from this admission you will deduce that the book was not written in this final, published sequence, but assembled in a patchwork fashion. It is quite possible that many readers will, in fact, approach it in a non-sequential *modus operandi*, dipping into and out of it, or skipping bits where the thread of the story gets lost; there are a lot of books I read this way (books of poems, especially, and specifically John Ashbery, whose work I have used in the past as a *sortes Virgilianae* when I got blocked, or the *Gospel According to John*, with its majestic opening: *In the beginning was the Word . . .*). At any rate, the noise and the action of these electronic keyboards is quite unlike the manual Imperials I learned on, whose spring-loaded machine-gun clunks resembled the chatter of linen looms, and both had *fasces* of visibly moving parts. The whole idea is like a 1930s SF flick dystopia, where phalanxes of nearly identical typists are overlooked by huge art nouveau clocks with blips for numerals, and are over-seen by white-coated centurions with clip-boards. The typing pool is the size of an aircraft hangar or a movie studio, and all of the girl extras who are acting the typists want to be Hollywood stars.

THE STAR FACTORY II

The stark reality of the Star, Factory is, on the face of it, more humdrum than the stories it has inspired. Located at 322 Donegall Road, between the streets of Nubia and Soudan, it is noted in the 1948 Directory as a 'boys' clothing manufacturers'.

But mention of its product summons up what seems, at this far remove, an antiquated, arcane world, where Reebok is not a sportswear label but the kind of antelope you might see depicted on a South African stamp. I have from this era a fully clothed vision of tweed suits, V-necked sleeveless woollen pullovers, floppy-collared flannel shirts, snake-clasp belts, and elasticated braces, whose slide adjusting mechanism sometimes cut into your collarbone. I sometimes think I still bear the consequence of knee-length socks, their ribbed garter scars. One could write a mini-treatise on the liberty bodice, defined by *Chambers Dictionary* as 'an undergarment like a vest, formerly often worn by children', whose name always struck me as an oxymoron, given its life-jacket, straitjacket shape, its dotted joins of rubber buttons and blanket-stitched seams.

In order to corroborate my memory of such clothing, I have resorted to my allotment of the family photographs, which I keep in an old wooden flute-box with two brass hook-and-eye catches. I thumb them open, and riffle through the sheaf of snaps: holidays, First Communions, or those inconsequential, important moments when one poses for the newly acquired box camera of a childless better-off uncle. Here is my Confirmation photograph, which shows me at about the age of eight (the Sacrament, then, was taken shortly after one had attained 'the use of reason', long defined by the Jesuits as seven). It would be 1956.

There are, in fact, two of us – perhaps this was an austerity measure, a photographer's special two-for-the-price-of-one deal – Roy McLoughlin and myself. In the left foreground, a pine table has been sanctified by a clean white tablecloth and a crucifix placed on it, supported by a glass jug. I have been arranged to stand almost dead centre, with my right hand brushing the cloth; Roy, being half a head taller, is behind me at my left shoulder, in the position usually attributed to Royal consorts. A makeshift shrine is poised on the dado rail of the wainscot immediately behind: a Madonna and Child, flanked symmetrically by two unlit candles in glass candlesticks, and two slender tulip vases holding sprays of mayflowers.

The improvised piety of the occasion shows in our wide-eyed faces and uncertain smiles. Our embryonic adult suits are manifestly new and stiff: three-buttoned jackets (it was *de rigueur* to fasten only the middle button) with wide lapels; short trousers. His is serge, mine is tweed. Every time I smell tweed, I get a whiff of that other era, or further back, to the First Communion: this was a nubbly Donegal suit, whereas the Confirmation was a fine houndstooth; yet, as I think about it, the aroma is generic, not specific, since one tweed summons up all other tweeds in a kind of domino effect. One would have thought that each tweed would emanate its own charisma, like Scotch malts with their local attributes of peat and heather, their different waters: so, the brand of sheep, the type of chlorophyll it grazes on, the weather, flecks of this and that, the dark interior of crofters' handloom cottages, all these must leave their redolent imprint; each bolt of cloth must be a web of DNA strands, and a trained dog could sniff one from another, but we cannot.

Or maybe not that we cannot; we just don't. One can admit the possibility of white-coated hierophants with flared nostrils – the parfumiers of tweed – mulling over dribs and drabs, like tea or whisky blenders; but no, smell is not a primary function of tweed, albeit a powerful one, which links moments of *non sequitur* in a time-evading narrative, as the last time reminds you of the first, and long olfactory shadows trail behind you like the remnants of a ticker-tape parade along the floors of canyon avenues in Manhattan, where, on a cold St Patrick's Day, swaying, saffron-kilted, tweed-jacketed pipe bands tread ponderously by, as light snowflakes fall.

The drum-major calls a lull; its sudden woof reminds me of the silence of a school yard when everyone is in, or when an annual photograph is being taken. This one, lying on the table where I'm writing, shows the class of 1958, I think, tiered on the five broad steps between upper and lower yards.

Imagining their dimensions again, I begin to see St Gall's Public Elementary School in all its different facets, adits, grades, corridors and stairwells, classrooms fugged with radiator-heat and the steam from damp gaberdines. There is a map of Ireland on one wall; on another, pinned to the display board, a diagram of the soul – an amorphous white blob with a black cancerous dot of mortal sin in it, and some grey venial smudges. Here, also, are our maps of how we got to school, which were that morning's exercise: our teacher, wearing his didactic hat, uses them as illustration to a principle of spiritual convergence, pointing out our different crooked radii. If you laid them one on top of another, they would form a predetermined black star.

What future detours have these pupils taken since? I travel my eye back to the yard steps. Our arms are folded, like footballers', as we gaze into the lens of then. Looking at these boys' faces, I can recognize them; but I barely remember half of their thirty-three names. I no longer see them now, apart from Roy of the Confirmation, who occasionally swims into my ken in after-office drinking confraternities in off-beat venues like the Elephant, or the Fly. On these premises, chance encounters seem fortuitous, or retrospectively predestined. We connect in asterisks or nodes – *node* being, among other related concepts, 'a point at which a curve cuts itself, and through which more than one tangent to the curve can be drawn'. Wandering through the mazy city, we also miss each other many more times, for our arrangements are not Filofaxed nor prior. When we do meet, we wonder when we last met in this haze of alcohol.

Lonely on a high stool, half-expecting a companion, the onset of a friendly argument, you stare into the whiskey mirror, or at the rank of spirit-level-bubbled optics, and contemplate their upside-down connected bottles with their labels printed right-way-up. You peruse the intersecting circles made by the base of your glass on the bar. You read the ashtray, and stub out another cigarette into its brand-name.

Kelly's Cellars, though relatively famous, was another favourite haunt. It was said to have a ghost, dictated, I suppose, by its antiquity and the whispered palimpsests of centuries of conversations. Kelly's is in Bank Street, formerly Bank Lane, which runs on one side of the long-since-culverted Farset, and it is a moot point as to whether 'bank' refers to the river, or to the Provincial Bank of Ireland on its left bank, or to the vast emporium of the Bank Buildings across the street from the Bank. Formerly again, it was known as Bryce's Lane, then as Crooked Lane, or as The Back of the River; it connects Chapel Lane (where the original electric lighting station for Belfast was situated) with Castle Place, which borders on Royal Avenue built on the demolished Hercules Lane, commemorated by the Hercules Bar (its sign shows the eponymous hero wrestling with Hydra) on the corner of Chapel Lane and Castle Street. The Castle itself has been well described by Marcus Patton, in his meticulous and comprehensive *Central Belfast: A Historical Gazetteer*:

The first castle of which we have real information was, so the

Plantation Commissioners reported, built on 'the Ruynes of the decayed Castle' and was to include 'a bricke house fifty foote longe which is to be adioyned to the sayd Castle by a stayrcase of bricke which is to be . . . two Storys and a halfe high . . . about which Castle and House there is a stronge Bawne almost finished which is flankered with foure half Bulworkes . . . the Bawne is to be compased with a lardge and deepe ditche or moate which will always stande full of water': they stated that it was 'in so good forwardness that it is lyke to be finished by the mydle of next Somer'. An English visitor in 1635 (quoted by Smith) noted that 'my Lord Chichester' had a 'dainty stately palace' so close to the river that 'the lough toucheth upon his garden and backside'. Maps of 1680 and 1685 show it as an Elizabethan castle with central courtyard, multiple chimneys, gables, and a central belfry; it was built of bricks from near Sandy Row. The Tax Roll of 1666 recorded the Earl of Donegall's castle as having 'fforty Hearthes', making it, as Benn remarked, 'the most magnificent dwelling in Ireland. at least in the matter of hearths'. The roll also describes 'the bowling green, the cherry garden, the apple garden . . . strawberries, currants and gooseberries', and 'women gathering Violats in ye Fields to sett in the Gardens' which extended 'to the edge of the sea'. In 1698, William Sacheverell confirmed that 'the gardens are very spacious, with every variety of walks, both close and open, fish ponds and groves'. These amenities were 'all Inclosed in a kind of Fortification, being Designed for a place of Strength as well as Pleasure', as Thomas Molyneux wrote in 1708.

Belfast Castle was destroyed by accidental fire on 25 April 1708, and three sisters of the Earl of Donegal were killed before 'the men of the town could gett in within the wals to help'. Apparently several rooms were still inhabited for many years after, including 'a fine parlour with black oak floor, wainscotted walls and huge chimney piece'.

Kelly's, indeed, with its low black oak counter and its apparent plethora of snugs and nooks and crannies, its wainscoted, white-washed walls, its pendulous pendulum clock, its open fireplace murmuring with glowing slack, could be a relic of that former ambience. 'It is the oldest surviving public house in the city', says Patton, 'still retaining something of the atmosphere of the heady days when the United Irishmen plotted here and Henry Joy McCracken crouched under the bar to escape pursuing redcoats. Souvenirs stored at the Cellars include the big key of the old Smithfield Gaol and an elephant's tooth.' Reading this, I thought I remembered there was a secret passageway from underneath the bar, or through a cellar, to the Presbyterian Church in Rosemary Street; but further study shows I've spun together two different yarns:

> If local legend is to be believed, the United Irishmen when plot-ting divided their time between these cellars and a secret room in the roof-space of the second Presbyterian Church in Rosemary Street . . .
>
> C.E.B. Brett, *Buildings of Belfast*, 1985

That the town Marshal's house had an underground passage is proven by a true story of a certain Campbell Sweeney, a drysalter of the town, who was confined in the cells of the building which was situated at the rere of the Donegall Arms Hotel, now Messrs. Robb's drapery establishment. A friendly servant girl employed at the place told him that if he got access to the yard he might get into the sewer, which opened into the river in High Street, and there make his escape. This Sweeney was able to do, and came up out of the sewer in the back yard of a house built on the site of the present Ulster Reform Club in Castle Place. Sweeney called out to a woman in the yard and asked her to acquaint the Town Sergeant, a man named Dick Moore, who was his friend. This being done, Moore got Sweeney dressed in the servant's clothes, and took him down High Street. Moore, where they went along singing loudly 'Rule Britannia,' was accosted by a soldier, and explained the presence of the uncouth female by saying that she was from the country and not up to the ways of the town. Down at the docks Sweeney got safely away in a vessel on which Moore's son was signed as a sailor, and, once away and still away, Sweeney never returned.

Cathal O'Byrne, *As I Roved Out*

I occasionally return to Kelly's. I like to sit there in an early-evening lull, when one can contemplate the plethora of bric-à-brac arranged on shelves, in niches and in alcoves: willow-pattern, Delft, dented brass half-gallon jugs, japanned tin boxes, guns, pictures, statuettes. A framed football team, with folded arms and centre-shaded, Brylcreemed hair, is hung immediately below the unreachable top shelf with its bottles variously full of rarely tasted, curious liqueurs and defunct brands of whiskey. Were they to exchange their hooped shirts for long white aprons, the footballers would appear perfect barmen; both trades share the collective 'team', realized as you watch the bar staff move into action on a jam-packed Friday night, confronted by a four-deep rank of eager punters brandishing big notes and tic-tac fingers. Professional barmen have served their time at making time. They show no stress under pressure. Their peripheral, fish-eye lens vision enables them to see everything at once, and know the order of its precedence. Moving rapidly yet languidly, seeming many-armed and ambidextrous as they simultaneously pour three pints of stout, strip the cellophane off a pack of cigarettes, while negotiating a Bacardi-and-coke and three rums-and-black and tallying the cost in advance, they still go to the inner, publicly unheard, relaxed tick of the wall-clock. After a flurry of orders, they stand before the reredos like priests, in a zone of free time, gazing into public space at the anticipated future.

It was in Kelly's that I drank my first pint of Guinness, not quite pleasurably amazed by its texture of thick black yeasty milk; and it was here that I was initiated into the ritual of going, half-jarred, to midnight Mass – St Mary's, in Chapel Lane, was just a short stagger up the street. Here, dazed by chanted Latin, incense, alcohol and candle-light, I felt myself an eight-year-old clothed by the Star Factory, barely kept from sleep by the coldness of my crisp, snowy, cotton, Christmas shirt, as I fingered its plastic collar-cartilages in their stitched slots.

MAGNETIC STREET

The typical Star Factory shirt tailed well below the bum, and could double as a sleeping-vestment. Robed in it, like Little Nemo, you felt you could flit through the bedroom window and glide above the rooftops with angelic connotations. I used to be adept at this dream-flight, but lost the power some time in late adolescence; perhaps there is a hormonal basis to this capricious skill. The flying dream is necessarily a recurrent dream, since the ability to do it depends on your remembering it was done before, and when it strikes you in the dream – usually, a mundane affair, as when you walk along a dream street replicated in the real world – you are astonished that you had forgotten it. Yet, the flying dream is not a lucid dream: if you know that you are dreaming, you will cease to fly; and knowing the full extent of your powers depends on an ignorance of your real state. Beginning to hover in this bliss, you see yourself in other retrospective loop-the-loops and spirals, seeking out the layered thermals of the city's altitudes.

When you fly, the mind acts on the disembodied body, like post-operative recuperation in a high magnolia hospital room, where a half-drunk bottle of Lucozade glows like a votive lamp on the bedside table. *Boh-dee and mind, boh-dee and mind, Lucozade refreshes, Lucozade refreshes boh-dee and mind*, the television jingle used to go; and remembering its beaded bubbles soaring through a glass of Lucozade to spit and blink within its rim, you saw them as the constant, orchestrated, upward flow of souls from Purgatory. I used to think that the soul did not reside in mind or body, which were subliminal to it, but occupied a total, other zone of self, a district not amenable to mind, and hence, the soul could never know itself; but I find that this proposition stands at a slightly heretical angle to official doctrine, as revealed by the *Catholic Encyclopaedic Dictionary*:

SOUL: The thinking principle; that by which we feel, know, will, and by which the body is animated. The root of all forms of vital activity. It is a substance or being which exists *per se*; it is simple or unextended, *i.e.*, not composed of separate principles of any kind; it is spiritual, *i.e.*, its existence, and to some extent its operations, are independent of matter; it is immortal (*q.v.*). The soul is the substantial form (*q.v.*) of the body. There are three kinds of soul, vegetative, the root of vital activity in plants; sensitive, the root of vital activity in animals; intellectual, the root of vital activity in man. The last contains the other two virtually (*q.v.*); the sensitive contains the vegetative virtually. The sensitive and vegetative souls are both simple, but incomplete substances, incapable of existing apart from matter; they are therefore neither spiritual nor immortal. See also IMMORTAL-ITY: INCORRUPTIBILITY: BODY AND SOUL, etc.

It seems to me that one of the roles of the soul – to co-ordinate our postulates of flying dreams – fits comfortably enough into this orthodoxy. The soul might have the independent eyes of the chameleon which, given the ability to fly, would resemble a dragon: I see its blinking gliding flight in visionary Morse across the city, so camouflaged as to be invisible, into whose creaking pterodactyl wings my hands fit like the gloves of virtual reality. Suspended high above the city like a British army dragonfly, I computate the angles and declensions of this aerial photography, alphabetizing unconnected streets mnemonically: Omar, Omeath, Onslow, Ophir, Orangefield, Orby, Orchard, Oregon, Orient. I could be a night-flight bomber, agent of an internecine blitz, and I got the names off an out-of-date Directory, and I can wipe them out with a few considered twitches of my release-mechanism: not the names, but the actual streets of two-up, one-down housing, their mantelpieces crowded with fragile souvenirs, their walls displaying popes and queens; not the names, which will reside when the streets are bombed into oblivion, and came from somewhere else, before the streets were named. We can never know the full nomenclature, which existed long before our time, evolving constantly beyond the individual, these gabbled, garbled stories which refuse to be oppressed.

Names have power; and on my flights across the city, I became aware of names more powerful than others. I should explain here that night-flying had two basic, complementary modes: the high flight usually performed with extended arms; and the low glide, sometimes done in upright stance, which had the compensatory bonus of a built-in invisibility option, so you could peer through bedroom windows undetected and feel your whereabouts by the Braille of cast-iron street-signs. Magnetic Street, for instance, emanated such a force-field that it proved impossible to cross in full high-flight mode; sometimes it exerted such a pull that the most I could manage was a feeble hover, a few inches off the ground. It was a place to be avoided; but in waking life I would pass it often, on my way to the Donegall Road Branch of the Carnegie Library (Magnetic Street lay almost equidistant between it and the Star Factory). Magnetic Street was a cul-de-sac, but immediately behind it lay my route, a laneway known locally as The Black Pad, whose name struck me with a vague, pleasurable terror: this crushed-cinder track, littered with broken glass, marked the beginning of Protestant territory. The area proclaimed itself by small details of street furniture: graffiti, obviously; more subtly, the galvanized iron flagholders bolted to the walls of terrace houses, defunct for that part of the year which was not the marching season. Even the colours of the flower displays in front windows could be read as code, these pansies of bruise-blue and black, those clustered reds of sweet william.

I had exhausted the Fall Road Library's stock of 'Biggles' books and, looking further afield for more stories of the intrepid British pilot, I explored the Shankill Road branch as well as the Donegall Road; though both lay in alien territory, they were agents of the same confederacy. Entering their tall portals, one became aware of the democracy of print, whose ink still lingered in the date-stamp redolence of pine shelves and brown linoleum. After acquiring a cache of 'Biggles', I liked to wander through the high dark stacks of the Adult section, where dusty sunbeams would illuminate the gold-blocked, arcane numbers of the Dewey Decimal Classification System. These libraries, for me, were the points of a star or a compass, important navigational beacons in the city I flew over nightly.

My experience of flying had led me to suppose that the somnolent brain contained thunderstorms of electrical activity that mirrored, by osmosis, the magnetic field of the earth. Magnets are the nearest thing we have to anti-gravity, and when you try to wobble together the like poles of a broken magnet, you feel their palpable disjunctive forces slipping in and out of one another's compass. Magnets affect clocks, and H.G. Wells' Time Machine, I suspect, was invented from magnetic principles; its likeness to a bicycle is not coincidental, since riding one is an epitome of balance, where avoirdupois seems cancelled.

The most impressive magnets were not the shop-bought horseshoe variety, whose power dwindled within days, exhausted by their iron contacts, but those chunky nuggets of broken car dynamos that looked like bits of meteorite, gun-metal dull and incredibly heavy. Such items were strong media of barter, equivalent to rare stamps or full sets of cigarette cards. Their flint-sharp edges wore holes in your pockets. Compact, neolithic, they were emblems of the great electromagnets in scrap depots, operated from the cockpits of tall cranes, which swayed bristling conglomerations of metal through huge volumes of air, depositing tons with a crash at the throw of a switch. Hearing that melismatic avalanche, I would try to analyse its junked components: bits of tractors, cars, bikes, storm-drain gratings, perimeter fences, radiators, corrugated iron roofs, a virtual trolley-bus, broken ships and sewer-pipes.

I am thinking, here, of Eastwood's Himalayan scrap-yard, whose site on the Andersonstown Road is now occupied by a shopping-mall. Close to it was St Agnes' Parochial Hall, a building not much bigger than a scout shed, which used to be the venue of a Saturday matinée film show, and I have always been puzzled as to why this French word for 'morning' should refer to a public entertainment or reception usually held in the afternoon; its other meaning of a woman's dress for forenoon-wear makes more sense. At any rate, the entertainment and the venue were pretty basic: the films were black and white serials or shorts – Charlie Chaplin, the Three Stooges, Batman, Roy Rodgers, and the like – and bare wooden benches were provided for sitting on. I believe that this show had a regular beginning and ending time, though it never did begin on time, and the projector was wont to break down frequently, thus postponing the end, and you realized where the expression 'the flicks' came from when you saw big upside-down numerals twitching on and off the drizzly screen.

Shows in big picture houses had an all-day-long schedule and the viewers could enter at any time, so that if they arrived in the middle of a feature, they could stay in until the beginning came up again in the complicated running-order of shorts, newsreels,

'B' movies and features, and could seam together the gist of the plot by remembering where they came in. An epitome of such a cinema was the Broadway, a mile or so down the road from the Parochial Hall, and made the Hall look truly parochial by its imposing art nouveau tiled façade outlined in red neon. I have a serial cinematic dream whereby the plush interiors of these establishments become incredibly complicated, with many foyers, ticket booths, shallow scalloped staircases, cocktail bars and powder rooms; the auditorium is a variously tiered, chambered Nautilus space lit by dimmable oyster-shell wall-lights, red exit signs, or the huge flickering silver presence of the screen itself, dominating the proceedings through a veil of cigarette-smoke, scarves of smoke floating up through the prism of projected light; and the overflowing ashtrays attached to the back of the seats are shaped like scallop-shells. It comes as no surprise that many cinemas are named Colosseum.

Those were the days of the communal understudied dream of cinema, of vast willing suspensions of disbelief, where people silently mouthed in retroactive advance the words that would come from the actors' lip-synch, and occupied their roles. Those were the days of snogging in the back rows, of ice-cream cones and Quality Street chocolates, of torch-bearing usherettes and cigarette-girls wearing pillbox hats and page-boy haircuts. Those were the days of cigarettes which people would proffer each other from flat opened packs, the days of books and boxes of matches and the daily whiff of sulphur, nicotine, and tar.

In about 1958, I saw *The Incredible Shrinking Man* in the Broadway Cinema. It absolutely terrified me. The plot is simple:

this guy is lying sunbathing on a yacht one day, somewhere off America, when an 'electric storm' brews up on the horizon, to the accompaniment of weird music; it passes over him like a rapid cloud of drizzle. The next day, or some time later, he notices that the cuffs of his shirt-sleeves droop half-way down the back of his hands. He thinks of making a complaint to the laundry, which, it would appear, has managed an antonym of shrinking. But they disclaim all responsibility, and things get progressively worse. Soon he is the size of a three-year-old boy, and his wife has to feed him on her lap. They find it increasingly difficult to relate to one another. After a while, as a tiny homunculus, he falls down the stairs into the cellar and gets lost. His wife assumes the cat has eaten him. He experiences many adventures in this enormous studio space where he absails from various worktop and table heights by way of a spool of thread, and fights a spider with a darning-needle. The mice are bigger than elephants. At the end of the picture, he finds an air-grille in the cellar and climbs through it to find himself in a lawn of bamboo forest size, and a Twilight Zone voice-over comes on with some big philosophical pronouncement about the measure of man beneath the galaxies. It's not entirely downbeat, since the Shrinking Man has a whole new microscopic universe to explore.

As I emerged dazed from the cinema, the habitual post-mat-inée glare of the afternoon seemed more dazzling than usual. I remembered how the sun had danced in the sky at Fatima. Negative time-lapsed clouds raced overhead. The edges of build-ings trembled within their shadows, as if flickered by the wings of lurking, fallen angels. A red trolleybus thrummed by like a passenger-bearing inferno. I held the hand of my younger brother Pat, but he seemed oblivious to the imminent catastrophe. The two-mile road home took an age to achieve,* as its gravity was stretched and pondered; its minor gradients became mountains of despair and valleys of fear. The overhead parallel trolley-wires met at infinity . . . 'Were you not scared?' I asked Pat. 'No', he replied. 'Were you?' I clutched his hand all the more tightly, realizing he was leading me.

Later that night I had what you might call a nervous break-down, though the term hardly existed then; adults were prone to suffer from 'bad nerves', or simple lunacy, and these syndromes did not apply to children. All evening I had been dreading going to bed; my parents noticed that I seemed to be more than usually preoccupied, as I sat in silent agony, but said nothing of it. I could say nothing myself because I did not know what there was to say. When bed-time did come round – so quickly now, as time forgot its previous funereal pace – I cowered behind the door in foetal position, and began to scream.

The room expanded and contracted and its angles warped and shifted as my parents loomed above me, their huge kind eyes filled with concern. I was struck by the magnified tick of the clock as it trembled on the mantel, working up its dark interior of cogs and ratchets. Creeping roses slanted into the mirror from the trellis wallpaper, and I could smell the votive glow of the Sacred Heart lamp. Rapid faces shimmered in the fireplace tiles,

---

*We had to walk, since we'd spent our bus fares on sweets.

and the empty grate – it was summer – was a solid breath of black soot. I felt bound by a square of the carpet pattern, and I don't know for how long I huddled there.

Eventually, relatively pacified, I was got up to bed. I remember the comforting weight of my mother on the coverlet, as she asked me again what was wrong, and I could only answer that it was because I had seen *The Incredible Shrinking Man*.

It took me years to get over this experience (whatever it was) and for a long time it took me about half an hour to go up the thirteen electrically lit steps that led to bed. Steeling myself for the lone ascent each night – by this stage, my parents had got tired of escorting me, and I had reluctantly accepted their attitude that I should be more grown-up – I would close the living-room door slowly on them, and stand for a while in the hallway. I would dip my fingers in the little holy-water font to my right. I'd cross myself. As if blind – but I dared not shut my eyes – I would feel my way along the wall of the hall till I came to the stairs, whereupon I would have to negotiate an interminable 180° turn to bring me to their foot. Squeezing myself against the staircase wall, I would take it one step at a time, all the while looking out from the corners of my eyes for possible tremors in the space-time fabric, and things that might creep out from it. My bedroom on the second storey seemed impossibly remote, but I would eventually get there, scuttling up the last few steps and across the landing to dive into bed and sink beneath the blankets.

It was a long time before I went to see another film.

THE GLASS FACTORY

It is Sunday, 19 April 1997, and I've just come back from the Queen's Film Theatre, where I saw *Orphée*, Jean Cocteau's free interpretation of the Orpheus myth, made in 1950. I first saw this film in about 1970 in this same cinema, a converted lecture theatre belonging to Queen's University, where I was a student; at that time, the QFT still retained its benches and fold-down desk-tops and, indeed, doubled as a lecture theatre by day. I wonder if this is still the case, though now it has rather plush air-craft-type seats (but no fold-down tables in their back-rests) and authentically dim red exit signs. In what I take to be a soon-to-be-abolished concession to my generation of film-goers, you are allowed to smoke in the foyer, but not, of course, inside. Then, in the past, you had gazed at the screen through a zone of smoke and, at salient points in the drama, a mini-choreography of struck matches would flare up throughout the auditorium, briefly illuminating the absorbed faces of the watchers. The sub-sub-plot of cigarettes was itself a habitual narrative or gestural prop both in and out of the film, proffered from monogrammed silver cases, dragged on thoughtfully or nervously, smouldering between the fingers of a heroine or villain or the person next to you, stubbed out viciously into overflowing cut-glass ash-trays, languidly dismissed from rolled-down automobile windows, ground out absentmindedly underheel, or cast into a gutter, where they might become important bits of evidence. suspects held in police interrogation cells were lavishly supplied with cigarettes to make them talk.

In *Orphée*, the female figure of Death has a severe nicotine addiction, and is wont to manipulate contemptuously fat caporals between her gloved fingers; in one scene, Orphée, ensconced in the house of Death, is told by her to 'Relax . . . my servants will bring you champagne and cigarettes', and two white-coated Indo-Chinese waiters appear from a closet, wheeling a trolley bearing these elaborately presented items. It is one instance of Cocteau's magical handling of space, that mirrors are portals to the underworld, and the poet's attic is approached by way of a trapdoor, or a ladder to the attic window. The ground-level garage houses a Rolls-Royce Charonmobile whose radio transmits enigmatic messages from down below: '*L'oiseau chant avec ses doigts*' (the bird sings with its fingers), for instance, reminding us of the winged emblem that surmounts the Acropolis portico of the Rolls-Royce radiator. Here, wondering if *cocteau* might mean anything in French, I turn to my edition of *Harrap's Shorter French and English Dictionary*, first published in 1940, reprinted in 1948, the year that

I was born, and find that the word does not exist there; but the near-echo of *cocotte* can mean 'a bird made out of folded paper', which is appropriate to the origami dimensions of the film. *Harrap's* spans the war years, and *Orphée* is, *inter alia*, an evocation of the French Underground movement; and its 'Zone' – through which one must pass to reach the Underworld from Earth – is a scenario of Second World War blitzed factories and warehouses.

The dereliction of this landscape is familiar to me from fairly recent hulks of bombed-out factories in Belfast; I could be at home in it, wandering its roofless arcades, looking out of glassless windows, squatting by a heap of rubbled bricks, contemplating their baroque, accidental architecture, imagining myself to be of toy-soldier size in order to crawl into its fractured interstices. In like fashion, I remember sitting on a kerbstone as a child, in a timeless ecstasy of boredom.

It has just rained, and the air beyond my skin is rinsed and sparkling. Little rills run through the alluvial ooze of the gutter to fall Niagarously into the iron depths of a storm-drain grating, whose upper rim is the edge of a minor Mississippi delta: how appropriate is the onomatopoeiac contour of this name, from the Chippewa *mici zibi*, 'big river', its majuscule important em announcing the sinuous esses, the dotted eyes, the occluded ox-bow lakes of the pees!

The delta-muck of the gutter is graphite-black, slick and gritty-thick when smudged between the thumb and fingers in a 'money' sign, reminding us of the fingertips of shopkeepers, grimed from their day's transactions, of the graduated Chinese-box compartments in the opened drawer of an ornamental brass-bow-fronted till, of the heraldic ding of its bell, and the prices popping up in the glazed display like miniature poker hands composed of the matchbox-sized playing cards you used to get in lucky-bags.

Gazing into the gutter, I imagined tiny sagas taking place within it, inspired perhaps by Hans Christian Andersen's 'Constant Tin Soldier', which was maybe one of the first stories I ever read in a book outside of school. I have the very worn book before me as I write, a Juvenile Productions Ltd., London edition of his *Fairy Tales*, which is practically falling apart, as its faded-orange, beat-up, cloth hard cover is nearly divorced from the text; many of its smudged-by-sweaty-fingers pages have become loose-leaf, and the whole thing bears the imprint of innumerable readings:

It now began to rain; every drop fell heavier than the last; there was a regular shower. When it was over, two boys came by.

'Look,' said one, 'here is a Tin-soldier! he shall have a sail for once in his life.'

So they made a boat out of an old newspaper, put the Tin-soldier into it, and away he sailed down the gutter, both the boys running along by the side and clapping their hands. The paper-boat rocked to and fro, and every now and then veered round so quickly that the Tin-soldier became quite giddy; still he moved not a muscle, looked straight before him, and held his bayonet tightly clasped.

All at once the boat sailed under a long gutter-board; he found it was as dark here as in his own box.

'Where shall I get to next?' thought he; 'yes, to be sure, it is all that Conjurer's doing! Ah, if the little maiden were sailing with me in the boat, I would not care for its being twice as dark!'

Just then, a great Water-Rat, that lived under the gutter-board, darted out.

'Have you a passport?' asked the Rat. 'Where is your passport?'

But the Tin-soldier was silent, and held his weapon with a still firmer grasp. The boat sailed on, and the Rat followed. Oh! how furiously he showed his teeth and cried to sticks and straws, 'Stop him! stop him! he has not paid the toll; he has not shown his passport!' But the stream grew stronger and stronger. The Tin-soldier could already catch a glimpse of the bright day-light before the boat came from under the tunnel, but at the same time he heard a roaring noise, at which the boldest heart would have trembled. Only fancy! where the tunnel ended, the water of the gutter fell perpendicularly into a great canal; this was as dangerous for the Tin-soldier as sailing down a mighty waterfall would be for us.

I cannot tell if I received this story first from reading or from listening, for my father used to cull such stories from *The Arabian Nights*, Grimm, Robert Louis Stevenson, Arthur Conan Doyle, and the like, and re-tell them to us children in Irish, which was the language of the home (the world beyond its vestibule was densely terraced with the English language, which I remember learning or lisping on the street, whose populations looked on us with fear and pity; yet we strange bilingual creatures, self-segregated from the mêlée, sometimes felt we had an edge on it, as we used our first language as a private code, in the way that the US intelligence services, in the Second World War, employed speakers of dwindling Native American languages. As English words and constructs seeped into our speech, our gradually bastardized Irish stood in daily correction by my father, and to this day I have a deep uncertainty about prepositions, those important little syntactical bolts which English uses in such confusing abundance). I can hear the smoky grain of my father's voice in the dark as I enter the colour of the world described by him.

One such favourite story was another of Andersen's, 'The Tinder-Box', which I loved for its mind-boggling dimensions and its hollow tree:

'What am I to do down in the tree?' asked the soldier.

'Get money,' replied the witch. 'Listen to me. When you come down to the earth under the tree, you will find yourself in a great hall: it is quite light, for above three hundred lamps are burning there. Then you will see three doors: these you can open, for the keys are hanging there. If you go into the first chamber, you'll see a great chest in the middle of the floor; on this chest sits a dog, and he's got a pair of eyes as big as two teacups, But you need not worry about that. I'll give you my blue-checked apron, and you can spread it out upon the floor; then go up quickly and take the dog, and set him on my apron; then open the chest, and take as many shillings as you like. They are of copper; if you prefer silver, you must enter the second chamber. But there sits a dog with a pair of eyes as big as mill-wheels. But do not you care for that. Set him on my apron, and take some of the money. And if you want gold, you can have that too – in fact, as much as you can carry – if you go into the third chamber. But the dog that sits on the money-chest has two eyes as big as round towers. He is a fierce dog, you may be sure; but you needn't be afraid, for all that. Only set him on my apron, and he won't hurt you; and take out of the chest as much gold as you like.'

So, I can hear my father's rendition of the soldier coming back from the wars, as he walks, *trip, trap, tripetty-trap*, whose metronomic onomatopoeia seemed to be a common feature of both languages. I have just re-read 'The Tinder-Box', and find that this vivid jaunty walk is rendered as 'One day a soldier came marching along the high-road – Left-right! Left-right!' – so the former locution is a typical embellishment of my father's; he was fond of introducing rhythmical runs, in the ornate alliterative manner of the Gaelic storytellers he had heard in Donegal; here, I have a sudden memory of dozing on my mother's knee, within a whitewashed interior lit by a popping gas-mantle and the smouldering glow of a turf fire, whose muffled perfume wafted in and out of the storyteller's droning recitation, interrupted, on occasion, by the gargle of his pipe, or the soft exhausted crash of turf collapsing on itself, and I would be well on my way to deeper sleep by the time the episode drew to a close, when I'd be carried homeward under the windswept stars.

It was always a pleasure, then, to wake in a strange bed in the morning, dazzled by Atlantic sunshine into momentary dislocation, becoming gradually aware of the bumpy damp mattress, light dappling the walls, and the far-off swash of the outgoing tide, where seagulls reigned their echolalia of white noise. Peering out of the tiny window, I could make out most of the parish: the low, white, telescopic houses set at odd angles to each other and in different gradients; the intervening crazy loopy roads of broken limestone, the contoured sheep-paths; sheep, grazing the mountainsides like clouds, or flocks of glacial stones; the deep, ruffled indigo of mountain lakes; the wind blowing the bog cotton this way and that in its galactic blossoming; one speck of kestrel overhead, riding the airy levels; the little Irish-green Post Office beside the pink pub and the blue B&B, the petrol pump, the milk-churns, and the pannier-bearing donkey; the church with a visible bell in its pedimented gable; the postman flying down a steep corkscrew on his push-bike, with his bag strung out behind him; turf-cutters out on the bog in small part-nerships, carving trenches of black oozy herring-bone, leaving little stooks or pyramids of cut turf in their wake; resorting at noon to scaldings of billy-can tea and buttered cut soda farls wrapped in damp linen tea-cloths; the three majestic rocks in the bay, diminishing like siblings towards America, since they feature in a local legend, where children are petrified. Indeed, the whole landscape is the stuff of legend, and every place-name bears a story.*

The pane I see all this through is made of that old bobbled glass with little dims and flaws embedded in it, quite unlike the broad clean picture-window glass of nowadays, which offers flat,

---

*This toponymic lore is known in Irish as *dinnshenchas*. 'The dinnshenchas reflects a mentality in which the land of Ireland is perceived as being completely translated into story: each place has a history which is continuously retold. The dinnshenchas is the storehouse of this knowledge, but the mentality which it expresses is to be found throughout all phases of Irish literature . . .' Robert Welch, ed., *The Oxford Companion to Irish Literature*, 1996.

uninteresting reflections. I have noted this former glass in the photographs of Willy Ronis, most specifically in his *Rue Laurence-Savart*, which focuses on an itinerant glazier. He is climbing a steep, granite-setted street, empty except for two conferring schoolboys in the background, and the declining sun bleeds his long shadow off the edge of the page. On his bent back he carries a trapezoidal frame with panes of various sizes laminated in it; together, they form ghostly symmetries of opaque light, which look as if they've slipped in from a glacial fourth dimension. It is an image that directly corresponds with Cocteau's Orphic Underworld, for a recurrent motif in the film is the apparition of a young glazier carrying similar material: '*Vitrier! Vitrier!*' he calls out in a hopeless trance, as he wanders below the glassless embrasures of derelict arcades and bombed factories.

The floors of the House of Death are strewn with fallen plaster, broken glass and crockery. Death regards herself in the mirror before plunging into it with gloved hands. Bubbles escape with a hiss from champagne glasses. The Underworld reflects the world above, seen through a glass darkly. Orpheus, forbidden to set eyes on his wife, catches a glimpse of her in the rear-view mirror of the Rolls-Royce; she vanishes on the spot. Glass is an aspect of death.

In about 1973, I worked in Central Belfast as a clerk in a branch of the Civil Service, Family Income Supplements, known as Fizz. It was at the height of one of the IRA's interminable bombing campaigns. At regular sporadic intervals throughout the week, there would be a bomb alert; buildings would be evacuated, and the staffs of various downtown office-blocks and multi-storeyed stores would traipse happily out of them, glad of this disruption. Pubs outside the danger-zone would be frequented, and spontaneous parties thrown in them. Sometimes people disappeared for days. Or, the crowds of shoppers, the regiments of clerks and salesgirls, the cabals of lawyers and bookies' runners would throng behind the fluttering white security tape that marked the demarcation of the zone: we were spectators of an imminent display of property-destroying pyrotechnics. The stilled streets were devoid of traffic, save for the parked bomb of the car and a protective barrier of static black-and-tan camouflaged armoured vehicles which looked incongruous in the unfoliaged city. The occasional approaching klaxon of a fire appliance interrupted the expectant calm.

Minutes or hours would pass before the device went off, and the delivery van became instant shrapnel, a rapidly-increasingly-exploded diagram of itself, visible in antiquated slo-mo newsreel footage or the eye of memory, as its wheels and engine-block and wings and gears and bonnet and boot and chassis and suspension and mirrors and interior trim and dashboard clock became history, like the flak of the Second World War or Battleship Potemkin, a shattered lens of spectacle. You felt the tangible shock of it on your face. Then there'd be a nearly simultaneous avalanche of glass, bursting and cascading from the windows of the buildings, crashing to ground level, till all of Royal Avenue was frosted with broken glass; and it was often rumoured that the glaziers and terrorists of Belfast had conspired in the coup.

The Glass Factory – to give it its full due, the Thermolux

Glass Company Limited – was situated at 2–20 Divis Street, on the other side of John Street from the back entrance of Barrack Street School. Behind the Glass Factory was a rectangle of waste ground bordered by the back-yard walls of small terraced houses. It was an interstitial unknown zone of the city, strewn with dog-turds, broken glass and isolated puddles that reflected the boringly moody weather of the time, the usual photographic darkroom clouds. This space was a gladiatorial or duelling arena for the students of Barrack Street, who'd assemble after school hours or in lunch-time to witness two big boys attempting to beat each other into a ritual pulp, as they made a great show of extricating themselves from the sleeves of jackets that were firmly grasped by their important seconds, who would parley to each other at the same time, setting up the ground rules of the physical debate. I am glad to relate that in one such contest, witnessed in about 1963, the underdog, a farmer's son from a townland beyond Ballynahinch, who was constantly interrogated for his rural accent and demeanour, won the battle hands-down by deviating from every unspoken rule in the book, as he gouged and spat and bit and kicked, getting a grip on most parts of his opponent's anatomy, and gaining the respect accorded to lunatics or geniuses.

Sometimes I would wander the back of the Glass Factory alone, mesmerized by its banality, stopping to gaze at a patch of yellow chickweed thrusting out from its soil of crushed coke and coal-dust, or a discarded brick embossed with its maker's name in bold Roman, or the broken amber shards of a beer-bottle. Here, squatting on a stone, or parading metronomically,

I might eat my packed lunch of sliced pan bread and Heinz Salad Spread, or Spam, or lettuce-leaf, which my mother habitually wrapped in a sheet of the waxed trade-named paper that the loaf came in.

McWATTERS' BAKERY

In the late sixties, there was a succession of jobs to be taken between school or university terms. Being the son of a postman, a word would be put in for me at Christmas-time, and I'd join the temporary army of the Royal Mail. Rising at dawn, I'd walk the mile or so down Stockman's Lane to the King's Hall, my footsteps echoing each other in the frosted air and the orange smog horizon beginning to evaporate into a chilly mauve or blue. For seven days, the Hall became a vast resounding parcel-sorting office, where Northern Ireland was divided into district-coded phalanxes of big wickerwork trolleys overseen by toponymical sages dressed in long tan drill coats, whose brains could instantly access a mental-synapsed Street Directory, guided by mnemonics like the one for a section of the Lower Falls: '*Bow*-legged *Baker* with a *Pound* of *English* and *Scotch Nails*'. These geniuses must have envisaged streets they'd never seen (for who could see all of Belfast, in its teeming terraces and factories and fractured loyalties?) and I thought of them as angels gliding high above the city, taking in its every aspect through their fish-eye lenses, recording the roll-call of the streets for Judgement Day, when the demolished and exploded urban fabric would be resurrected brick by brick from rubbish tips and landfills, and their galactic rubble swarmed before the Pearly Gates, mindful of their need to be reconstituted in their proper names and orders.

These overseers, adepts of blunt sarcasm, took pleasure in berating us students for our poor memories, and equal pleasure in responding instantly to our questions of directory, as the work took on a rhythm, and our calling out the names of streets became a chant of sailors guided by a master pilot, as he assigned them to their destinations. We sailed parcels through the air like World War flak into appropriate trolleys, and the atmosphere was heady with crushed chocolate and fruit, as Irish, Jerez, Advocaat and Scotch oozed out from their broken gift-wrapped bottles. A whole annual department of the Royal Mail was devoted to the compensation of this traffic lost in transit, and complicated tracking-forms devised for it by masters of bureaucracy.

Then, I loved the suburban 'walk', when I'd take the trolleybus to its terminus, and step out in to Drives and Avenues and Parks of new estates, where dawn dew or frost still shone on the privet hedges of front gardens, and dogs barked disconsolate welcomes. Each picture window would have its Christmas tree – some going for the real pine, others for brusque artificial monkey-puzzles, some for spinsterish snow-flake-patterned bonzais, all of them variously decorated with plethoras of glass and plastic baubles, winking fairy lights and sparkly tinsel. Opening sunburst-patterned squeaking iron gates, treading on the gravel walks, I'd approach the rippled glazed doors in a serial trance, seeing my reflection waver in them as I delivered envelopes through letterboxes that were wont to snap at my fingertips. Sometimes a radio would be playing in a back kitchen, or I'd hear the sound of lonely hoovering, or coffee percolating, as I wound my way from door to complex door in an arabesque of odd and even numbers.

The afternoon city shift was another thing, as dusk came early with a scent of oranges and coal-smoke, grocers' displays spilling on to pavements between beery pubs, haberdasheries, and poultry-merchants' windows filled with dangling plucked turkeys. Sometimes, as the bearer of goodwill to all, I'd be invited into the parlour of a bar on the Shankill Road, where a slacked fire emanated a huge orange plaque of warmth, and a bottle of Blue Bass and a Woodbine cigarette would be proffered to me, beneath the photograph of a young Queen or an icon of King Billy. I felt like a compromised spy as I accepted this commission.

In spring, there'd be work on building sites: labouring with tipsy barrows over the muck and sky-reflecting April puddles on narrow causeways of thick plank, wheeling the load up a precarious ramp on to the flimsy wooden deck of a hoist – when it started its cranky juddering ascent, driven by a phutting cloud-emitting diesel donkey-engine, you glimpsed daylight between the boards. Reaching the seventh storey, you experienced a twinge of hypsophobia, as you realized again that you would have to traverse the gap between hoist and floor on a single trembling plank poised high above the whole shebang below, which looked like a blitzed battlefield with cement-encrusted howitzers and dumper jeeps embedded in it between trenches. Putting this dizzy reconnaissance to the back of your mind, you took the aerial plunge and wobbled your full barrow over to the other side with a sigh of relief.

It was a great job when you were allowed to carry a Kango hammer, smaller electric cousin of the big-decibelled motor-biked-handled pneumatic drills controlled by little wiry men with bulging tattooed biceps. The Kango was built like a compact automatic weapon, and felt heavy-metal-snug as a snub gun in your arms as you cradled it. Its buck-lepping marsupial drill-power was brought into play to correct habitual design flaws, as when the apertures allowed in the cavity walls for electric sockets were misaligned, two brickies on either side having competed against each other to see who would finish first, and the relationship invariably got out of synch. Then the ghost-white plasterers would arrive with their hawks and trowels to cover it all up with a grey dawn skim, and no one would have known any different until the sparks came on the job and found the wiring-diagrams didn't correspond. Or perhaps it was the other way about. At any rate, it was especially pleasurable to drill through the fractional depth of the plaster into solid brick, feeling the Kango's blunt italic chisel-nib making impacts on it, sinking into it in steady irrevocables, till it burst into an emptiness of cavity with a sound like *scree*. Then I'd have a glimpse of myself in a mouse-dimension, scuttling through the Babel-towered intervallic levels, relaying messages from the Underground, stopping to

gnaw covertly on a length of enemy flex, oblivious of the conse-
quences.

When you blew your nose at snuffy intervals into a grey stiff
crumpled hanky, you'd find your snotters had been infiltrated by
cement-dust, stringy grits of it floating around in an ambient
spawn. The palms of your hands burned with lime, and the
knuckles of your toes were skinned by the unfamiliar metal caps
of industrial boots. You discovered muscles you had never
known, that pulsed with narrative aches and pains as you lay in an
exhausted reverie in bed, unwinding, rewinding the worked pattern of the day, the building taking shape within its scaffolding.

Then I would think of nightwatchmen's braziers, lumps of slag
burning through holes punched into a bucket on a tripod, the visible shimmer of acrid emanating blue heat; tin billy-cans boiled
on it, containing dust of tea-and-sugar emptied from pre-pack-
aged twists of paper; the glow of oil-fired red bull's-eye lanterns
dotting a no-go zone. The watchman, a great-coated veteran of
several wars, would relate sagas of the Boers to us children,
meanwhile extracting his supper from its wrapping of waxed
loaf-paper, sharing his unfamiliar sandwiches of corned beef and
pickle, thick-cut ham and palate-tingling mustard, thin-sliced red
cheese and cold burnt toast. Subsequently, he would smoke a
big Holmesian curved briar pipe, for which he'd rummage in
one of the fob pockets of his several waistcoats, as well as a tin of
Erinmore or Warhorse cut plug, and his smoker's pen-knife
attached to his watch-chain, with various devices for chopping
the stuff into fragments and tamping it into the bowl. A blue box
of Swift matches would appear from nowhere, and he'd take a

little splint from its magically open drawer, applying a red-tipped Hallowe'en flame to the packed tobacco in an aromatic gesture, as the fire caught, and drew, and gained his inhaled satisfaction. Then he'd embark on another episode of U-boat Baltic battle, by which time we'd be sunk on the verge of sleep in our beds, for our mothers had called us home hours ago, echoing our names down the long street; and I saw torpedoed convoys listing on the sea-bed, as various schools of thought swam in and out of their blasted hulls.

I worked for a summer or two in McWatters' Bakery, at 125–133 Cromac Street, in the Markets area. This was one of the many great bread manufactories to be found in Belfast at the time, whose economies seemed to depend on a traffic of casual labour – badly paid, I dare say, though it did not seem so to me at the time, and I still remember the thrill of receiving the weekly pay-packet, which had a clever slot that enabled you to tally the crisp notes before you broke its seal (there was a transparent window for the loose coins).

These big bakeries – Inglis's, Kennedy's, Hughes's, the Eglinton, the Ormeau, among others – maintained fleets of electrically powered bread-vans that purred in weekly rotas through the terraced streets, and their arrival at your doorstep was a great event. The breadserver would open the clever back door which swung up on two telescopic struts to make a rigid, rainproof awning under which he and the customer could do business and gossip in instalments. The interior of the van was revealed as a complex filing-system of sliding trays in which were shelved the batches of various plain and fancy breads, cakes, buns, and pastries;

dwelling momentarily within their remembered aroma, I'm trying to think of how one accessed the top shelves – they were, indeed, pulled out with a miniature version of the hooked pole used to reconnect to their overhead lines the accidentally disengaged trolleys of electric buses, but how they were brought to eye-level was another question I don't propose to go into, since the logistics of this apparently simple set of operations become more complicated the more they are examined.* All the same, it is a pity that this useful oven-to-door personal service has been largely discontinued, though I do not see how the line might have been profitably maintained in the face of supermarket competition.

I believe it was the ambition of the permanent bakers to gain command of one of these upwardly mobile outlets, since the working conditions and the opportunities for social intercourse

---

*The children's comic the *Beano* featured a near-relative of the bakery van, in its serial, 'General Jumbo'. Jumbo looked about eight, and was every young boy's role model then. From an issue of October 1953: "'The Army exercises are about to begin!" chuckled young Jumbo Johnson, as he stood proudly in Dinchester Park. "Very good, General Jumbo, sir," returned the plump, cheery-faced man beside Jumbo, and he began to strap a strange gadget on to Jumbo's left arm. The man was Professor Carter, Jumbo's greatest friend, and that gadget was the wonderful device by which Jumbo controlled an Army by radio. All his soldiers, tanks and planes were small, perfectly made models. They were all stowed away neatly in the Professor's van which was parked nearby.' The van, indeed, had a roll-top rear door, which was opened by a hooked pole to disclose a compartmentalized army. I remember being more fascinated by the van than by the gloveless gauntlet with its aerial and 'tiny knobs and buttons . . . cleverly-made controls', which puts one in mind of the radio wristwatches worn by spies in forties B-movies, or, more latterly, of Buzz Lightyear's interplanetary communications device.

Lying in bed after reading a 'Jumbo' episode by the light of a pocket torch, I would ponder the mysterious interior of the van, and I'd sometimes shrink myself to perfectly made toy soldier size in order to explore more fully its dimensions.

were much superior to those inside the factory, aspects of which resembled a vision of hell. The pan loaf bake-room was a particularly infernal chamber, with its glowing cast-iron gas-fired ovens connected by a miniature railway network of conveyor-belts on which clattered trains of dough-filled greased black loaf-tins; simultaneously, however, one sometimes thought of the process as a parable of death and resurrection, whose ultimate aim was the communion of bread with ourselves.

Here, the ambient temperature and humidity were such that you worked one hour on and one hour off; and the hour spent in the canteen (there was nowhere else to go, since I always worked night-shift on this duty) was passed in desultory camaraderie and boredom, between bouts of poker-playing and the relating of the many urban myths peculiar to the Markets area, in which great street-fighters and bar-room brawlers of the past were recalled vividly into the imaginative present, and the canteen then took on cantina connotations. All we lacked was drink, though it was not unknown for the occasional naggin bottle to be produced in a ceremonial gesture of bravado. It was here that I was taught how to roll hand-made cigarettes, which were especially popular with bakery workers, as they are with jailbirds, and it seemed the two were connected, since many of the casual staff had done some petty time or other. I am smoking a roll-up right now, as I write, and it is difficult to think of a time when I was unable to perform the fairly nimble roll-up operation, since I now do it on automatic pilot, and usually find myself with a lit cigarette between my fingers or lips without remembering how it or I got there.

And time was curiously skewed by the disparate dimensions of bake-room and canteen: sometimes the bake-room hour seemed interminable; sometimes it passed rapidly, as the rhythm of robotic work absorbed and hypnotized you, and you'd be surprised to see a proxy at your elbow, about to take over, as he nudged you out of whatever reverie you'd slipped into unwittingly. Even the canteen hour could drag, the talk declining into banal troughs or negative, exhausted silences. It was a joy, then, to go outside and stand on the empty dark quiet street, thinking of the sleeping denizens of Belfast, whose daily bread depended on our labours in the underworld; or perhaps there was an all-night corner shop which catered for the needs of night-shift refugees, a solitary lit outlet which combined, within its limited shelved space, the functions of grocer, confectioner, tobacconist and newsagent, and its aged attendant would be glad to see another soul wander in from the dark.

When not working nights, I'd sometimes be hired by day as a cleaner, for a lot of Augean work needed to be done around McWatters'. The gravy-ring contraption, for instance, which consisted of a long bath of boiling lard through which the dough-nuts were conveyed on a belt of sieve-wire, was habitually covered with a tacky congealed amber resin, nigh-impossible to shift. But generally, cleaning duties were regarded as easy numbers, since they afforded ample opportunities to skive, and you were usually assigned a mate, with whom you could pleasurably pass the time of day, smoking, playing cards in store-rooms, and exchanging late-adolescent philosophies.

One such assignment was the cleaning-out of No. 3 Flour Loft, which lay in a high remote annex of the factory, and had been disused for years. Here, ancient flour was drifted up the honeycomb walls of the chamber, and as we shovelled into it, thousands of dormant moths, grey-backed shellacky slivers of things, teemed into life and flight, swarming confusedly about our hands and eyebrows in a flitting pandemonium. Then we were given insecticidal spray-guns with bicycle-pump-action handles to enable us to zap the enemy, killing scores with a single squirt of drizzle. We'd rustle their fallen carcases into empty hundredweight bags.

Here, too, we discovered caches of old lading-bills, dockets and receipts, corroborated by near-pristine Georgian postage stamps overwritten with elaborate copperplate signatures, and I wondered how they'd got there from the Victorian wooden-panelled office whose bay window viewed the big cobbled roofed yard at ground level, where the delivery vans and breadservers' carts drew up to be serviced at loading-bays: it occupied an interesting dimension, since it ran at a slant between Cromac Street* and Joy Street, and could be approached from either iron-bollarded entrance or exit. Consulting the 1948 Directory, I see that Nos. 90–102 Joy Street are designated as the back entrance to the bakery, and note in passing that there are at least three Carsons in the street: John, at No. 9; James, baker, at No. 53; and Miss Jennie, at No. 86; all possible relatives of mine within this pretty Catholic enclave, since my father's father's father, a Protestant cabinet-maker from Ballymena who turned Taig when he came to Belfast looking for work and took Catholic wives, had

*From Irish *crom*, crooked.

sired a family of twenty-two, thirteen by the first before she
died, and nine by the second. So my father told me on my wedding day. But I confess I have not gone to the bother of looking up
the ramifications of this family tree.

The dockets, carbon-slips, and lading-bills appeared like mar-
riage, birth or death certificates, tallied in imperial aplomb. Awry
ranks of moths crawled over them. I felt a seethe of history
behind it all, authorized, and sealed, and signed on the heads of
kings, yet unacknowledged by the distant angels' hierarchies who
looked over us and out for us and after us, gazing through the
clouds of the city with their terrible eyes to detect our small
familiar-to-them movements in among the many terraces, and
corner shops, and churches, and rag-and-bone-yards floored with
dank brick and odorous public houses.

We were brought up to accept the Crown but not believe in it,
because its dominion had no power to extend beyond this temporal world, this Vale of Tears reiterated in our litanies and family
rosaries, as we dipped our fingers yet again into the cold stoup of
the holy-water font, and touched them to our cold foreheads.
Through the incense of Benediction, by way of gold-robed priests
intoning smoky Latin, in displays of star-shaped monstrances, we
could hear the tremors of another auditorium, where tiers of
saints and angels leaned slantedly to hear our every banal word,
for this communication is impossible in heaven, such is its huge
Vatican acoustic in which all the whispers sound the same, and
hallelujahs are a common parlance.

The white limbo of No. 3 Loft put me in mind of other work,
like that in Ross's* lemonade factory – 'Ginger Ale, Aerated and

Mineral Water Manufacturer's', to give it its full title. Here, in a high attic space, we were assigned one of those pointless tasks designed by prisoners of a work ethic, in which the appearance of work must be maintained, even when there is no work to be done: we were to shift a huge accumulation of old bottles from one side of the room to another.† Some of these were real museum-pieces: bottles of glazed clay, bottles of stone, bottles of pale green glass with air-bubbles embedded in them, bottles with names embossed on them, bottles with stone screw caps, and snappy spring-clip devices, bottles without long-popped corks: dusty, cobwebbed, empty bottles, eclectic regiments of slope-shouldered, drunk, dead soldiers. Regarding their profuse confusion, we wondered what principle of taxonomy might be applied to them, whether to sort them by colour, size, design, or apparent age; in the end, we contrived an ornate tableau inspired by chaotic principles, where, as we clunked and chinked them together in glassy rhymes, each juxtaposition suggested the next link, and interlocking snowflake patterns

---

* A quintessential Belfast name which was borne by other important establishments, of auctioneering, flax and tow spinning, and coal importing, respectively.

†This reminds me of a job I was once given as a casual clerk, when, in a long lull, I was required to transcribe, in my best handwriting, the entire *Northern Ireland Civil Service Code Book*, a street-directory-thick album of loose-leaf ring-bound pages abounding in paragraphs, sub-paragraphs, indemnifying codicils and clauses, all numeralled and alphabeticized, with typewritten emendations and addenda pasted into it. The Code Book purported to be applicable to every known human situation, and I enjoyed this fruitless labour as I wrote it out in a version of the roundhand I had learned for writing up a stamp collection, imagining myself to be a Celtic monk transcribing, and perhaps improving, a particularly desirable illuminated Bible.

became evident, for we burnished the bottles as we worked. Then, through the broad high attic skylight, a glancing ray of April sunshine – momentarily solid, with dust-motes drifting in it like the souls of moths – would illuminate the whole ornate array, twinkling its myriad glints of blue and green and clear and amber, till it looked like a starship Armada riding at anchor in the Coalsack Nebula, or a downtown Christmas tree composed of its own innumerable baubles of glass, and for a second I thought I detected a whiff of Norwegian fir in the high back room, as if green needles of it had been strewn on the pine boards of the floor.

It brought me back again to the Christmas post of Christmas past, and the sorting office of the General Post Office, where the legions of the city were divided into centuries and ranks of pigeonholes contained in upright formes. The high-ceilinged atmosphere was silted with a redolence of faded ink, gum, twine and rubber bands, illuminated by the technicoloured smell of stamps glimpsed on covers, accumulated and distributed: agate, bistre, carmine, deep blue, plum, purple, lilac, dull vermilion, milky blue, pale buff, orange, cobalt, slate, mauve, deep grey, deep red-brown, pale yellow-green, magenta, bright magenta, lemon, ochre, green, turquoise, Prussian blue, marone, pale violet, rose-red, chestnut. Most of these bore the head of the Queen of the British Commonwealth of Nations, so it was a nice momentary pleasure to come across a bit of correspondence from French India, Curaçao, Chile, Hejaz, Iceland, or The Vatican.

Once, some thirty years ago, I discovered a letter lodged in a forgotten crevice at the back of a pigeonhole, addressed to Belfast, Maine, USA, and postmarked 9 October 1948. It bore one of the Irish Republic airmail issues of that year, featuring the Angel Victor flying over various pilgrimage locations: the 1d chocolate, over the Rock of Cashel; the 3d blue, over Lough Derg; the 6d magenta, over Croagh Patrick; and the 1s green, over Glendalough. In all of these the Angel, in a series of dramatic Superman poses, fills most of the available sky, and carries a banner bearing the slogan, *Vox Hiberniae*, in Roman capitals; the names of the comparatively small places depicted below are given, of course, in Irish, in a stylized art nouveau half-uncial 'Gaelic' script. Trying to remember or visualize the value of the Belfast, Maine stamp, I am baffled. But it occurs to me now that, back in 1967, I indulged a momentary fantasy of Victor over Clonard Monastery, encompassing the whole of Belfast with his carrier-pigeon's aquiline angelic wings, recording all its architecture in the pupil-black orbs of his aerial Dresden vision: two-up-one-down terraced houses, shipyards, spinning mills, tobacco manufactories, tram depots, pubs, chapels, churches, ropeworks, barracks, corner shops, arcaded markets, railway stations, graving-docks, cinemas, post offices and photographic studios, much of it vanished now, into the maw of time, but still remnant in the memory of denizens and pilgrims like myself, and still extant in my father's mind.

When he comes home from work, he stoops over me with the slack enormous canvas bag at his paunch, and allows me to undo the thick tan leather straps from their glinting squeaky buckles. I plunge my head into the replicated coarse-weave gloom within, breathing its ample folds and crumples of absented correspondences. I detect a whiff of caramel or cinnamon behind it all, or clove-rock, suggestive nuggets of them stuck together in a quarter-pound bag with its serrated paper lips scrunched and twisted and sealed. Or the smell and glint of a bottle of Ross's lemonade or sarsparilla with its opaque screwed glass stopper, the metallic resonance of a small tin toy. Even when it is devoid of presents, I can discover in my father's bag a residue of string and thick brown rubber bands, the occasional stamp that has strayed from its envelope.

Now he is stretched out sleeping on the sofa because he'd worked the night shift before the morning walk. I take off his peaked cap and lose my head within its big dark crown. I get a chair to stand on to reach his coat from the hook on the back of the kitchen door. I drape myself within an amplitude of sleeve, cool linings that extend away beyond my fingertips, as the tail of the jacket reaches nearly to my heels or insteps, and sometimes skims the floor. I've remembered to sling the empty weight of the bag around me, feeling its hard leather strap cut into my left collar-bone, for I've taken off my sandals, and I've put my feet into my father's huge shoes, relishing their cold pilgrim insole contours that were formed by him before me. I stagger in them around the floor as he sleeps. I deliver important messages within this universe of room. His hands are clasped on his chest as he snores, and his nicotined fingers twitch in concert with his lips, which silently rehearse the story he's to tell me later on that night.

It's that night now. Like a boy with a Hallowe'en sparkler, he draws on the dark with a lit cigarette. The words are ghosted from his mouth in plumes and wisps of smoke, as I hold his free hand to guide him through the story, and we walk its underworld again.

ACKNOWLEDGEMENTS
AND PERMISSIONS

The author and publisher are grateful for permission to reprint lines from the following:

Donald Attwater (ed.), *The Catholic Encyclopaedic Dictionary*, Waverly Book Company, London, 1931; Jonathan Bardon, *Belfast: An Illustrated History*, Blackstaff Press, Belfast, 1982; Christian Barman, *Architecture*, Ernest Benn Ltd., London, 1928; Laurence Beesley, *The Loss of the* Titanic, Philip Allan & Co., London, 1912; Walter Benjamin, *Selected Writings, Vol. 1, 1912–1926*, ed. Marcus Bullock & Michael W. Jennings, the Belknap Press of Harvard University Press, 1996; C. E. B. Brett, *Buildings of Belfast*, Friar's Bush Press, Belfast, 1985; Rev. E. Cobham Brewer, *A Dictionary of Phrase and Fable*, new edition, Cassell & Co., n.d.; *Chambers 20c Dictionary*, new edition, Edinburgh, 1983; The Rev. Patrick S. Dinneen, *An Irish English Dictionary*, new edition, Irish Texts Society, Dublin, 1927;

F. L. Green, *Odd Man Out*, Methuen & Co., London, 1950; David Hammond, *Songs of Belfast*, Gilbert Dalton, Dublin, 1978; Robert Harbinson, *No Surrender*, Faber & Faber, London, 1960; Harold G. Henderson, *An Introduction to Haiku*, Doubleday Anchor Books, New York, 1958; Robert Humphreys, 'Whispering Death', from *Scale Models International*, April 1996; Capt. W. E. J. Johns, *Biggles and the Black Raider*, Hodder & Stoughton, London, 1953; Patricia Lynch, *Knights of God*, Hollis & Carter Ltd., London, 1945; Liam Mac Carráin, *Seo, Siúd, agus Siúd Eile*, Coisceim, Belfast, 1986; Chris McCauley, 'Star Factory', unpublished story, Derry, 1996; Eileen McCracken, *The Palm House and Botanic Garden*, Ulster Architectural Heritage Society, Belfast, 1971; James A. Mackay, *Eire: the Story of Eire and her Stamps*, Philatelic Publishers Ltd., London 1968; Maurice Maeterlinck, *The Life of the White Ant*, trans. Alfred Sutro, George Allen & Unwin Ltd., London, 1927; Alberto Manguel, *A History of Reading*, HarperCollins Publishers, London; John Montague, 'The Vikings', in John Montague (ed.), *The Faber Book of Irish Verse*, Faber & Faber, London, 1974, Cathal O'Byrne, *As I Roved Out*, The Irish News Ltd., Belfast, 1946; Noel O'Connell, *Father Dinneen – His Dictionary and the Gaelic Revival*, Irish Texts Society, London, 1984; Marcus Patton, *Central Belfast: An Historical Gazeteer*, Ulster Architectural Historical Society, Belfast, 1993; *Raphael's Astronomical: Ephemeris of the Planets' Places for 1922*, published by W. Foulsham & Co. Ltd., who owns the copyright; *The Reader's Digest Book of Strange Facts, Amazing Stories*, The Reader's Digest Association, London, 1975; *The Regent Priced Catalogue of the Postage Stamps of the British Commonwealth of Nations*, Robson

Lowe Ltd., London, 1934; T. Todd, *Stamps of the Empire*, Thomas Nelson & Sons, London, 1938, *The Sunday Missal for All Sundays and the Principal Feasts of the Year*, Browne & Nolan Ltd., Belfast, 1957 (copyright in Belgium, by Etabl, Brepols Turnhout); Julian Watson, introduction to *Belfast Frescoes* by John Kindness, Crowquill Press, Belfast, 1995; Wyn Craig Wade, *The* Titanic: *End of a Dream*, Weidenfield & Nicolson, 1980; Robert Welch (ed.) *The Oxford Companion to Irish Literature*, Oxford University Press, 1996; W. B. Yeats 'The Statues', in Norman Jeffares (ed.), *The Collected Poems of W. B. Yeats*, Macmillan, London, 1979, © A. P. Watt on behalf of Michael Yeats.